Do not be afraid

New Testament Studies in Contextual Exegesis
Neutestamentliche Studien zur kontextuellen Exegese

Herausgegeben von Johannes Beutler,
Thomas Schmeller und Werner Kahl

Vol./Bd. 6

PETER LANG
Frankfurt am Main · Berlin · Bern · Bruxelles · New York · Oxford · Wien

Johannes Beutler

Do not be afraid

The First Farewell Discourse
in John's Gospel (Jn 14)

PETER LANG
Internationaler Verlag der Wissenschaften

Bibliographic Information published by the Deutsche Nationalbibliothek
The Deutsche Nationalbibliothek lists this publication in the Deutsche Nationalbibliografie; detailed bibliographic data is available in the internet at http://dnb.d-nb.de.

ISSN 1616-816X
ISBN 978-3-631-61370-2

© for the English edition: Peter Lang GmbH
Internationaler Verlag der Wissenschaften
Frankfurt am Main 2011
© for the German edition: Verlag Katholisches Bibelwerk,
Stuttgart
All rights reserved.

All parts of this publication are protected by copyright. Any utilisation outside the strict limits of the copyright law, without the permission of the publisher, is forbidden and liable to prosecution. This applies in particular to reproductions, translations, microfilming, and storage and processing in electronic retrieval systems.

www.peterlang.de

Preface to the Series

The series *New Testament Studies in Contextual Exegesis* (NSKE) is dedicated to the publication of exegetical works which aim at enhancing a textually adequate understanding of the New Testament by taking into consideration the life-contexts, horizons of interpretation, and questions of the non-Western world. African, Latin-American, Oceanic, and Asian exegetes can, from their own perspectives, make significant contributions to the field of New Testament studies with respect to content and methodology. They might motivate their Western colleagues to critically reflect on their own history of interpretation and methodology, by enabling them to acknowledge the fact that any exegetical approach is contextually coined.

The contributions that appear in NSKE are works of critical exegesis. They are informed by methodological reflection. The authors consider the cultural embeddedness or contextuality of the New Testament writings as well as that of the exegetical perspective.

Taking into account that non-Western voices are not represented adequately in the exegetical discourse, the editors of NSKE intend to facilitate cross-cultural networking of exegetical research in a world-wide perspective, especially with respect to the transfer of scientific knowledge from the South to the North.

The editors

Prof. Dr. Johannes Beutler, Frankfurt
PD Dr. Werner Kahl, Hamburg
Prof. Dr. Thomas Schmeller, Frankfurt

Vorwort zur Reihe

Die Reihe *Neutestamentliche Studien zur kontextuellen Exegese* (NSKE) ist der Veröffentlichung solcher exegetischen Arbeiten gewidmet, die Lebenskontexte, Deutehorizonte und Fragestellungen der nicht-westlichen Welt für ein textangemessenes Verstehen des Neuen Testaments fruchtbar zu machen suchen. In ihrer je partikularen Perspektivität haben afrikanische, lateinamerikanische, ozeanische und asiatische Exegeten und Exegetinnen sowohl inhaltlich als auch methodisch einiges und zuweilen Entscheidendes im Bereich Neutestamentliche Wissenschaft beizutragen. Sie vermögen darüber hinaus, westliche Fachkollegen und -kolleginnen zur kritischen Reflexion ihrer Forschungsgeschichte und Methodik anzuregen, indem sie zur Anerkennung des Faktums der Kontextualität jeglichen exegetischen Zugangs nötigen.

Bei den in NSKE erscheinenden Untersuchungen handelt es sich um exegetisch-kritische Beiträge, die wissenschaftlich-methodisch verantwortet die kulturelle Einbettung bzw. Kontextualität sowohl der neutestamentlichen Schriften als auch der exegetischen Perspektive bedenken. Angesichts der Tatsache, dass nicht-westliche Forschungsbeiträge im exegetischen Diskurs unterrepräsentiert sind, liegt den Herausgebern von NSKE daran, die transkulturelle Vernetzung exegetischer Forschung in weltweiter Perspektive zu fördern, und zwar insbesondere in Hinblick auf den Süd-Nord-Transfer wissenschaftlicher Erkenntnis.

Die Herausgeber

Prof. Dr. Johannes Beutler, Frankfurt
PD Dr. Werner Kahl, Hamburg
Prof. Dr. Thomas Schmeller, Frankfurt

Original Foreword

The first steps towards this study were taken more than seven years ago. In a seminar in the summer semester of 1976, our group examined the Gethsemane tradition in the New Testament. In the course of this investigation, the significance of Ps 42/43 in the development of this tradition in the Synoptic Gospels and in John was elaborated. A preliminary conclusion to this study was able to be given in 1978/9 in *New Testament Studies* under the title of 'Psalm 42/43 im Johannesevangelium'. According to this approach, a good part of John 14 seemed to be dependent on the aforesaid Psalm tradition. But also the remaining verses of John 14 became much clearer than previously understood when seen as traditional material taken from the Old Testament and from early Judaism – in verses 15-24, taken particularly from Old Testament Covenant theology, and in verses 25-31 taken from the eschatological promises of the Exilic and post-Exilic prophets with regard to both language and concepts. A lecture at the annual conference of the Studiorum Novi Testamenti Societas in Toronto in August 1980 provided the opportunity for this hypothesis to be submitted for the first time before colleagues from within Germany and beyond. On that occasion the Deutsche Forschungsgemeinschaft readily gave their support.

It took more than a further three years for the book form that had then been suggested to be undertaken. Time and again, administrative duties in the Hochschule saw to it that the completion of the work was postponed. If I am now presenting the manuscript, it is in the full awareness that much remains to be said. Thus the interpretation of John 14 in the light of Old Testament, Jewish and early Christian traditions which is offered here should not be taken to exclude the possibility that the fourth evangelist was also influenced by pre- or early Gnostic concepts. The author would like only to express his agreement with the theory advanced by E. Haenchen in his 1980 commentary that Gnosis probably stood more at the end than at the beginning of the Fourth Gospel, particularly in the area of its reception history. Thus the present interpretation of John 14 from the point of view of Palestinian and biblical sources is not an exclusive one.

Thanks are due here, first to the Deutsche Forschungsgemeinschaft who made possible not only the Seminar lecture in Toronto but also the employment of a scientific collaborator throughout various semesters. My sincere thanks are due also to Angelica Strotmann, Karl-Werner Wilhelm and Katherine Wolff NDS for their help with the bibliography and the scientific apparatus. Thanks too to the Jesuit community at Schlump and the Protestant Theological Faculty in the University of Hamburg for their hospitality and support during the winter semester 1982/3 in which what is, in my view, the central chapter, chapter 3, developed. Among my Frankfurt brethren I would like to pay tribute in the first place to Dr. Norbert Lohfink who went through the said chapter 3 from the perspective of an expert in Deuteronomy. Finally, thanks are due to the editors of the 'Stuttgarter Bibelstudien' series and the management and operatives of the press who had the care of the manuscript during the process of printing.

Frankfurt am Main, March 1984   Johannes Beutler SJ

Foreword of the English edition

"Habt keine Angst" was published in 1984 and found its way into many libraries. For a long time it has no longer been in print. The present English edition gives access once more to my study of John 14 and exposes the text to the discussions of the past 25 years. At the same time it makes it accessible to the English-speaking public. A bibliography on John 14 since the year of the first publication was added and evaluated in the "postscript". In this way, the book has remained up to date.

The publication of the English edition in the series "New Testament Studies in Contextual Exegesis" may need some explanation. The approach chosen for the interpretation of John 14 in my monograph is intertextual. The chapter is interpreted in the light of Old Testament, Early Jewish and Early Christian texts and traditions. What comes to the fore is the strong influence of Jewish biblical and post-biblical tradition on the text of the First Farewell Discourse. This has its consequences for the place which we assign to the Gospel of John and its author(s) in the history of Early Christianity. Far from being close to early Gnostic groups, both text and author show strong connections to Jewish thought and movements in the Second Temple period. This justifies the publication of the manuscript in the series "New Testament Studies in Contextual Exegesis". I thank the co-editors of the series for their approval of the project and the staff of Peter Lang for their continued support and collaboration. Last and not least my thanks is due to the translator of the text, Dr Michael Tait, Mirfield, who also helped me in revising the additions to the translated text, and to Judith Breunig who took care of the indices.

Frankfurt am Main, 31 July 2010

Johannes Beutler SJ

Table of Contents

Original Foreword	7
Foreword of the English Edition	9
Table of Contents	11
I. Preliminary Literary Questions	13
1. The Context	13
2. The Literary Unity of the Chapter	14
3. The Structure of the Chapter	16
4. The Genre of the Chapter	18
II. The Announcement of Jesus' Departure as a Midrash on the Psalms (vv. 1-14)	23
1. The Structure of the Passage	23
2. Some Aporias	24
3. The Tradition behind the Passage	26
4. Redaction	43
III. The Threefold Promise of the Coming of Jesus in the Light of the Covenant Theology of the Old Testament (vv. 15-24)	49
1. The Structure of the Passage	49
2. Traces of Literary Strata	51
3. The Tradition behind the Passage	52
3.1 The Condition of Jesus' Promise: Love of Jesus, Keeping of his Commandments (vv. 15.21a.23b.24a)	52
3.2 The Content of Jesus' Promise (vv. 16-20.21b.23c)	58
3.2.1 The Coming and Abiding of the Spirit (vv. 16f)	58
EXCURSUS: The 'New Covenant' in the New Testament and in early Jewish tradition	60
3.2.2 The Coming and Abiding of Jesus and the Father (vv. 18.23)	64
3.2.3 Love, Life, Knowledge, Sight	70
Love	71
Life	72
Knowledge	74
Sight	75
4. Redaction	75

IV. The Eschatological Gifts of Jesus (vv. 25-31)	79
1. The Structure of the Passage	79
2. Literary Strata	80
3. Tradition	82
3.1 The Eschatological Gifts of Jesus	82
3.2 The Command to Leave	93
4. Redaction	95
V. Conclusions	99
Postscript: John 14 in Recent Research	103
Sources and Literature	111
Additional Bibliography	127
Index of Authors	135
Index of References	138

I. Preliminary Literary Questions

1. The Context

Up to the present day, exegetes are fascinated by the Farewell Discourses of Jesus in John as the sum total of his preaching according to the Fourth Gospel. On the one hand, as a catalogue of the literature shows, we have studies and spiritual sketches, which seek to take in the whole of the final discourse of Jesus from Jn 13,31 to the end of the High Priestly Prayer in 17,26; on the other hand, we have detailed examinations of individual passages or verses.

If Chapter 14 of John's Gospel has been chosen as the subject of the present study, this has been for two reasons: in the first place, this chapter is clearly a self-standing literary unit with a clearly recognisable beginning and end; secondly, this textual unit has not until now received the attention that it deserves.[1]

There is no direct transition from Chapter 14 to the discourse of Jesus in Chapters 15 and 16 together with the closing prayer in Chapter 17. The immediate connection with the signal for departure in 14,31 seems to be the route to the garden across the Kidron Brook in 18,1. Other proposals which imagine Jesus' further words in Chapters 15 to 17 to have been spoken while still in the Cenacle or on the way to the Mount of Olives[2] are not satisfactory. Moreover, transpositions within the Farewell Discourses[3] are not persuasive. A much more probable thesis sees Chapters 15 to 17 as later developments of an original Farewell Discourse of Jesus in 13,31-14,31.[4] From a formal point of view, something new begins with the Parable of the Vine in Jn 15,1-8. Questions from individuals, that is, named disciples, recede into the background. The theological emphasis shifts significantly from Christology and a theology of belief to ecclesiology and

---

[1] In recent times, only *Migliasso*, Presenza, has handled this chapter in book form. However, he remains exceptional on account of its strictly synchronic examination.

[2] For the first possibility, cf. *Schanz* 489; *Weiss* 418; *Calmes* 393f; *Knabenbauer* 454f; *Zahn* 576; *Pölzl-Innitzer* 418 *et al*; for the second, authors from *Godet* 298; *Westcott* 216 to *Haenchen* 479.

[3] For attempts of this kind, cf. *Bultmann* 350 n. 2 and Beiheft 43. *Bultmann* himself (349ff) puts Chapter 17 before Jn 13,31 and Chapters 15 and 16 (with 13,36-38) behind 13,35. *Brinkmann*, De priore, assumes that the original place of Chapters 15 and 16 was in connection with Jn 12,44-50.

[4] More conservative authors see or assume here later supplements of the evangelist himself. So *Durand*, Discours (1911) 322; *Lagrange* 397ff; *Huby*, Discours 74f; *Gaechter*, Aufbau, 203ff; *F.-M. Braun* 433; *Behler*, Abschiedsworte 155f; *Mollat* 26f; *Van den Bussche* 369f; outside Catholic research, *Strathmann* 213f; *Barrett*² 454f; *Lindars* 50f. Cf. *Hammer*, Stellung. Others think a secondary hand more likely. So first, *Wellhausen*, Erweiterungen 7-15 and Evangelium 79f. Since then, *Hirsch*, Studien 104-118; *Richter*, Fußwaschung (1965) 52ff and Fußwaschung (1967), 301ff; *J. Becker*, Abschiedsreden 215-246; *Thyen*, Johannes 343-356; also, but cautiously, *Schnackenburg* III 101ff.

the theme of brotherly love and unity against the background of the hatred of the world and impending persecution.

Though not quite so clear, there is a break and a definite new opening at the beginning of Chapter 14. Considerations of both form and content justify our seeing a new unit here. After the words to all the disciples in 13,31-35 that are made up of a small hymnic fragment (vv. 31f), a prediction (v. 33) and an exhortation to brotherly love (vv. 34f)[5], Jesus addresses himself to an individual, that is, Peter. In 14,1, the speech returns to the second person plural: the assembled disciples taken together are now the ones being addressed. Commands now take the place of predictions. A 'biographical apothegm'[6] relating to Peter gives way to the words of exhortation and comfort in Chapter 14; the latter discourse is held together interiorly and exteriorly by the command 'Let not your hearts be troubled' (μὴ ταρασσέσθω ὑμῶν ἡ καρδία, v. 1), which is only taken up again in v. 27 with the addition 'neither let them be afraid' (μηδὲ δειλιάτω). As has often been recognised,[7] these form an inclusion containing the chapter's leading idea. That Chapter 14 of John's Gospel is also a structural unity will be demonstrated in the following section. The break at Jn 14,1 is further confirmed by the insertion there of the Psalm tradition which is the subject of Chapter II of this work. According to our interpretation, this has been worked over in a midrashic fashion as will be further indicated. So, then, as the foundation for the Farewell Discourse of exhortation and comfort, a new literary genre is also begun in 14,1, still more clearly separating Chapter 14 from the last passage of Chapter 13 (vv. 36-38).[8]

2. The Literary Unity of the Chapter

If Jn 14 may be seen as a literary unity in respect of its demarcation from its context, the question remains whether it is a simple or a compound unity.

Since the intensive literary work on the Fourth Gospel at the beginning of the twentieth century, certain tensions have been observed within our chapter. Among these are the different views of the eschatological encounter with Jesus in vv. 2f on the one hand and in vv. 18f and 23 on the other. Related to that is the tension between the presentation of an impending coming of Jesus person-

---

[5] Verses 13,34f probably belong to the post-Johannine redaction, for the theme of the "new commandment" of brotherly love has no match in Jn 14; on the other hand, it is closely connected with Jn 15 (vv. 12-17) and the Johannine letters. Besides, 13,34f breaks the connection between 13,33, the mention of Jesus' "going", and 13,36, Peter's question as to where Jesus is going. The latter already occurred to *Wellhausen*, Erweiterungen 14 n. 1 and Evangelium 61. Cf., also, *Loisy*[2] 401; *Hirsch*, Studien 103. More recent authors speak explicitly of 13,34f as an interpolation: *Richter*, Deutung, 67; *Thyen*, Johannes 354; *J. Becker*, Abschiedsreden 220, and, in great detail, *Schnackenburg* III 59. Cf. *Onuki*, Abschiedsreden 208f.
[6] On the genre 'biographical apothegm', cf. *Bultmann*, Geschichte 26-38.
[7] Cf., for example, *Mollat* on 14,1; *R. E. Brown* 623.
[8] Cf., *infra*, section 4 of this chapter.

ally (vv. 3.18.23.28) or represented by the Paraclete (vv. 16f.26, even though the verb 'coming' is lacking here). The aforesaid sayings about the Paraclete seem, on their part, to be only loosely connected with their context in form and content so as to raise the question of their literary origin. Similarly, the numerous repetitions within the text can be taken as indications of literary stratification.

The older literary criticism tried to explain such tensions through the hypothesis of the reworking of a *Grundschrift* by a redaction.[9] In recent times, there belongs here the attempt of *G. Richter*,[10] to allocate the coming-again sayings of vv. 2f to a Jewish Christian *Grundschrift* which was then reinterpreted in verses 4-26 by sayings concerning the coming of Christ that are more strongly focused on the present. This interpretation would go back the evangelist, predominantly addressing Gentile Christians.

It is certainly just as difficult to see vv. 2f as fragments of an underlying written source taken out of their context like other words of Jesus in Jn 14, a source which *R. Bultmann*[11] and after him his pupil *H. Becker*[12] ascribe to a Gnostic source of revelation speeches. On the one hand, we have to observe here the argument from style,[13] on the other hand the theological kinship between the speech sections attributed, hypothetically, either to the source or to the evangelist.

On the whole, it seems sufficient to explain the grammatical and formal tensions in the text through the hypothesis of literary redaction of oral units of tradition. From *H. Windisch*, who viewed the Paraclete sayings as independent units of tradition,[14] there runs a line through to *S. Schulz* who sees in Jn 14 a Paraclete theme tradition joined to a coming again theme tradition.[15] With felici-

---

[9] This hypothesis can be divided into three different basic subdivisions. *H. H. Wendt*, Johannesevangelium 95-100.150ff.235f, claims that Jesus' words, which lie beneath the Farewell Discourse in Jn 14, are the oldest, apostolic component of John. More widespread is the second basic group which speculates that the oldest component of the gospel consists of the Johannine narratives or a part of them as opposed to the speech. Here, above all, we should mention *J. Wellhausen* – Erweiterungen 7-15 (1907) and Evangelium (1908), who not only distinguishes between the different successive strata in Jn 14 on the one hand and Jn 15-17 on the other hand, but also seeks to separate the basic component of the text in Chapter 14 from later redactions. Finally, the third basic type avoids regarding a specific kind of text as the oldest and takes as the *Grundschrift* both narrative and speech. In Chapter 14, this leads to complex divisions. Representatives of this type are, among others, *F. Spitta*, Johannes-Evangelium, especially 338-357, and *W. Soltau*, Evangelium.
[10] *Richter*, Studien, especially 360-373.
[11] *Bultmann*, especially 459-489.
[12] *H. Becker*, Reden, especially 105-109.
[13] This argument is especially associated with *J. Jeremias*, Literarkritik, and *E. Ruckstuhl*, Einheit 190-219. In fact, a re-examination of the stylistic arguments based on Chapter 14 shows that 'Johannine' stylistic features in the widest sense are to be found in almost every verse of the chapter and so its literary unity is reinforced.
[14] *Windisch*, Parakletsprüche.
[15] *Schulz*, Untersuchungen 142-158.

tous intuition, *M.-É. Boismard* recognises in vv. 15-23 three different models of reinterpretation of the coming again saying of vv. 2f which the evangelist would have put together out of oral tradition.[16] We will take up this hypothesis and use it as a basis for Chapter III of this work. The reappearance of key words from vv. 3-24 in vv. 25-29 will be explained in Chapter IV on redaction critical grounds.

3. The Structure of the Chapter

If Jn 14 can be viewed as a textual unity despite the tensions we have examined, the question of its structure is the next to arise. Older outlines attempt to divide the chapter partly with reference to aspects of the content,[17] or they proceed from formal division markers such as the interrogative interruptions of individual disciples.[18] A satisfactory division of the chapter would appear to require the combination of both aspects.

The decades since 1920 have seen the dominance of outlines which 1. identify the succession of sayings concerning the going away (ὑπάγειν, πορεύεσθαι) and the coming (ἔρχεσθαι) of Jesus in verses 1-14 and 15-24, and 2. recognize the clear break at the beginning of v. 25 together with the summary character of vv. 25-31. A pioneer here is *A. Loisy* in the second edition of his classic commentary.[19] Most important in German speaking circles is *R. Bultmann* who anyhow works less from Christological than from anthropological starting points in his division as far as v. 24.[20] While in verses 5-14 ('The Unity of Way and Destination'), the belief (πιστεύειν) of the disciples stands in the foreground, verses 15-24, according to Bultmann, are concerned with 'the loving relationship with the Son and the Father' with the framing key word 'love' (ἀγαπᾶν). Useful here is the classification of vv. 15-17.18-21 and 22-24 under the category of 'the Promise of the Paraclete', 'the Promise of the Coming Again of Christ' and 'the Promise of the Coming of Jesus and God'.[21]

It is not so convincing when *J. Becker*[22], followed by *R. Schnackenburg*,[23] still links verses 15-17 to the section on the 'going away' (πορεύεσθαι) of Jesus.

---

[16] *Boismard*, Évolution.
[17] So *B. Weiss* 396.403.412; *Holtzmann-Bauer* 243-251 and, above all, the French authors *Durand*, Discours (1910) 518f and Évangile 389; *Lagrange* 370f; *F.-M. Braun* 425.428-431.
[18] So, above all, the Anglo-Saxon research since *Westcott* LXV; cf. also *Calmes* 387-393; *Charlier*, Présence, especially 61-67; *Strathmann* 203f and *Wikenhauser* 263-280.
[19] *Loisy*² 44.52.403f.
[20] *Bultmann* 466-489.
[21] For the order after v. 14, cf., also, *Gallo*, Sermo Christi who sees Jn 15,1-8 as the centre of the Johannine Farewell Discourses and arranges Chapter 14 as strongly parallel to Chapter 15 in vv. 1-12a.12b-14.15-24 and 25-31.
[22] *J. Becker*, Abschiedsreden 223.
[23] *Schnackenburg*, Anliegen 95f. – The same break before v. 17 is also found in *Migliasso*, Presenza, especially 167-182.

In fact, as a survey of the contents confirms, there is already talk of some kind of new coming of Jesus in the first Paraclete saying. This means that, after the introductory verses 1-4, in which the 'going away' and 'coming' of Jesus are announced, and verses 5-14 which concern the 'going away' of Jesus, the fourth evangelist seems to offer in verses 15-17.18-21.22-24 three alternative models as to how the 'coming' of Jesus can be thought of and understood. This is also the proposal of the highly influential commentary of R. E. Brown[24] with which more recent works agree.[25] For the connection of the first Paraclete saying and its introduction (vv. 15-17) with the following and not the preceding material, linguistic reasons are not the least potent. As early as the commentary of R. Bultmann,[26] the varied distribution of the characteristic verbs within our chapter was noticed. While πιστεύω, 'believe' occurs some six times in verses 1-14, it is absent in verses 15-24. Conversely, ἀγαπάω, 'love', is encountered eight times in verses 15-24, while it is lacking in verses 1-14.[27] In addition to ἀγαπάω, in verses 15-17 we come across six further verbs[28] for the first time in Chapter 14. These to a large extent anticipate verses 18-24. There is a clear hook ('inclusion') between v. 15, with the theme of 'love' and the 'keeping' of the 'commandments', and verses 23 and 24 where the same theme, here expressed as 'keeping' the 'word' or 'words' of Jesus, is taken up again. As a transition, v. 21 speaks of the 'love' of the one who loves Jesus and keeps his commandments.

In addition to v. 15, v. 25, especially, presents an important caesura. Here Jesus seems to look back on all the revelations he has made previously and explains: 'These things I have spoken to you (λελάληκα, Perfect), while I am still with you'. To this there corresponds the other saying in v. 30: 'I will no longer talk much with you.' Since, then, in verses 25-31 a series of important themes are taken up again from vv. 1-24, such as the promise of the Paraclete (v. 26), the exhortation to fearlessness (v. 27), the announcement of the going away and coming again of Jesus (v. 28) as well as the theme of love (v. 31), we may see in these verses the conclusion of the chapter and thus of the first Farewell Discourse.[29]

---

[24] *Brown* 643-648.
[25] Thus, with variations on the Brown arrangement, *Schulz* 182-192; *Lindars* 470-483; *Blank* II 15.
[26] *Bultmann* 473 recognises, above all, the structural significance of πιστεύειν for verses 5-14 and of ἀγαπᾶν for verses 15-24.
[27] The observation can be put on a still broader basis. λαλέω, οἶδα, ὁράω, πορεύομαι and ὑπάγω occur only in vv. 1-14, γίνομαι, δίδωμι, θεωρέω and τηρέω only in vv. 15-24 – apart from the concluding verses.
[28] δίδωμι, εἰμὶ μετά, ἐρωτάω, θεωρέω, τηρέω, λαμβάνω.
[29] Cf., *infra*, Chapter IV.

4. The Genre of the Chapter

The previous section has shown that in Jn 14 we are faced with an artistic literary composition from start to finish. However, in New Testament literature we rarely come across forms that have not been influenced in one way or another by the 'ideal form' of an existing literary genre. Since the rise of form or genre criticism, therefore, the 'Johannine Farewell Discourses' either in whole or in part (such as Chapter 14 or Chapter 17) have been ascribed to the literary genre of 'Farewell Discourse' for which reference is made to parallels in very different areas of the history of religions.

Graeco-Roman examples of the farewell words or speeches of important men have been identified, particularly by *E. Stauffer*.[30] However, the examples adduced reveal few similarities of content and form both among themselves and in comparison with the New Testament. Similarly, the Gnostic parallels produced since *W. Bauer*[31] and *R. Bultmann*[32] offer little that is useful.

A more fruitful area of research would seem to be the genre as it is found in Old Testament, Jewish and New Testament texts that appear to be parallel. Here, *E. Stauffer* was early to assemble examples and evaluate them.[33] *J. Munck* widened the base of operations and placed the genre more precisely in this area with the aid of stricter criteria.[34] Since then, reference should be made, above all, to *H.-J. Michel*[35] and *F. Cortès*[36] for the New Testament Farewell Discourses and, for their Old Testament and Jewish models, to *E. v. Nordheim*[37] in addition to *F. Cortès*.

Modifying Munck's proposal, Cortès identifies three constant elements of content in the genre, above all in the intertestamental domain: 'The dying man (or the one faced with his decease) summons his relations to speak with them. 2. He delivers his exhortations. Among these, most prominent on account of their frequency are references to works of mercy, kindness, brotherly love and unity. 3. The discourse ends with a few sentences on the future of the community or the end of time.'[38] Considerations of content are supplemented by formal ele-

---

[30] *Stauffer*, Abschiedsreden 29f. But cf., also, among others, *Schnackenburg* III 63f.

[31] *Bauer*² 201f; ³207f refers to the Corpus Hermeticum, the end of Tractate I, and Mandaean sources for Jesus' Prayer in Jn 17. Cf. *Dodd*, Interpretation 420ff for the additional reference to Tractate XIII of the Corpus Hermeticum.

[32] Similarly, *Bultmann* 374 with n. 2 and Exegetica 87f for the Prayer of Jesus in Jn 17.

[33] *Stauffer*, Theologie 327-330.

[34] *Munck*, Discours, especially 159-169.

[35] *Michel*, Abschiedsrede 35-72.

[36] *Cortès*, Discursos.

[37] *v. Nordheim*, Lehre.

[38] *Cortès*, loc. cit. 54. In the first place, *Cortès* draws his examples for the definition of the genre "Abschiedsrede" according to form and content from the intertestamental field, that is, from the apocryphal and pseudepigraphic Jewish literature, principally the Test XII (106-297). According to *Cortès*, the genre is developed only rudimentarily in the Old Testament

ments which take their place beside them: 1. 'The summons' (qr'/καλεῖν) of the children and grandchildren; 2. the 'charge' ($ṣwh$/ἐντέλλεσθαι) of the commands to be observed; 3. the form of address 'my children' (τέκνα [μου]), in connection, above all, with the prediction for the future.[39] Moreover, according to *Cortès*, the literary genre is infused with an apocalyptic element: prediction for the future on account of the pressure of the present;[40] the element of midrash: reinterpretation or actualisation of biblical texts;[41] and a sapiential element:[42] 'the search after a true understanding of oneself and one's relation to things, to one's fellow men and to the Creator'.[43] The address '(my) children' almost certainly owes its origin to this element.[44] It was made the centre of attention in the studies of E. v. *Nordheim*,[45] who also tried to bring the elements of content identified by *Cortès* into a meaningful arrangement.[46]

We pass over those authors who seek to derive the genre of the Farewell Discourse of Jesus from its post-Easter *Sitz im Leben* in the community,[47] and enquire into the development of the genre's elements of form and content in the Johannine Farewell Discourses. Here, the question can be limited once again to Chapter 14 as 'Farewell Discourse', as was the case in Section 1 on the 'Context' (with verses 13,31-33.35-38 as transition and introduction).

The second and the third of Cortès's three elements of the genre according to content are to be found clearly evidenced in our texts while the attendant elements of style are not lacking: Chapter 14 – as the words of Jesus before his 'going away' (ὑπάγειν, πορεύεσθαι 13,33.36; 14,2-5.28) – is dominated by his exhortations which, as we shall see again, focus on faithfulness to the covenant, the new covenant in Jesus. This is true, above all, of the central section of the chapter in which the talk is of 'love' for Jesus and the keeping of his commandments (ἐντολαί vv. 15.21) or 'words' (λόγοι = *dbrjm* v. 24).[48] Certainly

---

itself with the exception of the (late) book of Tobit, Chapters 4 and 14 (71-105). The same goes, with some modification, for the NT with the exception of Paul's speech at Miletus in Acts 20,17-38 (385-485). For the latter, cf., also, *Dupont*, Discours, especially 11-21 on the genre of the Farewell Discourse.
[39] *Cortès, loc. cit.* 56-61.
[40] *Cortès, loc. cit.* 62ff.
[41] *Cortès, loc. cit.* 64ff.
[42] *Cortès, loc. cit.* 66-70.
[43] *Cortès, loc. cit.* 66.
[44] *Cortès, loc. cit.* 69.
[45] *v. Nordheim*, Lehre 239f.
[46] *v. Nordheim, loc. cit.* 229-237.
[47] Cf., among others, *Hoskyns*[2] 495; *Dodd*, Tradition 54; *Lindars* 468f; *Schneider*, Abschiedsreden 109f; and *Grundmann*, Wort 62ff.
[48] Cf., *infra*, Chapter III.3. The thesis advocated there, that the section Jn 14,15-24 is consistently and thoroughly stamped with the covenant theology of the Old Testament, that is from the Deuteronomic and Deuteronomistic theology, finds, with respect to the genre of 'Farewell Discourse', an interesting parallel in *Michel*, Abschiedsrede 55f who reckons this genre to have arisen in the circle of the Deuteronomistic school.

ἐντέλλεσθαι ('charge') occurs only as a command of the Father with respect to Jesus (v. 31), but it nonetheless belongs significantly to the word-field of the chapter. The exhortation to brotherly love occurs only in the probably secondary 'overture' section 13,34f, but it is essentially grounded in the 'commandments' of Jesus as is indicated by the further development of the Johannine redaction in 15,9-17 (there also ἐντέλλομαι vv. 14.17).

The chapter is also dominated by predictions which refer to the relationship of Jesus with his disciples and their future destiny. At the beginning, in 13,33, stands the genre's characteristic address 'little children' (τεκνία) with a statement about the impending 'going away' of Jesus and the effect of this on the disciples. However, predictions of this kind are found throughout Chapter 14 (cf. vv. 2f.7a.12ff.16f.18-20.21-23.26.28) in connection with which apparently present sayings such as that on the coming of the adversary (v. 30) can also belong to the predictions: the coming of the 'ruler of this world' is, in fact, an eschatological event.

According to *Cortès*, an element of intercession can also belong to the genre of Farewell Discourse.[49] It occurs in our chapter both with respect to the prayer of the disciples in Jesus' name which the Father will fulfil (vv. 13f) and with respect to the prayer of Jesus to the Father to send the disciples on earth an advocate who will take on the role of Jesus (vv. 16f; cf. 26). To the extent that he becomes the representative and successor of Jesus, one can see in him an expression of the genre above all in its Old Testament predecessors.[50]

A direct reference to the death of the departing Jesus which, according to *Cortès*, can belong to the genre as a supplementary feature,[51] does not occur clearly in our text, but Jesus' departure is hinted at all the way through, up to the closing verses, and the introductory words in 13,1ff clearly present the speech and action of Jesus in the room of the Last Supper as the testament of the revealer and redeemer who is going to his death.

Among the contacts with the other genres, that with the genre of midrash appears to be of especial significance for the interpretation of Jn 14. According to *Cortès*, the genre of Farewell Discourse in the full sense appears first in the literature of Israel at a time when the Canon of Scripture was already more or less closed. Thus the post-biblical Jewish literature not seldom used as starting points the Old Testament account of the deaths or translation of godly men to fashion them into formal Farewell Discourses. Already in the Targum for the beginning of Jacob's blessing in Gen 49,1f, we come across a narrative, haggadic midrash on the exhortatory and predictive words of Jacob and the reaction

---

[49] *Cortès*, Discuros 372-376 offers it as one of the incidental elements of the Farewell Discourse genre.

[50] Cf. the reference to the successor in Deut 31; 1 Sam 12,1f; 1 Kgs 2,1-9; 1 Chron 28,1-28. Cf. also *Munck*, Discours 155f. *Cortès* overlooks this point.

[51] *Cortès*, Discursos 381-383 alleges the reference to death as one of the incidental features of the genre.

of his sons.[52] For its part, the apocryphal and pseudepigraphical literature deals with the dying moments or last farewells of the leading holy men of Israel. *Cortès* gives the example of the development of the Farewell Discourse of Abraham in Gen 25,5 in *Jub* 20,1-20; of the last words of Isaac in Gen 27,1-45; 35,27-29 in *Jub* 36,7-10; 37,4; or of the notice of the translation of Enoch in Gen 5,24, cf. 22, in the pseudepigraphical literature, for example in *1* (Ethiopian) *Enoch* (93,2) and *2* (Slavonic) *Enoch* (XIIf).[53] *J. Munck* has drawn similar examples from Hellenistic-Jewish literature.[54]

In interpreting Jn 14, therefore, we have to be open to the possibility that here too in this Farewell Discourse of Jesus, composed by the pen of John the evangelist, midrashic techniques have been used. This is true, not only in the sense that the words of Jesus (perhaps those about his approaching end, about the coming of the Son of Man etc) have been worked over in a homiletic manner and so brought into their present form as a Farewell Discourse of Jesus, as Lindars now thinks,[55] but also in the sense that traditional material from the Old Testament could have and has been worked over in this Farewell Discourse of the Lord within the circle of his disciples. Here, we must also reckon with the possibility that not only haggadic, that is narrative, techniques have been employed, but also halakhic ones, that is, techniques focused on the exposition of the Law. The great importance which is awarded to the word-field of 'love' of Jesus, 'commandments' and 'keeping' the commandments or 'words' of Jesus in the central section, vv. 15-24, is confirmation of this hypothesis. Besides this, we have also to reckon with the employment of prophetic and wisdom traditions. The course of the individual exegeses in the following chapters should strengthen this working theory.

---

[52] *Cortès, loc. cit.* 298-365 and the tabular summary.
[53] *Cortès, loc. cit,* 64-66.
[54] *Munck,* Discours, especially 158f.
[55] *Lindars* 468f.

II. The Announcement of Jesus' Departure as a Midrash on the Psalms (vv. 1-14)

Having placed the first Johannine Farewell Discourse in its context and looked into the question of its literary unity, its formal structure and its literary genre, we can now get down to the analysis of the individual texts themselves. As was shown in Chapter I, John 14 can be divided into three sections composed of verses 1-14, 15-24 and 25-31. The working hypothesis which forms the basis of the following investigations runs as follows: that behind verses 1-9 (14) of John 14 in particular there lies an early Christian tradition which interprets the Passion of Jesus in the light of Ps 42/43. For verses 15-24, another complex of themes from the Old Testament can be specified as constituting the basis of the section, namely the covenant theology of Deuteronomy.[1] In the closing verses (25-31), themes from the previous sections are taken up again but enriched by a third complex which must feed on the prophetic tradition of the eschatological gifts of salvation.[2]

As pointed out in the previous chapter, verses 1-14 of John 14 are determined by his ascension: Jesus goes to the Father and as a result it is important to remain linked to him in faith. This is now to be developed more closely in several stages.

1. The Structure of the Passage

It seems that the questions of Thomas (v. 5) and Philip (v. 8) help to introduce the revelatory words of Jesus. The question of Thomas shows non-understanding, the one of Philip misunderstanding.[3] This formal criterion, however, is clearly not sufficient to reveal the principle on which our section is being constructed. Further indications of language and content must be taken into account. Thus, the catchword 'believing' (πιστεύειν) binds together the whole section from v. 1 to vv. 10-12 to which vv. 13f are attached through conformity of meaning. The "going away" (πορεύεσθαι) of Jesus in vv. 2f is also pursued in the following verses by means of the synonym of the ὑπάγειν of Jesus from vv. 4f which is connected with the catchword of the "way" (ὁδός). The latter for its part holds together vv. 4-6. The "coming to the Father" of vv. 6f, which is used almost synonymously with 'to know the Father (or Jesus)' and 'to have seen him (or Jesus)' or 'to be shown' them, leads to the following verses (vv. 6-9).

Verses 10-14 seem to be held together by the unity of the Father and the Son with an extension through connecting catchwords in vv. 12ff: what it means

---

[1] Cf., further, in Chapter III.
[2] Cf., *infra*, Chapter IV.
[3] Cf., on the genre of misunderstandings, *Leroy*, Rätsel. Cf., also, n. 87 *infra*.

for Jesus to be in the Father and the Father in him (v. 10a) is explained through the union of the Father and the Son in word (v. 10b) and work (vv. 10c-11). The catchword "works" leads consequently to a saying on the "works" carried out through faith in Jesus (v. 12) and then returns to the "doing" of Jesus (ποιήσω twice) in reply to the prayers of believers (13f).

There is actually no continuation within our section of the theme of the "coming again" of Jesus in v. 3. As already indicated and as is to be shown in the following chapter, its development through different models of reinterpretation of the early Church's parousia expectation is to be located in verses 15-24. Thus verses 1-3 are arranged at one and the same time on an ascending and a descending course: from the thoughts of the "going away" of Jesus and of his "coming again". In this way, since the theme of the "going away" and "coming" of Jesus will also be taken up again in the concluding verses 25-31, they serve as an introduction for the whole chapter in which these two chief motifs are developed, first individually and then together. Verse 4, with its connection to both sides can then be seen as a transition.

Thus the following structure may serve as a basis for our ensuing investigation:

vv. 1-3   Statement of theme: The "going away" and "coming again" of Jesus
vv. 4-6   Jesus the way to the Father
vv. 7-9   Whoever sees him sees the Father
vv. 10-14 The union of Jesus and the Father in word and work

2. Some Aporias

The starting point for the new tradition-historical interpretation of, in particular, the opening verses of Jn 14 which is being presented in this study is a row of aporias of language and content. They are already present in a concentrated manner in v. 1.[4] A, largely psychologically motivated, transition from the words of Peter with respect to the announcement of Jesus' 'going away' (13,36-38) to 'Let not your hearts be troubled' in 14,1 is unsatisfactory.[5] It may explain this transition up to a certain point, but where else does the Fourth Evangelist show himself to be concerned with psychology? Could there not be a theological reason behind the warning in the face of the disciples' 'distress'? But if this should turn out to be the case, what could it be?

---

[4] Cf., in this connection, *Beutler*, Psalm 42/43, especially 47f.
[5] So, among others, *Holtzmann-Bauer* 243f; *Bauer*[3] 177; *Bernard* 531; *de la Potterie*, Voie 914; *Sanders-Mastin* 272; *Schulz* 183. The psychological state of the disciples is vividly portrayed by *O. Schaefer*, Sinn 210f, and *Haenchen* 474.

Within v. 1, then, the oddities and questions pile up: Why is there no agreement between ὑμῶν (your, plural) and καρδία (heart, singular)?[6] Is the repeated πιστεύετε (πιστεύειν = 'believe') in v. 1b to be understood as a statement,[7] a command[8] or a question?[9] How are we to explain the fact, only here in John, that 'belief' (πιστεύετε εἰς) refers to God and only then to Jesus?[10] And how is it that, again in distinction from the linguistic usage of the rest of the Gospel of John, the verb here has the sense of "trust" ('do not be troubled', cf. v. 1a)?[11] Finally: what connection exists between v. 1a and v. 1b? And further: what is the link between Jesus' command in v. 1 and his saying about the many "mansions" in (his) Father's house in v. 2? Is it newly created by Johannine redaction as has been accepted right up to the most recent work of G. Fischer,[12] or could it have been part of the evangelist's tradition? The same question arises in connection with the link between 'Father's House' and 'mansions' in v. 2a.[13] In v. 2b, we have to explain both the connection of εἰ δὲ μή, εἶπον ἂν ὑμῖν ('if it were not so, would I have told you?') with either the preceding[14] or the following[15] material, and also the sense of ὅτι: is it to be translated here with "that"[16] or "because"?[17] On the answer to this depends the further question whether we

---

[6] The connection of ὑμῶν and καρδία is mostly explained as a Semitism. So *Schlatter* 291; *Lindars* 470; *Brown* 618.
[7] Only rarely is the repeated πιστεύετε read as an indicative: thus *Behler* 91; *Sanders* 320, n. 4. More commonly is it the first πιστεύετε which is translated as indicative with the second as imperative: so *Lagrange* 372f; *Lightfoot* 257.272; *Wikenhauser* 263; *Brown* 617. Bultmann 463 n. 1, understands πιστεύετε as indicative, in fact, on both occasions, but he formulates the first as a question (cf., *infra*, n. 9). Nevertheless 'the sentence is of course an indirect exhortation' (*ibidem*).
[8] The majority of interpreters tend towards a double imperative, from *Westcott* 200 through *Loisy*² 404 and *Barrett*² 456 to *Schnackenburg* III 61, *J. Becker* 460f and *Haenchen* 474.
[9] Cf. *Bultmann* 463 who formulates the first πιστεύετε as a question: 'Do you believe in God?'
[10] Cf. *Schnackenburg* I, Exkurs 7: Das joh. Glauben, especially 510. Only Jn 12,44 and 5,24 (with the verb πιστεύειν but construed with the dative) come at all close.
[11] So *Loisy*² 404; *Barrett*² 456; *Schnackenburg* III 65. For the opposing position, cf. *Bultmann* 463 n. 2. He rejects the sense of "trust" because John does not know of such a believing. *Brown* 618 refers to the Hebrew word for 'believe' with the root 'mn whose meaning as steadfastness and imperturbability he would like to transfer to the doubled πιστεύετε.
[12] *Fischer*, Wohnungen 20-27.
[13] *Fischer*, Wohnungen 295ff, regards this linking of motifs as a creation of the evangelist.
[14] *Westcott* 201; *Barrett*² 381; *Wikenhauser* 264; *Brown* 617, among others, allot it to the preceding material.
[15] *Zahn* 553; *Holtzmann-Bauer* 244; *Bultmann* 464 n. 3; *Schulz* 183; *Becker* 457 allot it to the following material (v. 2c).
[16] So, among others, *Holtzmann-Bauer* 244; *Zahn* 553; *Bultmann* 464, n. 3; *Strathmann* 198; *Lindars* 471; *Becker* 457; *Haenchen* 470.
[17] Cf., among others, *Weiss* 397; *Barrett*² 457; *Wikenhauser* 264; *Behler*, Abschiedsworte 95; *Morris* 636.639.

have a statement[18] or a question[19] in v. 2b. The frequency of aporias precisely in the first couple of verses justifies the undertaking of a new tradition-critical investigation here. It will also shed light on some peculiarities in the following verses which until now have been awaiting a satisfactory explanation. To these belong the "Way" motif in verses 4-6, the arrangement in v. 6 of the three images and concepts used to describe Jesus, 'Way', 'Truth' and 'Life' as well as the connection between the "Way" motif and that of "seeing" God in vv. 7-9. That verses 10-14 only develop the idea of the unity of Jesus and the Father as set out in the previous verses will be further demonstrated below.[20] Thus, in fact, the new interpretation of the section from its beginning is supported by the aporias which are encountered there.

3. The Tradition behind the Passage

Most of the aporias exhibited here can be accounted for if we can posit a common tradition behind the section Jn 14, 1-9 (14). Behind this tradition, in its turn, lies Psalm 42/43 understood as a witness to Jesus and his Passion.[21] That here we have an instance of a double psalm is a conclusion that is now generally accepted by Old Testament scholarship.[22] The psalm is constructed symmetrically: at the end of each of the three strophes, after four or five verses, respectively, there occurs a refrain: 'Why are you cast down, O my soul, and why are you so disquieted within me? Hope in God; for I shall again praise him, my help and my God' (Ps 42,6.12; 43,5).

It is well known that, in order to demonstrate the compatibility of the suffering and death of Jesus with the will of God, the early Church had recourse not only to the 'Law and the Prophets' but also to the Psalms (cf. Lk 24,27 with 24,44 where the 'Psalms' are expressly mentioned along with the 'Law and the Prophets'). In this connection, the most commonly used psalms are Ps 22, 'My God, my God, why hast thou forsaken me?' and Ps 69 'Save me, O God'. But Ps 42/43 was apparently also used early as a Passion Psalm. This happened above all in the Gethsemane tradition. According to Mk 14,34 (= Mt 26,38), on the Mount of Olives, Jesus says to his disciples: 'My soul is very sorrowful, even to death'. At least in its first half (περίλυπός ἐστιν ἡ ψυχή μου), this formulation appears to be taken from Ps 41,6.12; 42,5 LXX where it says: 'Why are you cast down, O my soul?' (ἵνα τί περίλυπος εἶ ψυχή).

---

[18] Among others, *Zahn* 553; *Loisy*² 404f; *Behler*, Abschiedsworte 95; *Lindars* 471 go for a statement.
[19] Among others, *Holtzmann-Bauer* 244; *Bultmann* 464 n 3; *Schulz* 183; *Becker* 457; *Haenchen* 470 opt for a question.
[20] Cf., *infra,* section 4, pp. 45-47.
[21] Cf. *Beutler*, Psalm 42/43, especially 48-54.
[22] Cf. *Kraus*, Psalmen I 318; *Dahood*, Psalms I 255.

In Anglo-Saxon exegesis, the suggestion was early made that in Jn 12,27f, the fourth evangelist may allude to the Synoptic Gethsemane tradition, and so, like Mark in Mk 14,34 pick up an expression from Ps 41,7 LXX:[23] the νῦν ἡ ψυχή μου τετάρακται ('Now is my soul troubled') of Jn 12,27 corresponds to the πρὸς ἐμαυτὸν ἡ ψυχή μου ἐταράχθη ('my soul has been troubled within me') of the psalm. That here we are reminded not only of Ps 6,4 (f) – with the following σῶσόν με ('save me')[24] - but at the very least also with Ps 41 LXX is reinforced by the fact that Ps 41,7 LXX is employed in two other places in the wider context of the Johannine Passion narrative as already suggested by *Bernard*[25] and *C. H. Dodd*.[26] Here we have the accounts of Jesus' being 'troubled in Spirit' before the grave of his friend Lazarus in Jn 11,33 and in the face of his own death before the departure of the betrayer in Jn 13,21. We have attempted to show elsewhere[27] that the unusual reflexive ἐτάραξεν ἑαυτόν (literally: 'he troubled himself'), which in this form has no parallels in the Old and New Testaments, can most easily be explained with reference to Ps 41,7 LXX, something which receives confirmation through its reappearance in the clear context of the Passion of Jesus in Jn 13,21. There, anyhow, it seems that the evangelist has substituted πνεῦμα ("spirit") for ψυχή ("soul") as the seat of Jesus' emotions as, among others, *C. H. Dodd* already guessed.[28] In fact, Dodd shows moreover a linguistic connection with Jn 14,1 (27) where the expression is simply changed into the plural and καρδία ("heart") substituted for ψυχή.[29] Behind the use of the poetic line from Ps 41,7 LXX in the Johannine Passion narrative, and already with Mark and his parallels, *C. H. Dodd* sees an early Christian testimony which knows of Ps 42/43 (41/42 LXX) as a Passion psalm.[30] Precisely the fact that Mark could have recourse to Ps 41,6.12; 42,5, whereas John went for Ps 41,7 LXX shows, according to *Dodd*, that for both evangelists (or their tradition), it was not a single scriptural citation but the whole psalm which lays behind the Passion of Jesus.[31]

Dodd[32] finds at the end of Jn 14 in the already discussed[33] 'Departure Signal': 'Rise, let us go hence' (ἐγείρεσθε, ἄγωμεν ἐντεῦθεν Jn 14,31, cf. Mk 14,42; Mt 26,46: ἐγείρεσθε ἄγωμεν) confirmation of the fact that a Gethsemane tradi-

---

[23] Cf. *Bernard* 436; *Dodd*, Interpretation 373.408 n. 11. 425; Tradition 69f.80.130; *Brown* 475; *Lindars*, Apologetic 99 n. 2.
[24] Cf. *Lindars, loc. cit*; *Freed*, Psalm 42/43, 65ff.
[25] *Bernard, loc. cit.*
[26] *Dodd*, Tradition 33.37f for Jn 13,21.
[27] Cf. *Beutler*, Psalm 42/43; 40-44.
[28] *Dodd*, Interpretation 223; Tradition 37 with n. 3.
[29] *Dodd*, Tradition *loc. cit.*
[30] *Dodd*, Tradition 33.38.
[31] *Dodd*, Tradition 38; but *Lindars, loc cit.*, is sceptical.
[32] *Dodd*, Interpretation 406-409; Tradition 72.
[33] Cf., *supra*, Chapter 1, Section 1.

tion stood at the disposal of John the evangelist which also found a place in Mark.

In both cases, Jesus' command is based on the 'coming' of the adversary – in Mark, the approach of the betrayer (14,41b), in John that of the 'Ruler of this world' (14,30). In both cases, there is also a connection with Jesus' readiness, to go to his 'hour' (Mk 14,41) or to carry out his Father's commandment (Jn 14,31). The reference to his 'hour' occurs in another, related, context in John (Jn 12,27f; 17,1). As in the Synoptic Gethsemane tradition, in John too, Jesus uses the prayer-address "Father" on this occasion. Similarly, the evangelist lets Jesus pronounce the saying about the 'cup' which the Father has given him to drink in the arrest scene in the garden (Jn 18,11; cf. Mk 14,36 par.).

There is thus no doubt that the fourth evangelist is aware at least of the content of the Gethsemane tradition of the Synoptics and that he has employed elements of its tradition at various points in his own Passion narrative.[34] It is also indisputable that, in connection with the tradition of Jesus' agony in the garden, John knew of Ps 42/43 (41/42 LXX) and adopted it in his Passion narrative and, in fact, always where he speaks of the "distress" of Jesus (Jn 12,27; 11,33; 13,21).

But it seems that we can go a step further. The "troubling" of hearts is also the subject in Jn 14,1.27. C. H. Dodd notices the parallel to the already mentioned texts and observes: 'John seems prepared to use ψυχή or πνεῦμα indifferently as an equivalent for נפשׁ. In xiv. 1, καρδία is used with ταράσσειν, without difference of sense (cf. Ps. xxxvii. 11, ἡ καρδία μου ἐταράχθη)'.[35] What has escaped Dodd is the fact that there are good grounds for the use of Ps 41/42 in Jn 14,1.27 also. Only here we no longer have speech in the first person singular which Jesus takes from the prayer of the psalm as he goes to his Passion in Jn 12,27; the words no longer even refer to him, as in Jn 11,33 and 13,21, but are in the second person plural, referring to his disciples: 'Let not your hearts be troubled'. This seems to be a taking up of Ps 41,7 LXX, but there also seems to be an allusion to the refrain Ps 41,6.12; 42,5 LXX (as already in the Synoptic tradition): 'Why are you cast down, my soul, and why are you disquieted within me?' (ἵνα τί περίλυπος εἶ ψυχή καὶ ἵνα τί συνταράσσεις με;). The conversion into the plural can be explained by the new use of the psalm: no longer is it concerned with the 'trouble' of Jesus. After the departure of the betrayer (Jn 13,30), the 'hour' of his "glorification" of the Father and by the Father has arrived (Jn 13,31f: νῦν ['Now']). No longer fear and pain and the power of evil threaten Je-

---

[34] Cf., *infra*, Chapter IV, 3.2 with n. 62.

[35] Dodd, Tradition 37 n. 3. Freed, Psalm 42/43: 65, refers also to Job 37,1; Pss 54,5; 108,22; 142,4 LXX for the connection of ταράσσεσθαι and καρδία. Although these texts could have influenced the linguistic expression of Jn 14,1, their mobilisation for the elucidation of Jn 14,1-14 as a whole is less helpful. The latter, in fact, reveals itself to have further numerous contacts with Ps 41/42 as will be shown in the following. For the reason why the evangelist probably substituted καρδία in Jn 14,1.27 for ψυχή in Ps 42f, cf. the following.

sus himself, but rather his disciples. The variations in the formulation lead to the understanding that for the evangelist, the psalm tradition was known not only in its Greek but also in its Hebrew or possibly Aramaic form. When ψυχή ("soul") appears here replaced by καρδία ("heart"), this could go back to the context of Jn 14,1: in the short exchange between Jesus and Peter in Jn 13,36-38, the subject is Peter's alleged readiness to "give up" his "life" for Jesus. In semitising fashion, ψυχή is used twice here for "life". Here too, in the background, lies the Hebrew נפשׁ "breath of life". Since the word has now been used twice in this sense in verses 13,37 and 38, the evangelist could not use it in 14,1 in its stricter Greek meaning as seat of the emotions. Thus the substitution by καρδία seems defensible. The word crops up again in this sense in (the probably post-Johannine) Jn 16,6.22.

The decisive reason why we consider that the tradition of Ps 42/43 is to be detected behind Jn 14,1a is the striking closeness of the following sentences in John to the theme and expressions of this very psalm. Let us remind ourselves of the various aporias which exegetes have until now located in the half verse 14,1b. They all become clear and are satisfactorily resolved when we take into account that behind this half verse lies the second line of the refrain in our double psalm Ps 41,6.12; 42,5 LXX: ἔλπισον ἐπὶ τὸν θεόν ('trust in God'). Here too, of course, John has not taken over his source word for word: 'trust in God' becomes 'believe in God and believe in me'. Why? Just as the substantive ἐλπίς ('trust', 'hope') is absent from the Fourth Gospel (and indeed from the first three), so also the verb is scarcely encountered. It is used only once, namely in Jn 5,45 where the subject is Moses 'on whom you set your hope' (εἰς ὃν ὑμεῖς ἠλπίκατε). Otherwise it is the verb πιστεύειν ('believe') that dominates the vocabulary and the thought of the evangelist. In the fourth gospel, it is focused throughout on Jesus and his mission in connection with which the predominant construction is πιστεύειν εἰς ('to believe in').[36] Precisely for this reason the evangelist had to change his pre-text into πιστεύετε εἰς τὸν θεὸν καὶ εἰς ἐμὲ πιστεύετε ('believe in God and believe in me'). The closeness of the Greek πιστεύειν to the ἐλπίζειν of the LXX would have made this transposition easy.[37] For the fourth evangelist, to trust in God means to believe in him, and to believe in God means to believe in Jesus. The underlying Hebrew version of the psalm with the verb *bṭḥ*,[38] 'to feel oneself secure, to be carefree', 'to rely on something

---

[36] In John, it is found altogether 36 times out of 98: cf. *Schnackenburg* I 508.510.

[37] Cf. *Bauer*, Wörterbuch 1311f, at least for the religious use of the word. If *Freed, loc. cit.* (68) would like to reject any idea that πιστεύειν and ἐλπίζειν are synonymous in the sense of 'trust', on the grounds of the weak meaning of ἐλπίζειν in Jn 5,45, equally it has to be pointed out that in that place it is a question of only the negative sense of "trust". It does not follow that this can make a contribution to the positive use of the concept in John.

[38] Cf. *A. Jepsen, bṭḥ* in ThWAT I (1970) 608-615, here: 610. Moreover, the LXX renders the Hebrew *bṭḥ* in the negative sense of trust in created things with πεποιθέναι, but in the positive sense as trust in God for the most part with ἐλπίζειν.

or someone' would have made possible the transposition in Greek from the one to the other.

At the same time, we would now have found an answer to the aporias in v. 1: not only have we been able to produce a tradition which binds together the two half verses and which is able to explain the transition to Chapter 14 and from 14,1a to 1b, without having to have recourse to psychology; but we can also resolve the linguistic difficulties in 14,1. The lack of congruence between ὑμῶν ("your") and καρδία ("heart") can be interpreted as a Semitism, but is still better explained as the adoption of a pre-text with a singular subject. The question as to whether the first πιστεύετε constitutes a statement, a question or a command allows itself to be clearly decided in favour of a command, and so the second πιστεύετε would be decided in the same sense (= "believe"). Moreover, John's departure from his normal linguistic usage, in which he consistently uses πιστεύειν for 'believe' and not 'trust', finds an adequate explanation in the recourse to our psalm text, provided that we also realise that through the καὶ εἰς ἐμὲ πιστεύετε ('and believe in me') the connection with the usual Johannine linguistic usage is to be found.

We now come to verse 2. For the purposes of our tradition-historical hypothesis, we next have to explain the connection between verses 1 and 2, the command of Jesus to steadfastness and belief, and his saying about the 'many mansions' in the 'house' of his 'Father'. Are here just motifs from various religious and tradition critical origins strung together, as generally supposed,[39] or do these sentences form an already pre-Johannine and closely woven set of motifs from a single text that is to be expounded here?

We shall concentrate first on Jesus' saying in v. 2a, 'In my Father's house are many mansions'. Both the expressions employed here have met with an abundance of possible meanings, something which is reflected in the unusual number of monographs devoted to this verse. Basically the way in which this double expression is interpreted by authors can be shown to tend in two different directions. One group of authors understands both the saying about the 'Father's (that is, God's) house' as well as that about the 'mansions' situated in it against the background of Gnostic concepts. Among these belong the studies of *Bultmann*,[40] *Widengren*[41] and others. They understand the 'Father's House' as

---

[39] This hypothesis is so general that *Fischer*, Wohnungen is even able to confine his investigation to Jn 14,2f. Similarly *Freed*, Psalm 42/43: 69f in connection with the expressions: 'my Father's house' and 'mansions'. In fact, *Freed* identifies two places which have linked both expressions as in Ps 42/43 (Ps 54[55],15f; Gen 24,23), but the παροικίαι in Ps 54[55],15f do not refer to the dwellings of God and the *bjt-'bjk* and *mqwm* in Gen 24,23 cannot be thought of in any way as 'house' or 'dwellings of God'. Nevertheless, it is interesting that Freed considers that Ps 54(55) embodies elements of Jn 14,1 and 2 (68). However, for the use of this psalm for Jn 14,1.2. one would have to observe what is said above (παροικίαι are houses for wicked men) as well as the fact that Ps 54(55) produces no further motifs for Jn 14.
[40] *Bultmann* 462ff.

'House of Life' or 'Kingdom' through which the successful souls pass as stages on their heavenly journey to consummation. In fact, in his voluminous monograph on Jn 14,2, *G. Fischer* has succeeded in showing that this concept is probably secondary in the Gnostic texts and dependent on the speculations of Jewish apocalyptic thought.[42] In biblical material, however, evidence for the 'House of God (of the Father)' with reference to heaven is difficult to find. A reference to the temple appears to be much more likely. This is so not only because the nearest parallel to our text in John, in 2,16, has this sense: 'You shall not make my Father's house a house of trade', a meaning confirmed by the concluding citation from Scripture: 'Zeal for thy house will consume me' (v. 17; Ps 69,10), but also because elsewhere in the Old Testament 'House of God' consistently signifies the temple.[43] How then does it come to refer to 'heaven' and the 'mansions' therein, the meaning that seems to be presumed here?

Again, these 'mansions' give rise to an analogous problem of meaning: are they to be understood as 'staging posts' on the heavenly journey (of the Gnostics),[44] as 'camping sites' during the liberation of God's people in their new Exodus,[45] as rooms in an otherworldly palace[46] or just as the existence of Christians in the realm of faith? [47] With these questions also, our tradition historical hypothesis may be of further assistance.

Earlier it has fallen to the genre criticism of the Psalms to point out that Ps 42/43 represents two different genres simultaneously.[48] On the one hand, it is an 'individual lament', and as such can be the expression of the lament of the 'suffering righteous'. In this sense, it is clearly used by Mark, if not encountered before as an early Christian 'testimony'. The evangelist John was able to use it in this way for the 'troubling' of Jesus when he alluded to Ps 41,7 LXX and 41,6.12; 42,5 LXX in Jn 11,33; 12,27; 13,21. But, at the same time, the psalm embraces elements of another genre: it is also related to the 'pilgrimage song': it is the expression of the desire of an Israelite who is sojourning a long way off

---

[41] *Widengren*, Maison 12-15; cf. *Bauer*[3] 178. In a metaphorical, not necessarily Gnostic sense the „House of the Father" is understood by *Schaefer*, Sinn, and *Aalen*, Reign, 238f.

[42] *Fischer*, Wohnungen, II. Hauptteil, 115-298.

[43] Cf. *H. A. Hoffner, bjt*, in ThWAT I (1973) 629-638; here, 634f.

[44] Cf. *Widengren* 9-12; in a non-Gnostic sense, *Westcott* 200.

[45] Thus, with reference to Deut 1,29-33, *Guilding*, Gospel 87f; *Boismard*, Évolution 520f; *de la Potterie*, Voie 514f; *Estalayo Alonso*, Vuelta 30-33, who sees here a particular closeness to the Targum. Cf., *infra*, for v. 2b.

[46] Cf. *Bernard* 533; *Sanders-Mastin* 321; *Lindars* 470.

[47] *Schaefer*, Sinn 213: Jesus speaks here of 'his Father's kingdom of power and love which embraces heaven and earth'. According to *Gundry*, House 70, we are faced here with 'spiritual positions in Christ' both in the hearts of the believers and also with God. *Heise* too, Bleiben 100, speaks of the 'Room' or 'House of Love' in which the many mansions are situated.

[48] Cf. *Gunkel-Begrich*, Einleitung 193.310 with n. 19; *Kraus*, Psalmen I^2 318. In the fifth edition 1978, 473, Kraus arranges the Psalm under the 'Gebetslieder'.

under Mount Hermon (cf. Ps 41,7 LXX) and longing for the sanctuary of Jerusalem as the place and centre of help against his enemies. It is in this situation that the one who prays can say: 'These things I remember, as I pour out my soul: how I went with the throng, and led them in procession to the *house of God*, with glad shouts and songs of thanksgiving, a multitude keeping festival' (Ps 42,5). And in the third strophe of the double psalm it says: 'Oh send out thy light and thy truth; let them lead me, let them bring me to thy holy hill and to thy *dwelling*!' (Ps 43,3). A survey reveals that this is the only psalm which mentions together the 'house of God' and the 'dwellings' of the Most High. Can we make bold to think that in these elements of Ps 42/43, which is now being understood as a Pilgrim Song, we can see the continuation of the psalm tradition we have postulated for Jn 14,1?

Linguistically the taking up of 'House of God' and 'dwelling' near God can be wholly justified. Indeed, the fourth evangelist speaks of the οἰκία τοῦ πατρός μου ('my Father's house') while the LXX version of the Psalter uses the more or less synonymous οἶκος τοῦ θεοῦ ('God's house'). In fact, οἰκία occurs instead of οἶκος through a preference of the fourth evangelist as well as to indicate, through a lexical nuance, a dwelling of some spaciousness (cf. Jn 8,35). That Jesus calls God his 'Father' is conspicuous not only in the other places in the Fourth Gospel where he speaks of the temple as 'God's house' or his 'Father's house' (cf., *supra*, for Jn 2,16) but also on further occasions (cf. Jn 5,17f; 8,19; 10,18.25.29.37 and frequently). The designation of the 'mansion' in Jn 14,2 comes even closer to the description and idea in the double psalm. First of all, different from most translations, the psalm has the plural not the singular. The Septuagint speaks of σκηνώματα and so reproduces the Hebrew *mšknwtjk*. The expression in Hebrew means simply 'dwelling', in Greek 'tent', 'tabernacle' or 'dwelling', and causes one to think of the Exodus tradition of the Ark of the Covenant and the 'Tent of Meeting' in P.[49] In the New Testament and in John, the expression μοναί / μονή, here and in the parallel at 14,23, is unique. Commentators hold different views as to whether John found it lying in the tradition[50] or coined it himself in view of his preference for μένειν = 'abide' as a theological term.[51] The way shown by us indicates a mediating solution: the fourth evangelist found in his psalm tradition the saying about the σκηνώματα or *mschknwtjk*, that is, the tabernacle or 'dwellings' of God, and coined his neologism simply by analogy with his customary usage, not least in the Johannine Farewell Discourses.

---

[49] Cf. *A. R. Hulst*, schkn dwell, in THAT II (1976) 904-909; *Liddell-Scott*, Lexicon, under σκήνωμα, σκήνημα and σκηνή.

[50] Thus, apparently, *Boismard*, Évolution 518-521, who understands vv. 1-3 as tradition, and *J. Becker*, Abschiedsreden 221, who recognises an 'Offenbarungswort' of the Johannine community tradition in vv. 2f (*ibid.*, for older authors).

[51] *Brown* 619; *Schnackenburg* III 69; cf. *Heise*, Bleiben 93.

However there remains a difficulty: how on earth could a psalm which speaks in a very personal way of the longing for the earthly sanctuary in Jerusalem as the place of help become the expression of a longing for the heavenly sanctuary, for the 'house of God' and its 'mansions'? Here a development can be shown which can make such a transposition understandable in the light of contemporary Jewish texts. In the first place, apocalyptic Judaism knows of the 'dwellings' of the righteous with God in the age to come.[52] Then, rabbinic Judaism already shows an early tendency to refer, either in whole or in part, what were originally meant as thoroughly this-worldly sayings from Scripture to the age to come. Thus, in the Targum to the Psalms, the early translation of the Psalms into Aramaic for use in the post-Exilic synagogue services, promises for the future can be taken in relation to the age to come, the future world, by means of glosses. In this way, statements which refer to 'God's house' can also be understood in an eschatological way. Thus before the saying in Ps 65,5 'We shall be satisfied with the goodness of thy house, thy holy temple!', the Targumist inserts the preface: 'The righteous will say'.[53] Thus the initial reference to the earthly sanctuary subsequently – after the destruction of the second temple[54] - receives an eschatological adjustment. Similarly, statements about God's 'dwelling' in his sanctuary in Jerusalem can also experience a new, eschatological meaning. Ps 46,5 speaks about the sanctuary in Jerusalem: 'There is a river whose streams make glad the city of God, the holy habitation of the Most High.' In the Targum this becomes: *'Nations like rivers and their sources will* come and make glad the city of God; *and they will pray in the house of the* sanctuary *of the Lord*, in the tabernacle of the Most High'.[55] If the original psalm describes the earthly Jerusalem as surrounded by life-giving streams (an admittedly rather Utopian picture), it thus now becomes the portrayal of an eschatological pilgrimage of the nations to Mount Zion, as expected in apocalyptic circles. A similarly free development of the statements about God's 'house' and his 'dwellings' is to be encountered in other parts of the Targum to the Psalms.[56]

---

[52] The evidence is gathered and evaluated by *Fischer*, Wohnungen 137-178; for the conceptually contrasting Qumran texts, 179-185.
[53] Reproduced after the Polyglot of *Walton* III 182.
[54] The Encyclopaedia Judaica IV 849, cf. 842, puts the Targum on the Psalms later than the other Targums although it contains older traditions. Cf. *Stemberger*, Geschichte 83. *Bacher*, Targum 471, and *Le Déaut*, Introduction 132-136, argue for a not so late origin and a Palestinian origin.
[55] Text and (Latin) translation from *Walton*. I have italicised the words added to the Hebrew text of the psalm.
[56] Ps 65,5 becomes 'God's house' in the Targum as the place of the benefits of eschatological salvation through the fact that it adds the words 'and the righteous will say' before the sentence 'We shall be satisfied with the goodness of thy house, the goodness of thy temple!'. In another context, Pss 63,5 and 116,13 find themselves with glosses which refer to the world to come. Cf. *Beutler*, Psalm 42/43: 50 with n. 1.

The paraphrase of Psalm 42/43 in the Targum still does not permit us to recognise an eschatological significance for the sanctuary. This is certainly the case, however, in the – admittedly later – midrash on the Psalms. This stems from post-Talmudic times but includes material that goes back to the golden age of rabbinic exegesis, the time of the emergence of the Talmud.[57] Here the 'dwellings' of God are now referred to the end time. Psalm 43,3 is cited and paraphrased as follows: 'Therefore it says: send thy light and thy truth that they may lead me, bring me to thy holy mountain and to thy dwelling, as it says in the account of the exodus from Egypt: "bring them and plant them on thy own mountain etc." (Ex 15,17), so will they also come in the future to thy holy mountain and to thy dwellings, for it says in v. 4: I will come to the altar of God'. That with 'the future' the 'age to come' is intended is neatly expressed in the more recent English translation by *W. G. Braude*.[58] In the period immediately close to the composition of the Fourth Gospel, that is to say, at the beginning of the second century A.D., a text from Sifre brings us to the oldest Jewish commentary on Deuteronomy. Here the subject is the seven classes of the righteous who have found their dwellings close to God in the Garden of Eden. They are arranged in concentric circles around the 'face' of God in the Holy of Holies. The starting point is Deut 1,10 where the commentator seems to have heard the 'this day' as an allusion to the seven day week: *"And behold, ye are this day as the stars of heaven for multitude* (1:10): Behold, you are as eternal as the day. Hence the Sages have said: There are seven groups of the righteous in Paradise, one higher than the other: the first, *Surely the righteous shall give thanks unto Thy name; the upright shall dwell in Thy presence* (Ps. 140:14); the second, *Happy is the man whom Thou choosest, and bringest near* (Ps. 65:5); the third, *Happy are they that dwell in Thy House* (Ps. 84:5); the fourth, *Lord, who shall dwell in Thy Tabernacle?* (Ps. 15:1); the fifth, *Who shall dwell upon Thy holy mountain?* (Ps. 15:1); the sixth, *Who shall ascend into the mountain of the Lord?* (Ps. 24:3); the seventh, *and who shall stand in His holy place?* (Ps. 24:3)"[59]

This text is remarkable from three points of view: it knows of different dwelling places of the righteous with God; it situates them in the Garden of Eden, that is, in Paradise;[60] and, without exception, it argues for this from the psalms, in part those which expressly concern 'God's house' or his 'tent'.

The same idea is known also to a text from the midrash to Psalm 11, §6, which *H. Strack* and *H. L. Billerbeck* cite in immediate connection with the

---

[57] Cf. *Braude*, Midrash I XI f. XXXI; *Strack-Stemberger*, Einleitung 294f.

[58] *Braude*, Midrash I 445.

[59] *Ljungman*, Sifre 25f; English text according to Sifre: a Tannaitic commentary on the book of Deuteronomy / transl. from the Hebrew with introd. and notes by *Reuven Hammer* (Yale Judaica Series 24), New Haven [etc.]: Yale University Press 1986, 34f; cf. *Strack-Billerbeck* I 209.

[60] Cf. *Volz*, Eschatologie § 49,4 (pp. 413-418).

foregoing text.[61] There it says at the end: 'If the man was righteous, the words "Clear a place for such-and-such a righteous man" are spoken before him, and he passes from dwelling-place to dwelling-place until he beholds the face of the Presence. Therefore it is said *The upright shall behold his face* (Ps 11:7)'. Here the thought is clearly of the situation of the soul after death as being in the Garden of Eden, as the context shows.

We now have sufficient material for comparison to be able to understand why the fourth evangelist could have recourse to Ps 42/43 when he wished to give a biblical foundation to Jesus' promise of the preparation of heavenly mansions for his own. Already during the lifetime of the fourth evangelist, that is, not long after the destruction of the Second Temple, people seem to have begun to interpret eschatologically those texts in the Psalter that speak of the temple, 'God's house', and his 'dwellings'. Two models can be differentiated: either these texts were interpreted in a general way with reference to the future in which God would allow the temple to be rebuilt or they were referred to the final situation of the righteous in which they would find a place for themselves after their death in heavenly 'dwellings'. That Ps 42/43 was included under such interpretation is shown at least by the late midrash on the Psalms at Ps 43,3.

The fourth evangelist could develop Jesus' word of promise about the 'many mansions' out of the passion psalm 42/43 already quoted in Jn 14,1 in this way since the genre of this psalm was, in fact, not only an individual lament, and, at that, a lament of a suffering righteous individual, but also, at the same time, a pilgrimage song, the expression of the longing on the part of Israelites dwelling far from Jerusalem after the sanctuary in the holy city as the place of help in tribulation and necessity. The evangelist would have been able to discover the 'many' mansions in the plural *mšknwtjk* of the psalm. We found parallels for this in the rabbinic theologoumenon of the seven dwelling places of the righteous in the Garden of Eden. We were generally struck by the fact that, in his adoption of Ps 42/43, the evangelist apparently had greater recourse to the Hebrew text of the Psalter and its Jewish significance than in v. 1. Apparently, in this new interpretation of the double psalm, his work is theologically more independent than in his adoption of the psalm as a testimony for the Passion of Christ.

From v. 2b to 3 inclusive, the evangelist seems to have drawn on other sources from a tradition historical point of view. In his voluminous monograph, G. Fischer has assembled valuable material for these verses.[62] His linguistic conclusions are to be followed when, with the varying consent of more recent authors, he puts the εἰ δὲ μή ('if it were not so...') clause with the following, understands the ὅτι as recitative (and so reproduces it with a colon) and takes

---

[61] *Strack-Billerbeck* I 209f.

[62] *Fischer*, Wohnungen 35-36.

the ensuing saying, 'I go to prepare a place for you' as a question.[63] It can be shown that John uses other back references which at the same time, from the point of view of content, carry the thought forward (*Fischer* refers here to Jn 11,40, but also possibly 10,25; 6,36; 10,36; less obviously 16,15; 8,24; 6,65; 16,17b). It is more difficult to accept the suggestion of his teacher *R. Schnackenburg* to restore a ὑπάγω before πορεύομαι: 'Haven't I said to you before: I am going away?'[64] Also, *R. E. Brown's* omission of the ὅτι before πορεύομαι has too feeble a textual basis to be entertained seriously.[65] Thus we stick with the traditional text in the translation most used today: 'If it were not so, would I have told you: I am going to prepare a place for you?' Moreover, Fischer rightly emphasises the difference between ὑπάγω and πορεύομαι in John:[66] while the first verb is stronger denoting the moment of separation ('go away'), the second rather brings a positive element to expression ('go there'), as is shown by the following statement: 'I am going [there] to prepare a place for you'.

It is, of course, disputed whether and how far in this repeated expression at the beginning of v. 3 the evangelist produced an independent formulation or remained more tightly bound to his tradition. *G. Fischer*[67] sees the fourth evangelist rather working independently here, even when echoes of similar formulations in the New Testament can be produced. Another view sees an Old Testament tradition lying behind this verse. It was first advanced by Aileen Guilding in her book, 'The Fourth Gospel and Jewish Worship'.[68] Her conclusion would have the fourth evangelist dependent for his themes and motifs in the more extensive speeches of Jesus in his gospel on the cycle of feasts in the synagogue and the corresponding (reconstructed) lectionary. For John 5 and 14, she claims as probable the common background of the Jewish New Year festival. The beginning of the book of Deuteronomy is the Torah reading for this feast every third year. There we encounter the passage: '...the Lord your God bore you, as a man bears his son, in all the way that you went until you came to this place. Yet in spite of this word you did not believe the Lord your God, who went before you in the way to seek you out a place to pitch your tents...' (Deut 1,31-33). For 'seek' the LXX uses here the verb ἐκλέγεσθαι; the Hebrew original speaks rather

---

[63] One group of authors puts the εἶπον ἂν ὑμῖν with the preceding material ('I would have told you') and understands the ὅτι as causal: *Weiss*[8] 472; *Westcott* 201; *Mollat* 178; *Behler* 95; *Brown* 619f who omits the ὅτι; *Morris* 639 and *Barrett*[2] 457 who take the εἰ δὲ μή clause as a parenthesis; other authors place the εἶπον clause with the following material and thereby take it as a question: *Heitmüller* 148; *Bernard* 534; *Bauer*[3] 178; *Bultmann* 464 with n. 3; *Strathmann* 202; *Schulz* 182f; *Sanders-Mastin* 320 with n. 6; *Lindars* 471; *Becker* 457-460; *Haenchen* 470; *Clarke*, Jn 14,1-4: 41f; as a statement: *Zahn* 553; *Loisy*[2] 404f (v. 3 is then ascribed to the redactor); *Schaefer*, Sinn 213 with n. 5.

[64] *Schnackenburg* III 66; cf. *idem*, Anliegen 97.

[65] *Brown* 619f.

[66] *Fischer*, Wohnungen 75-84.

[67] *Fischer, loc. cit.* 85-89.

[68] *Guilding*, Gospel 69-91, especially 87.

of 'spying out'. The thought is thus only related. While *A. Guilding* cites this text as simply one of other putative synagogue lections as the possible tradition-historical background for Jn 14,2f, *M.-É. Boismard*,[69] *I. de la Potterie*[70] and *V. Estalayo Alonso*[71] hold the significance of this text to be pre-eminent for the correct understanding of Jn 14,2f. However, the difference from the Johannine presentation should not be overlooked: while the Deuteronomy text speaks of God spying out or choosing provisional camp sites in the desert for his journeying people, Christ here is going to prepare a lasting dwelling for his own in the presence of God. The one picture is not easily explained in terms of the other.

However another observation of *A. Guilding* is to be noted: the lectionary texts for the Jewish New Year festival consist not only of readings from the Law and the Prophets (the so-called Haftarot) but also from the Psalms. Now, the New Year festival on 1 Tishri and the surrounding days are dominated by the Pilgrimage Songs. Guilding includes here Psalms 23; 25-27; 73 and 122 with the themes of 'God's House' and of the 'dwellings' therein, as well as the 'search' for the 'countenance of God'[72] These references appear significant in the context of our investigations, even if the author does not cite Ps 42f under the relevant festal psalms.

It can thus be said in conclusion about this verse that the focus in v. 2 remains entirely on the next world: at the time of his departure, Jesus refers his disciples to the heavenly sanctuary of the Father of which, according to contemporary Jewish interpretation, the Pilgrim Songs of the Old Testament were already speaking – not least our friend Psalm 42/43 – and goes on to promise, what he supposes to have already announced to the disciples, that he will prepare a place for them there. Sayings like Jn 12,32 would probably have also played a role in this: 'and I, when I am lifted up from the earth, will draw all men to myself'. It is, therefore, improbable to hold with *H. J. Holtzmann*[73], that the introductory ἐάν with which the evangelist in v. 3 takes up again the expression at the end of v. 2, is to be understood as hypothetical, even if this remains possible from the grammatical point of view: 'And *if* I go and prepare a place for you...' Already W. Bauer, in the same commentary series, rightly corrected this into a temporal understanding:[74] 'And *when* I go and prepare a place for you...' For that Jesus is going away, is no longer in doubt after the announcement of his 'departure' in Jn 7,33-36; 13,33.36-38,

It is more difficult to interpret Jesus' 'coming again' in Jn 14,3b than his 'going away'. Since in John a second coming of Jesus after Easter is mentioned

---

[69] *Boismard*, Évolution 520f.
[70] *De la Potterie*, Voie 914f.
[71] *Estalayo Alonso*, Vuelta 30-33; according to him, the Targum of Deut 1,33 comes even closer to Jn 14,2f in that here the 'preparation' of a camping site is spoken of.
[72] *Guilding*, Gospel 87f.
[73] *Holtzmann-Bauer* 244; similarly *Schaefer*, Sinn 214 ('even if').
[74] *Bauer*³ 178.

only in Jn 21,22, a context ascribed by many to the post-Johannine redaction, the viewpoints on the πάλιν ἔρχομαι ('I will come again') of Jn 14,3 are widely divergent. One opinion is that the expression permits no other reference than that to the Parousia.[75] Another opinion sees Jesus speaking here of his coming in the hour of the death or martyrdom of the believers.[76] B. *Lindars* would like to leave open whether Jesus is speaking here of his Parousia or of his coming in connection with this resurrection.[77] According to S. *Schulz*, the subject here would be the coming of Jesus in the Spirit-Paraclete – corresponding to vv. 16f and 26 with their context.[78] According to R. E. *Brown*,[79] R. *Schnackenburg*[80] and G. *Fischer*[81], on the other hand, Jesus is speaking here of his coming to his own in a general and timeless sense in which a reference to the Parousia is no more to be detected or even expressly excluded.

The decision which interpretation to prefer here, must take account also of the following words, above all Jesus' announcement that at his new coming he will 'take' his own with himself (παραλήμψομαι ὑμᾶς πρὸς ἐμαυτόν). The linguistic expression does not lead us to think immediately of a 'rapture'. John uses the word for the 'taking' of Jesus in both a positive (1,11) and a negative (19,16) sense. The most common meaning in the Synoptic Gospels is that of 'taking with oneself'. This seems to be supposed also in some texts which come close to rapture: the story of the Temptations (Mt 4,5.8) and a saying of Q about the Parousia: 'There will be two women grinding together; one will be taken and the other left' (Lk 17,35, par Mt 24,41). However, in Jn 14,3 there is a glimmer of that meeting with Christ, who appears on the clouds, as it comes to expression in I Thess 4,17. R. *Schnackenburg*[82] has convincingly compared the three phases which are found in the Johannine and Pauline texts: to the 'descent' of the Lord 'from heaven' in Paul corresponds the 'coming again' in John, to the 'we shall be caught up...to meet' of Paul corresponds the 'I will take you with me', and to Paul's conclusion 'so we shall always be with the Lord' corresponds John's 'where I am, you may be also'. It is not clear, therefore, why Schnackenburg understands the saying about the 'taking' of the disciples at the new coming of the Lord so completely as part of the Johannine realised eschatology and so spiritualises it and wishes to interpret it as the coming of the Lord in faith. The recurring ἔρχεσθαι= 'come' used by Christ (vv. 18.23.28) would justify such an

---

[75] So, among others, *Zahn* 555; *Heitmüller* 148f; *Bernard* 535; *Clarke*, Jn 14,1-4: 43; *Hoskyns* 454, but with a reference to the many-sided coming of the Lord already in the present of the believers; similarly, *Schaefer*, Sinn 214f.
[76] Thus, *Kundsin*, Wiederkunft 213.
[77] *Lindars* 471.
[78] *Schulz* 183; likewise *Sanders-Mastin* 320.
[79] *Brown* 626f.
[80] *Schnackenburg* III 70.
[81] *Fischer*, Wohnungen 90-98.
[82] *Schnackenburg* loc. cit.

interpretation, but not, however, the idea of the 'taking with him' of the disciples which ill suits such a transferred understanding. Even if the expression is to be interpreted as one in a series of sayings like Jn 12,24 which speak only of being with Jesus, even in suffering and death, here in Jn 14,3 the sense should be understood rather as that of 17,24: as being with Jesus in his glory.

Precisely the wider context of our passage supports the idea that the statement in Jn 14,3 about the new 'coming' of Jesus and of his 'taking' the disciples 'to himself' is not purely to be taken as a realised eschatological statement concerning the existence of believers: as we have already seen[83], verses 1-3 in Jn 14 seem to serve as an introduction to the rest of the chapter in which the central sayings of Jesus about his imminent destiny are displayed one after the other: first his impending 'departure' in vv. 4-14, then his new 'coming' in vv. 15-24. If it were clear from the beginning how this 'going' and 'coming' should be understood, then the succeeding explanation would not be necessary. This would also have been necessary, then, for the second theme of the new 'coming' of Jesus because precisely here the early Christian apocalyptic understanding of the eschatological coming of the Son of Man, as Paul assumes it also in 1 Thess 4,17, is only with difficulty brought into harmony with the eschatological conceptual framework of the community of the fourth evangelist. That this, for its part, was anything other than homogeneous is shown by the different, though neighbouring, sketches of the coming again of Christ in verses 15-24.[84]

Thus the evangelist is clearly bound to his tradition also in Jn 14,3b-c. Only here, his presentation draws on other sources than in Jn 14,1-2a, namely on a tradition about the eschatological coming on the clouds of heaven of the Son of Man who takes his own to himself, as appears also in 1 Thess 4,17.

In verses 4-6, the evangelist makes extensive use of his own verbal and conceptual material. In fact, if the subject in verses two and three was the πορεύεσθαι ('going away') of Jesus, this verb, as we saw, is almost synonymous with the word ὑπάγειν, and both words in the sense of the 'going away' of Jesus to the Father are precisely Johannine favourites.[85] Moreover the twofold new start without any connecting element in vv. 5 and 6 in the exchange between Jesus and Thomas is to be reckoned among the Johannine peculiarities of style.[86] Finally, the words 'truth' (ἀλήθεια) and 'life' (ζωή) belong among the key Johannine concepts. Even the interruption of the revelatory speech of Jesus through the question of a disciple who expresses lack of understanding (or misunderstanding) and so leads to the deeper insertion which Jesus makes to his

---

[83] Cf., *supra*, Chapter 1, Section 3.
[84] Cf., *infra*, Chapter III.
[85] Cf. *Ruckstuhl*, Einheit 204.
[86] Cf. *Ruckstuhl, loc cit.* ('epic asyndeton')

message, may be put down to the characteristic stylistic technique of John.[87] Here, therefore, it has in view neither the figure of Thomas nor the disciples nor a parallel between Thomas and the 'Jews' who give voice to the same misunderstanding in 7,35f; 8,22, but serves only the progress of the revelatory discourse. Thus 'way' (ὁδός) turns out to be the only new key word here. It occurs on this one occasion in the three successive verses 4-6 and otherwise not at all in the Gospel and Letters of John, except in Jn 1,23 where, parallel to the Synoptic tradition, it is quoted from Is 40,3 for the appearance of the Baptist as the one preparing the way. More recent authors such as *B. Lindars*[88] and *V. Estalayo Alonso*[89] would be right, therefore, when they also conclude to tradition for the employment of the motif of the way in Jn 14,4-6.

Basically, two possibilities of interpretation seem to offer themselves. One group of authors, especially in the German speaking sphere, thinks, in connection with the revelatory saying of Jn 14,6, especially of the Gnostic concept of the Revealer who shows those who believe in him the way to the Light World of illumination.[90] Another interpretation, particularly in the Anglo-Saxon world, thinks rather of the Jewish wisdom idea of the 'Way' of 'Truth' shown by God which leads to 'Life'.[91] From our conclusions here so far, we feel encouraged to look in this direction. Here again we have two possibilities. Either we look for Old and New Testament parallels for the 'Way' motif used in a religious way – alone or together with the concepts of 'Truth' and 'Life' – as happens consistently in the commentaries, or we ask ourselves whether the saying about the 'Way' in this text perhaps constitutes a tradition-historical link with other elements of Jn 14. If we only take as a working hypothesis that this is a possibility, the double Psalm 42/43, already used by us as an explanation of Jn 14,1-2a, can also shed some light on the question.

First of all, we were led to the conclusion that the psalm has found its usage here by John in its character as Pilgrim Song. It is the expression of the singer's longing for the sanctuary – by which the psalmist himself understood the earthly sanctuary of Jerusalem, the worshipper of the early rabbinic period more and more the world to come or the other world with God. Against this background, the 'Way' motif in Jn 14,4-6 is no longer so very surprising. Indeed

---

[87] Cf. *Leroy*, Rätsel 54f, precisely on the theme of the unfamiliar purpose for the interruptions of Jesus; disciples' questions also belong to the progress of the dialogue or the revelation discourses in the Corpus Hermeticum: *Dodd*, Interpretation 13.44.
[88] *Lindars* 471.
[89] *Estalayo Alonso*, Vuelta 22.
[90] Cf. *Heitmüller* 149; *Bauer*[3] 179; *Bultmann* 466-468, according to whom John is demythologising a mythical, innerworldly idea of the way; similarly *Wikenhauser* 265; *Schulz* 184f.
[91] Cf. *Bernard* 537; *de la Potterie*, Voie 917-926; *Brown* 628ff; *Lindars* 473; more cautiously, *Hoskyns* 455f ; *Barrett*[2] 458, who refer, above all, to the self-understanding of the early Christians as 'the Way' (Acts 9,2; 19,9.23; 22,4; 24,14.22) and Jesus as the 'access' to the Father (Rom 5,2; Eph 2,13.18; 3,12; Heb 7,25; 10,19-21; 1 Pet 2,5; 3,18).

it is already presupposed in the use the evangelist makes of the motifs of 'going away' and 'coming'.

Our glance falls here above all on Ps 43,3 where it says: 'Oh send out thy light and thy truth; let them lead me, let them bring me to thy holy hill and to thy dwelling! (more exactly, thy dwellings)' For 'lead' here, the Septuagint uses the verb ὁδηγεῖν = 'lead the way'. It is noteworthy that it is God's 'Light' and 'Truth' that are to lead the worshipper to the sanctuary. It is exactly in this sense that 'Truth' appears to be used in Jn 14,6 as *I. de la Potterie* has demonstrated in some detail;[92] it is thus not the goal, as is the 'Life', and therefore also not to be interpreted in a Hellenistic-Gnostic but in a Jewish way as the revelation of God that leads to the goal. Of course, when *I. de la Potterie* stresses that he knows of no Jewish or Jewish-Christian text which identifies the 'truth' with the 'reality of the divine',[93] this statement can and must now be modified by the midrash to Ps 43,3. It is precisely in the midrash to the text in the psalter that we have already put forward that the 'Light' and 'Truth' of God are interpreted as Elijah and the Messiah. *Strack-Billerbeck's* translation in the Excursus on Elijah reads: 'Oh send out thy light and thy truth Ps 43,3. Thy 'light', that is the prophet Elijah from the house of Aaron of whom it says: the seven lamps shall give light in front of the lampstand Num 8,2 (the light as symbol of the priesthood). And "thy truth". That is the Messiah ben David as it says: Yahweh swore to David a sure oath from which he will not turn back Ps 132,11'.[94] The text is post-Christian,[95] and also it does not put the 'reality of the divine' but, in fact, the Messiah on the same level as 'the Truth', something which cannot be without significance in explaining the context of Jn 14,6.

The theme of 'Life' also belongs to the vocabulary and field of ideas of Ps 42/43. According to 42,3, the worshipper is 'thirsting for the living God' while in v. 9 he 'prays to the God of (his) life'. Taken by themselves, these texts mean little. They fit together only as jigsaw pieces in the larger picture which suggests itself to us.

Still disputed among the exegetes is the relation implied by the ordering of the three concepts 'Way, Truth and Life' in Jn 14,6. Precisely on the assumption that the concept of the 'Way' was provided to the evangelist from tradition history here, by contrast with his usual vocabulary of salvation, everything suggests that the second and third concepts are (Johannine) explanations of the first. The majority of more recent commentators[96] also incline to this view, so departing from the thought of Augustine who looked on the three concepts as the steps

---

[92] *De la Potterie, loc. cit.*, especially 929-942.
[93] *De la Potterie, loc. cit.*, 923.
[94] *Strack-Billerbeck* IV/2, 791.
[95] Cf., *supra*, p. 34, for the dating of the midrash on the Psalms.
[96] Cf., apart from the commentaries from *Holtzmann*, 245, to *Lindars* 472, also *Schaefer*, Sinn 215 (with *Bengel*) and *de la Potterie*, Voie 915-917.

in a process in which the human person was being led by Christ as the 'Way' through the 'Truth' to the 'Life'.[97]

That 'no one comes to the Father, but by me' in 14,6b would again be a Johannine development of the positive statement of 14,6a. The exclusive claim of the Johannine Jesus to the Way to the Father finds here its pre-eminent expression.[98]

That our postulated influence of the tradition of Ps 42/43 reaches beyond the opening verses of Jn 14 seems clear above all in verses 7-9. Here the inner-Johannine thought process is clear, provided that one does not have recourse to the very doubtful hypothesis of the taking over of a source of Gnostic revelation discourses.[99] In fact, it fits in well with the perspective of the fourth evangelist if, in the sense of his realised eschatology, he is now placing the 'seeing of God' in the perfecting of the righteous in the hour of faith and looks on it as realised in the 'seeing of Jesus'. However, this must arouse our curiosity since the evangelist otherwise uses expressions bound to tradition when he speaks of 'seeing God'. This appears to be the case not only at the end of the Prologue at Jn 1,18 but also in the controversy with the Jews in Jn 5,37, where, on both occasions, it is clear that it is to the Moses and Sinai tradition that allusion is being made.[100] It is to be expected, therefore, that also in Jn 14,7-9, the evangelist is speaking with a look back at the tradition of 'seeing God', realised in the 'seeing of Jesus'. Nevertheless, by contrast with Jn 1,18 and 5,37, no allusion to the Moses and Sinai tradition can be recognised here. Instead, the emergence of the theme can be explained as a development of the tradition of Ps 42/43. Thus there is first the longing of the distant worshipper for the sanctuary. In Ps 42,3 this finds its expression in the cry: 'My soul thirsts for God, for the living God. When shall I come and behold the face of God?' Quite early on, this formulation must have struck an offensive note in Jewish ears, and so the Masoretic Text, followed by the LXX, changes the psalmist's question into the weakened: 'When shall I come and appear (be seen) (before) the face of God'. However, the older reading is still preserved and rightly restored by many modern translators and commentators.[101]

The shift from 'knowing' to 'seeing' God in Jn 14,7 thus finds its tradition-historical explanation, but so too the demand of Philip in v. 8: 'Lord, show

---

[97] Against this understanding of *Augustine* and other Fathers of the Church, cf., expressly, *Lindars* 472; *de la Potterie*, Voie 908-915.

[98] Cf., above all, *Gollwitzer*, Christus.

[99] According to *Bultmann*, 469f at least v. 7a and part of v. 10 belong to the posited source; according to *H. Becker*, Reden 106, v. 6 (apart from the introduction), v. 9c and v. 10bc.

[100] Cf. Ex 24,10f: Moses and his companions see the God of Israel; Ex 33,18-23; Deut 4,12 men are forbidden the possibility of seeing the face of God.

[101] Cf. the Einheitsübersetzung, the Zürcher and the Jerusalem Bible; *Kraus*, Psalmen I^5 470.472 with reference to some Hebrew mss. as well as to the Targum and the Peshitta; *Anderson*, Book of Psalms I 330 among others. Quite different *Dahood*, Psalms I 253 ('to drink in deeply the presence of God').

us the Father, and we shall be satisfied'. Philip has thus not understood the foregoing saying of Jesus. So he expresses himself with a similar kind of misunderstanding as Thomas before him in v. 5. But he thereby takes up the content of the question which the enemies twice pose to the worshipper in Ps 42: 'Where is now your God?' (Ps 42,4.11). Both strophes of Ps 42 take their dramatic poignancy precisely from this piercing question. So then Philip's demand is decisively turned back by Jesus in v. 9: whoever was with Jesus could arrive at the recognition of his nature, and so it could become apparent to him that whoever sees him has also seen his Father, that is, God. The thought is still Johannine; however, not only through the motif of 'seeing God' but also through the demand to be shown him, it should go back to the evangelist's tradition complex which has already been indicated.

In the following verses, such a complex is no longer discernible. For the unity of Jesus with his Father in vv. 10f, the authors refer to texts like Deut 18,18f[102] or the Synoptic parallels Mk 11,23f and Mt 21,21f for the certain hearing of prayers made in faith.[103] However, in other respects, Johannine theology is very directly in evidence as the linguistic formation of verses 10-14 shows.[104].

4. Redaction

So then the evangelist is to different degrees dependent on tradition in the first fourteen verses of John 14. At its strongest, it is evident that he has had recourse to tradition in the first three verses. Here we encounter the greatest differences from his vocabulary and from his usual world of theological concepts and ideas. However, in this whole section, the evangelist remains more than a redactor assembling random blocks of material; he is rather an author in his own right, as can be shown in the following paragraphs.

Verses 1-3 turn out to be the introduction if not to the whole chapter then at least to verses 4-14 and 15-24. The psalm tradition that we have elaborated does not concern the Christological statements about the 'going away' and 'coming again' of Jesus in vv 2b-3b which form the structure; on the contrary, it precedes it. Nevertheless, not only does it have the function of an exhortation of the disciples, but it also forms its own part of a Christology: that of the 'suffering righteous' figure going to death and that of the worshipper longing for the (heavenly) sanctuary. However, these aspects now appear to be subordinated to the characteristic ideas of the Johannine Christology of the 'Son' (or Son of Man, Son of God) who comes from the Father and goes back home to the Fa-

---

[102] *Brown* 632; cf. *Schnackenburg* III 82, on v. 13.
[103] *Schnackenburg* III 80, on v. 12.
[104] Johannine here are, among other things, ἀπ' ἐμαυτοῦ (10), ἀμὴν ἀμήν (12), πιστεύειν εἰς τινα (12), ἐκεῖνος = αὐτός (12), ὑπάγειν = πορεύεσθαι = go to the Father (12), resumption (11,14). Cf. *Ruckstuhl*, Einheit 203ff.

ther[105] (cf. Jn 3,13.31f; 6,38; 8,23.42; 12,46; 7,33-36; 13,1.3.33.36-38; 16,5f.17.28!; 17,13). Of course, the concept of Jesus' 'coming again', which in all probability is similarly taken over from the tradition, is integrated into the Johannine thought with more difficulties. It seems premature to recognise a Johannine reinterpretation of the early Christian concept of the 'coming' of the Son of Man in the clouds of heaven already in v. 3bc.[106] Rather this idea seems to have been taken up in a deliberately open fashion as an opportunity to reinterpret it in different ways within the Johannine thought world. This happens in verses 15-24.[107] Before this, the significance for his disciples of Jesus' 'going away' is dealt with in verses 4-14.

In verses 4-6, the evangelist returns first to the question already posed by Peter in 13,36 as to where Jesus is going. The tradition (possibly our psalm tradition), provides only the key word 'way' which is now interpreted in a Johannine fashion in v. 6: Jesus is the 'way' to the Father, in that he is the 'truth' revealed by him and the 'life' that is made possible through him (in faith). Thereby two key Johannine concepts are employed for interpretation. If the concept of 'truth' is still bound up with the Johannine revelation theology,[108] so, with the concept of 'life', the evangelist now leads on to the notion of the full possession of salvation, as, among others, the parallel to the revelation saying in Jn 11,25 shows (cf. also 6,35; 8,12). The 'way' concept is developed in v. 6 to the extent that in the second half of the verse the subject is the 'coming to the Father'. However, this idea is immediately reinterpreted in the following verses.

In verses 7-9, the 'seeing' of God seems to be the motif which John has taken here from a (we mean, his) tradition. To it corresponds the 'letting see' or 'showing' which Philip demands. This idea too can take us back to our psalm tradition. The 'seeing' of the Father or Jesus which has its roots in tradition is now linked up with the evangelist's characteristic theme of 'knowing' Jesus or his being sent or his descent (cf. Jn 1,40.48; 6,69; 7,26f; 8,28; 10,14.38; 14,20; 16,3; 17,3.8.23.25) or, as the case may be, 'knowing' the Father (cf. Jn 8,55; 10,15; 16,3; 17,3.25). At the same time, the tense is important: following the reading that is rightly preferred today,[109] 14,7 is still future: 'If you have known me, you will know my Father also'. However, in that case, the sequence of tenses changes abruptly in the second half of the verse, and the text can proceed: 'Already now you know him and have known him'. With this present and perfect, we arrive at John's realised eschatology as it comes to expression in Jn

---

[105] More recent studies start out above all from the concept of sending: cf. *Meeks*, Man from Heaven; *Borgen*, God's Agent (mentioned by *Brown* 632); *Miranda*, Vater.
[106] Cf., *supra*, Section 3.
[107] Cf., *infra*, Chapter III.
[108] Cf. *de la Potterie*, Vérité; Voie (cf., *supra*, Section 3) ; *Ibuki*, Wahrheit.
[109] Cf. *Nestle-Aland*^{26} and *The Greek New Testament* with *Tischendorf* against *Westcott-Hort*, *v. Soden* and *Nestle* who read here a present *irrealis*. The pros and cons of the current reading are provided in detail at *Schnackenburg*, Johannes 14,7

4,23; 5,25 ('the hour is coming, and now is'). The perfect continues in v. 9 where Jesus is able to declare: 'He who has seen me has seen the Father'. Thus what Jewish piety awaited from life after death, precisely on the basis of its understanding of the psalms, is promised by the Jesus of the Johannine Farewell Discourses to his disciples and to those believing in him here and now.

Those believing in him: in fact, at the beginning of v. 10, the evangelist brings us back to the theme of 'belief'. If first of all there is a question – rather reproachful with its introductory οὐ ('not') – to an individual disciple, from out of it there comes a command to all the disciples. The content is the same in both cases: 'that I am in the Father and the Father in me'. Nevertheless, one may detect a discrepancy in this 'reciprocal *Immanenzformel*': Jesus originates from God in his whole being and existence; conversely, the Father speaks and acts through the Son. It is not to be wondered that at this level we can no longer provide any biblical parallels or tradition-historical influences in the strict sense. Here, we clearly have to do with a Johannine development of the, at least partly given, concepts of the ability to see and to recognise the Father in the Son. However, the sequence of thought in v. 10b-c now creates certain difficulties. It might be a return to the abbreviated repetition of an idea that is encountered elsewhere in John. Jesus speaks and acts in full dependence on his Father as Jn 8,28f shows. Thus then the operation of the Father is recognisable in his word as well as in his activity, as is indicated by the appropriate parallel of Jn 15,22 with 24 (perhaps post-Johannine). Besides, it is in fact the case that the words of Jesus are works,[110] and his works have the nature of word or revelation[111]. However, this involves the evangelist's distinguishing the two, as the following v. 11 shows.[112] The command to believe if not because of the words then because of the works makes us think of 10,38 (cf. the 'testimony' of the works for the sending of Jesus in 5,36; 10,25[113]). In no way is there any appeal here to reason where faith is lacking, but, if necessary, to a mediated form of belief which still needs 'signs', in any case to some form of belief. Thus the words and works of Jesus should lead to belief in his unity with the Father in word and deed whereby by 'works' is probably meant all the deeds of the Giver of Life which are reported in detail in the Fourth Gospel (4,46-54; 5,1-30; 9; 11,1-47; but cf., also, 2,1-11; 6,1-15.16-21).

Among the more recent commentators it was probably *W. Bauer* who was the first to recognise the key word connection between vv. 10f and vv. 12ff. with the key words 'belief' and 'works'.[114] Such is evidently the case here. Thus there

---

[110] *Lagrange* 377; cf. *Westcott* 203; *Brown* 633.
[111] *Bernard* 542; *Bultmann* 471; *Brown* 633: they must be recognised in faith as worked by God. Thus, we must wonder at the rationalistic viewpoint of *Holtzmann* who sees in them the 'visible proof' of the revelatory claim of Jesus (246).
[112] So, correctly, *Schnackenburg* III 78.
[113] Cf. *Beutler*, Martyria 259f. 293-298.
[114] *Bauer*³ 181.

is little sense in regarding verses 12-14 as an opening to the following verses on the coming of the Paraclete and Jesus himself.[115] From the point of view of content, of course, the works which the disciples work through faith in Jesus are not unconnected with the works of Jesus but appear as their extension, even identical with them. To what extent they can be 'greater works' than those of Jesus is something which has received no agreement among exegetes. Certainly it is not a question of more spectacular works than those reported in the Fourth Gospel (with the healing of the man born blind in Chapter 9 and the raising of Lazarus in Chapter 11).[116] Rather the success of the early Christian mission which breaks through the boundaries of the people and land of Israel which had been observed by Jesus.[117] *R. Bultmann*,[118] followed by *A. Wikenhauser*,[119] *R. E. Brown*[120] and *R. Schnackenburg*[121] think, of course, not only of the breaking through of the spatial limits of the activity of Jesus but still more of the time limits imposed on it. The meaning is supported by v. 12c: 'because I go to the Father'. Through the arrival of Jesus at the eschatological hour of his 'exaltation' and 'glorification', the activity of the divine Spirit can now come to its full completion (cf. 7,39). For this activity, *Bultmann* makes particular reference to Jn 16,8-11.[122]

Also verses 13 and 14 appear to be linked to the preceding material by key word connection, in fact with 'doing', v.12 and v. 13, and also with 'Father'. Verses 13 and 14 are further linked to each other through 'asking'. What asking 'in the name of Jesus' means in v. 13 is disputed by the exegetes. Influenced by the monograph of *W. Heitmüller*, the older authors think of the prayer which takes place by mentioning the name of Jesus.[123] Since, however, that is nowhere else the case in John, more are now of the opinion that here a prayer 'in union with Christ' and his will is intended.[124] The reference to the glorification of the Father through the Son probably indicates, then, not only the goal but also the limits of Christian prayer.

---

[115] Cf., *supra*, Chapter 1, Section 3 for the corresponding suggestion of *Becker*.

[116] Cf., among others, *Heitmüller* 150.

[117] Cf. *Holtzmann* 480; *Bauer*³ 181, who includes the wonders of the early Christian missionary activity.

[118] *Bultmann* 471f. Cf., already, *Loisy*² 408.

[119] *Wikenhauser* 267.

[120] *Brown* 633.

[121] *Schnackenburg* III 81.

[122] *Bultmann* 472.

[123] *Heitmüller*, Im Namen Jesu; *idem*, Commentary 150; *Zahn* 561f; *Loisy*² 409; *Lagrange* 379f; *Bauer*³ 181; *Bultmann, loc. cit.*

[124] Cf. *Hoskyns*² 457f; *Wikenhauser* 268; *Brown* 633-636, all three with reference to 1 Jn 5,14; somewhat otherwise *Schnackenburg* III 82 (with reference to *Behm*, read: *H. Bietenhard*, ὄνομα κτλ., in: ThWNT V [1954] 242-283, here 260f) who here again thinks of the Old Testament messenger principle in connection with Deut 18,18: the one who proceeds in the name of another, is endowed with his authority, and the one who calls on him can claim this authority.

Precisely after the idea has thus rather definitively retraced its steps to the Father, the sequel in v. 14 is surprising. If one follows the reading presented recently in the text of *K. Aland* and the *Greek New Testament*, the thought of v. 13 receives a new, definite intensification: Jesus himself (designated through ἐγώ ['I']) will hear the prayers which are addressed to him (the με ['me'] is stressed). Thus, with another looking back, his unity with the Father in deed shows itself once more, and the thought from v. 10 on rounds itself off as far as content also is concerned.

III. The Threefold Promise of the Coming of Jesus in the Light of the Covenant Theology of the Old Testament (vv. 15-24)

After the first three introductory verses which announced the two principal themes of John 14 – the going and coming of Jesus - the subject in vv. 4-14 was the imminent departure of Jesus and the abiding relationship with him in faith. Psalm 42/43, which the chapter had already taken as its point of departure, has shown itself to be the constant background. In what follows, the promise which already sounded in the Johannine working out of the 'way' motif, namely that Jesus is the already attained goal for the believers, that in him one already has a share in the eschatological vision of God, is now more clearly developed. With that, the perspective is inverted: Jesus speaks no more of the coming of the believers to him and through him to the Father, but of his own coming, of the coming of the Spirit-Paraclete, and of the coming of the Father to the believers or, to put it more exactly, to the one who loves Jesus and who keeps and does his commandments or words. Through this it appears, once more, that we may recognise here an Old Testament tradition – this time rather a whole complex of motifs - as the foundation of the whole section.

1. The Structure of the Passage

The section is first marked out by its characteristic vocabulary. The most common verbs and nouns are ἀγαπάω 'to love' (8 times), τηρέω 'to keep, guard' (4 times), εἶναι ἐν 'to be in' (something or someone, 4 times), πατήρ the Father (4 times) γινώσκω 'to know' (3 times), θεωρέω 'to see' (3 times), λόγος the 'word' (3 times), κόσμος the 'world' (3 times), ἐντολή the 'commandment' (twice), ἔρχομαι 'to come', ἐμφανίζω ἐμαυτόν 'to reveal oneself' and ζάω 'to live' (each twice). It is striking that the group of especially frequent words 'to love' and 'to keep' the 'commandments' or the 'words' of Jesus constitutes a word-field that only occurs in certain verses, namely vv. 15.21.23f. We can call these 'framing' verses.

That this description is correct is shown also by an examination of the syntax of the section. In general, short main clauses predominate, joined together by καί or δέ. Subordinate clauses are encountered relatively rarely, and the same goes for participial constructions and appositions. Subordinate constructions occur piled together, above all, in vv. 16-17 where we find a final clause, apposition, a relative clause and a causal clause within a single complex sentence. If one disregards for a moment the twofold ὅτι 'that' in vv. 20 and 22 and the causal ὅτι-clause in v. 19c, there remains, as an outstanding syntactical phenomenon, the fivefold conditional complex in the 'framing' verses that is rendered twice (vv. 15.23b) with a conditional clause with ἐάν 'if', three times

(vv. 21.24) with a generalising participle. The 'framing' verses thus betray their own style not only in vocabulary but also in syntax.[1]

Like the previous section, this one too is distinguished by the contrast 'I'- 'we'/ 'you'(s) -'you' (p). The third person (generally the singular) is seldom present. Apart from the introduction of the speaker at and after the interpolated question of Judas vv. 22f and apart from the mention of the 'world' (vv. 17.19), the 'Father' (vv. 16.20.23) and the 'word' (v. 24), it is encountered, only in vv. 16f where it is used with the 'Father' in addition to the 'Paraclete', identified, through apposition, as 'Spirit of Truth' (here we find in one place the threefold use of the third person: the 'Father', the 'Paraclete' as 'Spirit of Truth' and the 'world'). The special position of theses two verses which has already attracted our attention is confirmed by this consideration.

The clauses and their components are so related temporally that the conduct of the 'world' is expressed in the present, the behaviour of the disciples/believers in the present (thus throughout ἀγαπᾶν ['love'], regularly determined, of course, by ἐάν ['when'] or a participle, and twice τηρέω ['keep']) or the future (so τηρέω twice)[2], the activity of the Father, of Jesus himself and the Paraclete almost always in the future.[3] Here the characteristic emphasis on condition and promise which defines the passage is showing itself from another perspective.

This shift is particularly apparent from an analysis of the content of the sequence of thought. The 'framing verses' (15.21ab.23b; 24a constitutes a negative counterpart) are followed by the respective announcements of a promise: in vv. 16f the 'gift' of the Paraclete from the Father to which the proclamation of the coming again of Jesus is immediately attached in vv. 18-20, and the love of the Father and of Jesus and the self-revelation of Jesus in v. 21b as well as, after the change of subject of vv. 22.23a, the promise of v. 23c that the Father and Jesus 'are coming' and will take up their 'dwelling' with the one who fulfils the condition of v. 23b. Thus one can certainly speak here of an ascending 'Trinitarian structure'[4] attaching to the promise of Jesus even if Jesus' activity never appears to be separated from that of the Father.

---

[1] *Pesch*, Markusevangelium II 58 recognises in connection with *K. Berger* the genre of 'command sentence': 'condition in the protasis, imperative or prohibition with regard to behaviour in the apodosis'. It is used above all in the 'framing' verses vv. 15.23b, although here the imperative is also conveyed by the future.

[2] As in v. 23b, also in v. 15, we read with $Aland^{26}$ and the *GNT* the future, in v. 24 with $Aland^{26}$ the present.

[3] Exceptions in this case are constituted only by ἔρχομαι 'I come' v. 18, ζῶ 'I live' v. 19, and the threefold εἶναι ἐν 'be in' in v. 20. To this we could add μένειν in v. 17 of the above-mentioned edition of the text.

[4] Cf. *Boismard*, Évolution 519; *Brown* 642 speaks of a 'triadic pattern'.

2. Traces of Literary Strata

Already preliminary to any literary and tradition critical hypothesis, our section gives occasion to the hypothesis of literary strata. Thus, we encounter here words and groups of words which are seldom or never encountered elsewhere in John or in the New Testament: ὁ παράκλητος 'the advocate' (only Jn 14.16.26; 15,26; 16,7; 1 Jn 2,1), ὀρφανός 'orphan' (only Jn 14,18; Mk 12,40; Jas 1,27), ἐμφανίζω ἐμαυτόν 'I will manifest myself' (reflexive only at Jn 14,21f) or μονή 'home' (only Jn 14,2.23). Also, τὸ πνεῦμα τῆς ἀληθείας, 'the Spirit of truth' is encountered only in the Paraclete sayings of the Farewell Discourses (Jn 14,17; 15,26) as well as 1 Jn 4,6. Finally, there is the word-field of 'love' and the 'keeping' of the 'commandments' or 'words' which is confined to this section of John's Gospel. The New Testament parallels will be dealt with in the tradition history part of this chapter (cf., *infra*, 3.1).

Lesser peculiarities of expression can also be traced to links with tradition. They are met with especially in the 'framing verses'. There, beside 'keeping' (τηρεῖν) the commandments or word (or words) of Jesus, appears 'having'/'holding' (ἔχειν, v. 21). Similarly striking is the change from the 'commandments' (ἐντολαί vv. 15.21) to the 'word' (λόγος v. 23) and the 'words' (λόγοι v. 24) of Jesus.

Moreover, the conspicuous repetitions in our section are a sign of literary strata. The most important example in this case is once again the 'framing verses' (15.21a.23b.24a). Striking also is the parallel between v. 17, according to which the world does not 'see' the Spirit, and v. 19 where it does not 'see' Jesus. Corresponding is the parallel theme in v. 18 of the 'coming' of Jesus and v. 23 of the 'coming' of Jesus with the Father. Here we are already coming into contact with the theological problem of the different outlines given to the early Christian belief in the expected 'coming' of Jesus.

That here we are faced with parallel statements, probably of different origins, is confirmed by the double appearance of the motif of 'abiding': according to v. 17, it is the Spirit who abides with or in the disciples, according to v. 23, it is the Father and Jesus. Finally, the 'indwelling' sayings are to be found divided between different texts: on the one hand they are associated with the Spirit-Paraclete (v. 17, cf. v. 16), on the other hand, with the Father and Jesus (v. 20, cf. v. 23).

That especially in v. 16 traditional material has been adopted is shown by the overloaded construction, the unusual subject in the third person (the Paraclete) and the frequency of the third person in this double verse as we have already seen (cf., *supra*, section 1).

However, traditional material may also lie behind v. 18, with its presentation of the 'orphans', unique in John. A similar explanation is demanded for the unusual μονή 'dwelling' in v. 23. If we also include the 'self-revelation' of Jesus in v. 21d, we can say then that clearly traditional material is used in the promise sayings. This might also go for the word-field of the 'framing verses' as has already been shown. In the following, we go on to examine, separately from each other, the conditions of Jesus' promise in the 'framing verses' and the content of his promise. This procedure is also justified by the partly independent nature of the syntax of the promises which comes to expression especially in v. 18. In the course of the investigation, it will be shown that the origin of the condition and the content of the promise of Jesus are not as different as perhaps we might have supposed at first.

3. The Tradition behind the Passage

3.1 The Condition of Jesus' Promise: Love of Jesus, Keeping of his Commandments (vv.15.21a.23b.24a)[5]

According to the 'framing verses' of our section (vv. 15.21a.23b.24a), Jesus makes his promise depend on his disciples 'loving' him and 'having, keeping' his 'commandments' or 'word' or 'words'. The supposition that here we have a word-field that already lay before the fourth evangelist is strengthened through a glance at Jn 14,31, the only place in John's Gospel where the subject is the love of Jesus for the Father. Here too it is said that, as an expression of this love, Jesus acts as his Father has commanded (ἐνετείλατο) him, that is according to his 'commandment' (ἐντολή).

That ultimately, behind the love for Jesus in Jn 14,15-24, stands love for God and faithfulness to his commandment (cf. v. 24!) is something confirmed also by the First Letter of John, as will be shown below in connection with 1 Jn 4,7-5,3.

It is to the credit of *E. Malatesta*, in his voluminous thesis,[6] that he has uncovered the tradition history, not only of the so-called 'indwelling formulae', but also of the internal connection of the 'love of God' and the 'observing of the commandments' in the First Letter of John. In what follows, we should try to make use of his stance in interpreting the first Johannine Farewell Discourse, especially the whole of our section vv. 15-24, and therein, first, the 'framing verses'.

'Love of God' and 'observing' his 'commandments or 'words' is a theme that pervades the Old Testament from its earliest layers right up to the latest writings in the post-exilic period. The tradition historical provenance of the word-field and thought complex could be given within the Bible in the Deca-

---

[5] More fully for the connection between love for God and observing of his commandments in the Old Testament, in the intertestamental literature and in the New Testament in a forthcoming publication.
[6] *Malatesta*, Interiority.

logue,[7] where, in the promise attached to the prohibition against the worship of strange gods and the manufacture of graven images, it says: 'For I, the Lord, thy God, am a jealous God and visit the sins of the fathers upon the children (and) on the third and fourth generation of them that hate me and show mercy unto thousands in them that love me and keep my commandments' (Ex 20,5f; Deut 5,9f).[8] The connection between 'love' for the Lord and the 'observing' of his 'commandments' appears to have even older, extra-biblical roots as has probably been shown by the research of the 1960's and 1970's into the vassal treaties of the Ancient Near East.[9] Accordingly, the Johannine word-field might have some very Ancient Near Eastern roots.

The link between the 'love of God' (or 'fear of God) and the 'observing of the commandments' is taken up and developed most strongly in the book of Deuteronomy. Here, in almost all the places in which 'love of God' is the subject, the 'observing' of his 'commandments' or 'ordinances' or the 'hearing' of them or of his 'voice' is also mentioned. The texts are located first in Chapters 5-11, which N. Lohfink has taken as a basis for his book 'Das Hauptgebot' (Deut 5,10 Decalogue; 7,9; 10,12; 11,1.13.22; for 6,5, see below), then in Chapter 19 (v. 9) as well as in the closing thirtieth chapter (vv. 6.16.20) where blessing and curse are bound up with faithfulness or disobedience to the commandment of Yahweh. Even when, as in Deut 13,4, the 'observing of the commandments' is not expressly mentioned, it is to be found in the context (13,5).[10]

In the different layers of Deuteronomy, it is not simply a question of promulgation of the law but above all the development of the 'chief commandment' as it comes to expression in Deut 6,4ff and has become the daily prayer of the Jews since early times. It is the commandment of the unique worship of Yahweh which stands as the 'chief commandment' (cf. Mk 12,28), as the 'fundamental law' of Israel. Thus here too and precisely here (Deut 6,5), the com-

---

[7] The 'observing of the commandments' is rendered in the MT by *šmr mṣwt*, in the LXX by φυλάσσειν τὰ προστάγματα. *Moran*, Background 84f, traces it back behind the Decalogue to Jdg 5,31 with the description of Israel as those 'who love him (God)'.
[8] The wording in the Decalogue is the same in the MT in both places as far as the 'and' in brackets. In the LXX, there are some trifling differences which do not concern the ending τοῖς ἀγαπῶσιν κτλ.
[9] Cf. *Moran*, Background; comprehensive summary in *Lohfink*, Hauptgebot, especially 108-112, cf., *infra*, n. 10; *McCarthy*, Treaty 81.160 n. 6. 288.
[10] According to Lohfink, Hauptgebot 65, one can speak of a Deuteronomistic principle of word order: The word pair *šmr* – *'śh* ('observe' – 'do') forms the kernel. At the head stands 'hear' (*šm'*) and learn (*lmd*), followed by 'observe' (*šmr*) and 'do' (*'śh*); 'walk in the way' (*hlk bdrk*) and 'turn from the way' (*swr mn hdrk*) form the end. Love (*'hb*) is regularly the precondition. 'The leading role of *šmr* goes back as far as the covenant tradition outside Israel' (68). Already there, 'these words' describes the content of the obligation (cf. 69).

mand to 'love God' is bound up with the command to keep his commandments, though here too the word is only in the context (cf. Deut 6,1; 'words', v. 6).[11]

In connection with our investigation, it is important that the 'chief commandment' is the fundamental prescription of the 'covenant' which Yahweh has concluded with Israel. In the book of Exodus in its present state, the subject of the 'love' of God and the 'observing' of his 'commandments' appears in the Decalogue (Ex 20,6) which is the commandment obligation imposed by Yahweh at the conclusion of the covenant on Sinai (cf. Ex 19,5; 24,7f). As integral component of the conclusion of the covenant, then, the Decalogue is encountered again in the book of Deuteronomy (5,6-21) where the conclusion of the covenant at Sinai/Horeb is expressly called to remembrance and actualised for the present.

Love for Yahweh and the observing of his commandments is expressly linked with the 'observing' of the 'covenant' and the 'obtaining' of his 'mercy' by Yahweh himself in Deut 7,9 – a text which should have an echo after the Exile as will be seen presently.

The close connection between 'love' for Yahweh and the 'observing' of his 'commandments is also found in the Deuteronomistic school. Here we should mention Joshua's exhortation to the Reubenites in Jos 22,5.[12] We can compare the related text, 1 Kgs 3,3. If, in these places, a more general Deuteronomistic reference is being made to Deuteronomy and its preaching language, a post-Exilic text, probably originating from the Chronicler,[13] namely a prayer in Neh 1,5, goes back directly to Deut 7,9 in connection with 7,21. In this way, the connection of the motif complex of the 'love' of Yahweh and the 'observing' of his 'commandments' with the concept of the covenant reveals itself to be still alive in these later portions of the Old Testament. Still later on, an echo of this latter text extends to Dan 9,4, itself the beginning of a prayer with a liturgical imprint, which might have been added secondarily to the already late book of Daniel.[14]

Within the Wisdom literature of the Old Testament the collection of motifs that we are examining is taken up especially in the book of Sirach where (2,15f) it says: 'Those who fear the Lord will not disobey his words, and those who love him will keep his ways. Those who fear the Lord will seek his approval, and those who love him will be filled with the law'. The love of God

---

[11] The significance of the connection between 'love for God' and 'keeping the commandments' in the Deuteronomic and Deuteronomistic theology for the corresponding connection in John is indicated in: *Mollat* 180 (in a note with citations); *Brown* 644; *Lacomara*, Deuteronomy 73-77; *Pancaro*, Law 431-451; *Cortès*, Discursos 434-436.

[12] For the Deuteronomistic provenance of the section, cf. *Noth*, Studien 228; *Hertzberg*, Josua, Richter, Ruth 121f.

[13] Cf. *Galling*, Chronik, Esra, Nehemia 218; *Myers*, Ezra, Nehemiah 95f.

[14] Cf. *Hartmann-DiLella*, Daniel 248, cf, 245f. Bel 38 G/Θ and 1 Macc 4,33 speak again of those who love God. The participial style makes one suspect influence from the Decalogue.

now appears to be individualised and left to the decision of the individual. Correspondingly, there is no longer a visible link with covenant theology. However, precisely in its generalising formulation (participle with article in the nominative) which is equivalent to a conditional clause, it comes close to the Johannine text.[15]

The connection of the 'love for God' with the 'observing of the commandments' under the influence of Deuteronomy seems to have found a privileged place in the biblical and post-biblical testaments.[16] This is shown in the demand for the love of God in the Farewell Discourse of Joshua (Jos 23,11).[17] That here the chief commandment of the unique worship of Yahweh is meant especially is shown in the following verses. In the Deuteronomistic redaction of the Testament of David[18], love for God is not expressly mentioned in connection with the keeping of the commandments, but, in its way, it reminds one slightly of allusion to the chief commandment (1 Kgs 2,3f). The connection of both elements is found in what *Cortès* regards as the earliest clear example of the genre in Tobit 14[19] where, almost immediately after the mention of the 'love of God' (v. 7), there follows: 'Keep the Law and the commandments' (v. 9).

Among the pseudepigraphical writings of the Old Testament, *Jubilees* and the *Testaments of the Twelve Patriarchs* show clear examples of the two motifs. In *Jubilees*, most important is the Testament of Abraham (20,7), though there is a trace of the connected motifs also in the Testament of Isaac (36,5ff). In the *Testaments of the Twelve Patriarchs*, both motifs are to be found linked in *TestBen* 3,1.[20] However, the exhortation to the love of God and faithfulness to his commandments otherwise dominates the *Testaments of the Twelve Patriarchs*. In some places, the command to love God is linked with that of loving the neighbour or brother (*TestIs* 5,1f; 7,6, as a statement; *TestDan* 5,3; cf. *TestBen* 3,5) which seems to be here a pre- or extra- Christian connection.[21] In other spots, we find the command to love God on its own,[22] and the same goes for the exhortation to the love of neighbour or brother[23]. Finally, the exhortation to ob-

---

[15] The 'love of God', in a transferred sense, if also without direct connection with the 'keeping' of the 'commandments', remains a frequent theme in Sirach: 1,10 v.l.; 7,30; 31(34),16(19); 47,8.22.
[16] Cf. *Michel*, Abschiedsrede 50.
[17] On the Deuteronomistic origin of the Farewell Discourse of Joshua (Jos 23,1-16), cf. *Noth*, Studien 7ff; *Hertzberg*, Josua, Richter, Ruth 129f.
[18] Cf. *Noth*, Könige I 29f. According to him, v. 3f is 'certainly a Deuteronomistic insertion'.
[19] *Cortès*, Discursos 104.
[20] A direct influence of the NT on these texts is to be excluded because the formulation is different from that of John and the Letters of John (φυλάξατε ἐντολάς instead of John's τηρεῖν 'keep, observe').
[21] *J. Becker*, Testamente 27f locates them in the Hellenistic-Jewish synagogues; cf. *Burchard*, Liebesgebot 55-57.
[22] *TestGad* 5,2; *TestBen* 4,5.
[23] *TestRub* 6,9; *TestSim* 4,7; *TestGad* 6,1.3; *TestJos* 17,2; *TestBen* 3,3f (cf. Charles's Index).

serve the commandments – mostly in key places – pervades each of the Testaments.[24]

It is worth noticing that, in the Essene texts from Qumran, the Deuteronomistic theme of 'love' for God and 'observing' the 'commandments' remains present, to some extent bound up with the covenant motif: in the Damascus Document (CD 19,1f), Deut 7,9 is directly taken up and referred to the members of the 'community of the covenant'. The promise of the Decalogue is adopted in the following column of the Damascus Document (CD 20,21) where, in place of the expression 'and who keep his commandments', there appears the abbreviated turn of phrase 'and who have regard for him'. The promise is encountered in a lesser form also in the Qumran Hymns (1QH 16,13; cf. 16,7 = DSS 1QH 8, p. 157f) where the commandments of God appear in the context as 'statements of his covenant' (16,15).[25] There remains a certain reticence at Qumran to speak of the love of God other than in the traditional connection. This is confirmed by a glance at the use of the substantive 'love' in the Essene texts from Qumran.[26]

The same strong tradition connection appears in the New Testament when the subject is 'love for God'. Generally speaking, in terms of frequency and importance, the theme of love for God is relatively rare in the New Testament. As in the prophets, the love of God for men is much more to the fore. In addition, there is the love of brother and neighbour.

In the Synoptic Gospels, the theme of love for God is encountered especially in Jesus' answer to the question of the scribe concerning the 'first commandment' (Mk 12,30 par Mt 22,37; Lk 10,27). The Q Tradition is aware of the chief commandment (Deut 6,13 A) in the account of the Temptations (Mt 4,10 par Lk 4,8). The connection with the basic commandment of God is also preserved in both places where Mt (24,12) and Lk (11,42) alone speak of 'love'.[27]

Paul is also a witness to and interpreter of the tradition in the few unambiguous texts where he speaks of 'love for God'. In Rom 8,28; 1 Cor 2,9 he has

---

[24] Cf., in varying formulations, *TestLev* 13,1; 19,1; *TestJud* 13,1; 23,5; 26,1; *TestZab* 5,1; *TestGad* 3,1; *TestAs* 6,1.3; *TestJos* 18,1; *TestBen* 10,3.5.

[25] Two further texts which speak of the love of God recall the chief commandment through the phrase 'with all the heart (and with all the soul)' (1QH 14,26; 15,10).

[26] The word refers either to God's love for the ancestors or the Fathers (CD 8,15.16; 19,28.29) or the community (4QDib Ham 2,9 = DSS 4Q504-506 Fragments 1-2 col. IV [Puech col. XV] 4-5, p. 1015) or the love to be exercised in the community whereby it is mostly mentioned with equivalents such as 'righteousness', 'compassion' etc (1QS 2,24; 5,4.25; 8,2; 10,26; CD 13,18). Also the 'loving' and 'hating' of 1QS 9,16.21 refers to fellow men as indicated by the context.

[27] According to *Frankemölle*, Jahwebund 284f , ἀνομία 'lawlessness' is the antithesis of δικαιοσύνη 'righteousness' as the definition of behaviour in conformity with the Law. With the increase of lawlessness, love, as the basis of the relationship with God and the neighbour grows cold. Cf. *Schweizer*, Matthäus 295. Lk 11,42 (Q) describes as 'love of God' the essential commandments of God over and against the small commandments about tithes.

recourse to the typical participial style of the Decalogue.[28] In the remaining text, 1 Cor 8,3, the chief command is standing at least in the background because of the context (the unicity of God, v. 4). In the only text outside the gospels and the letters of John where the New Testament speaks of love for Jesus (1 Pet 1,8), this is placed in parallel with faith, and is thus intended with respect to the fundamental relationship with Jesus.

Also in John's gospel, the passages, where love for God or for Jesus is the topic, can be explained most easily in the light of the chief commandment. Jn 5,42 sets love for God parallel to the search for the glory which comes from the one God. Besides, this (v. 44) is the only occasion in John's gospel where the adjective 'only' (μόνος) appears to be referred to God.[29] In Jn 8,42, Jesus sets love for God in contrast to the pretended claim of the Jews to have God as their 'one Father (v. 41).[30] In Jn 14,31, we have already been struck by the connection between Jesus' love for the Father and his fulfilling of the latter's 'commandment'.[31] There still remains Jesus' question concerning Simon Peter's love for him in Jn 21,15ff. It can be understood as a question about the recognition of Jesus as of the 'one' shepherd in the sense of Jn 10,16 – only again in Jn 10 do we come across the word-field of 'shepherd', 'sheep, and 'tend'.[32]

The theme of love for God in the First Letter of John appears clearly to be bound up with the observing of the commandments and therewith with the complex from the covenant theology which we have examined. This is particularly the case in the section 1 Jn 4,7-5,3. Criterion of the love of God is the love of the brothers (4,7-21) and the fulfilling of the commandments (5,2f).

The well-founded study by *E. Malatesta*[33] has set forth the basic structural significance of the theme of communion with God in the New Covenant for 1 John. In fact, the word διαθήκη ('covenant') is absent in 1 John. However, the promises concerning the New Covenant of Jer 31,31-34; Ezek 36,24-28; 37, especially vv. 26-28, are clearly active and important there.

Thus, the first result of our examination of the 'framing verses' Jn 14,15.21a.23b.24a is this: the Jesus of the Johannine Farewell Discourses is clearly speaking here on the basis of a biblical, Jewish and Christian tradition,

---

[28] The same formulation occurs again in Jas 1,12; 2,5. Otherwise, 'love for God' appears again in the epistolary literature of the New Testament only in the post-Pauline 2 Thess 3,5.
[29] Only comparable is the address to the Father as 'the only true God' in the – probably post-Johannine – High Priestly Prayer in Jn 17,3.
[30] The tradition critical interpretation of the text is supported by the observation that only here in John is God spoken of as the 'one' God, as also in the Old Testament Deut 6,4 is the most influential of the few texts which speak of the unicity of God with the aid of the numeral 'one'. Cf. N. Lohfink, 'ḥd (except II 1a), in ThWAT I (1973) 210-218, here 212ff.
[31] Cf., *supra*, in this section.
[32] For the last text, cf. *Schnackenburg* II 377: 'The one flock is realised through the one shepherd. Thereby the prophecy of Ezek 37,24 on the universal scope of the new covenant is fulfilled'.
[33] *Malatesta*, Interiority.

which has its oldest roots in the language of the treaties of the Ancient Near East, of the Decalogue and of Deuteronomy, which since that time has been determined by the 'chief commandment' of Deut 6,4ff, but which also in other tradition variants appears close to the Decalogue. This has passed through the Wisdom and Testament literature as well as liturgical texts, those at Qumran included, until it has reached the New Testament. There it is evidenced in the Synoptics, in Paul and in the other epistolary literature. The Johannine parallel texts (cf. Jn 5,42; 8,42, less unambiguously the post-Johannine text Jn 21,15ff) show a clear relationship with the 'chief commandment' of Deut 6,4-13 (with its acknowledgement of the unicity of God) and thereby with the covenant theology of Deuteronomy. This is further developed in the First Letter of John in the sense of the theology of the 'New Covenant' after the promises of Jer 31 and Ezek 36f.

3.2 The Content of Jesus' Promise (vv. 16-20.21b.23c)

3.2.1 The Coming and Abiding of the Spirit (vv. 16f)

Not only the condition attached to the promise of Jesus of his threefold coming in Jn 14,15-24 but also the content of this promise itself seems to be understood in terms of Old Testament covenant theology. In the first promise (vv. 16f), Jesus promises the divine gift of the Spirit-Paraclete as an abiding gift to the disciples who love him and keep his commandments.

We have already made a provisional division between language and thought that is Johannine and tradition that is probably pre-Johannine (cf., *supra*, 2). This can now be refined. To the evangelist we can probably ascribe, first, the introduction to the promise, by which he links the condition and the promise: 'and I will pray the Father'. There, not only the description of God as 'Father'[34] but also the verb 'pray' is Johannine.[35] The description of the Paraclete as 'another, second' may also go back to the evangelist. It is conditioned here by the idea that Jesus himself is now taking his farewell but will clearly remain as advocate for his own with the Father (cf. Heb 7,25; 9,24; 1 Jn 2,1). At the same time, the description of the Paraclete as 'Spirit of truth' appears linked with the tradition, but reshaped by John. It is met with repeatedly within the Johannine Paraclete sayings (Jn 14,26; 15,26; 16,13), and there too appears each time as an added phrase in apposition.

---

[34] While in the Synoptic material, God is spoken of relatively seldom as Father (Mk 3x, Q 4x, Lk's special material 4x, Mt's special material 31x), John uses it 100 times. Cf. *O. Michel*, πατήρ in: EWNT III (1982) 125-135, here: 126 = EDNT III (1993) 53-57, here 53.

[35] It belongs to the thematic of this chapter, in the immediate context, with the verb αἰτέω v. 13f. Among the evangelists, ἐρωτάω in the sense of 'pray' is used in a preferential way by Lk (Lk 9x, Acts 6x) and Jn (12x). Mk and Mt use it only once. Cf. *W. Schenk*, ἐρωτάω, in: EWNT II (1981) 144f, here: 145 = EDNT II (1991) 57-58: 57.

The expression itself is stereotypical, as is shown by parallels in the New Testament (1 Jn 4,6; cf. Herm[m] 3,4),[36] in Qumran (1QS 4,21)[37] and in the Testaments of the Twelve Patriarchs (TestJud 20,1.5).[38] This excludes neither that elements of the formula belong to other word fields (as will shown for 'Spirit') nor that the evangelist makes more or less free use of the formula. Finally, the opposition of the 'world', which can neither 'receive' nor 'see' and 'recognise' the Spirit-Paraclete, and the disciples who are able to do so, seems to be formulated by John on account of its correspondence with both the other promises (vv. 19.22) and its connection with Johannine dualism (cf., already, the Prologue, Jn 1,4.10-13), at least in the text as we have it, which similarly does not exclude reference to the tradition.

As probable components of the pre-Johannine tradition in this text, there remains, first of all, the 'giving' of the Paraclete by God, then the description itself of 'Paraclete' (perhaps also as 'Spirit of truth' – wholly or in part), as well as the promise of his 'being with' (μετά) the disciples, his 'being with' (παρά) and 'being among/in' (ἐν) them, and, indeed, 'for ever'.

The probable pre-Johannine tradition that we have described yields a word-field which has a clear counterpart in the Old Testament, namely the promise of the New Covenant, of the 'everlasting' covenant and the covenant of 'peace' in Ezek 36,26-28; 37,26-28; cf. 11,19-21.[39] Already the 'giving' finds its threefold correspondence in Ezek 36,26ff (cf. *wnttj* 2x in v. 26, *'tn* in v. 27; LXX 3x δώσω). The 'Spirit' is twice mentioned as the content of God's giving in Ezek 36,26ff; in v. 26, it is described as a 'new Spirit'; in v. 27 God promises: 'I will put my Spirit within you', and, as the sequel: 'and cause you to walk in my statutes and be careful to observe my ordinances'. Here it is a question of the spiritualising of the Law which is prepared for in the promise of the 'New Covenant' in Jer 31,31-34 and further developed by Ezekiel.[40] The spiritualisation takes place here through the fact that God gives the Israelites a 'new heart' of flesh and pours out his Spirit into their inward parts (*bqrb*). To this promise runs parallel the announcement in Ezek 37,26ff that God will erect his sanctuary for ever among (*btwk*) the Israelites and make his dwelling among (*'l*) them. That both the Ezekiel texts are concerned with the promise of the 'New Covenant' is clear from the dependence on Jer 31,31-34; from the presence in both

---

[36] Cf. *Bauer*, Wörterbuch 71.
[37] Cf. *H. Braun*, Qumran I 131f. There also for 1QS 3,18-24.
[38] Cf. *Beutler*, Martyria 274.301; *Porsch*, Pneuma 231, as well as generally on the literary background of the Johannine Spirit of truth 228-236.
[39] For the significance of the promise of Jer 31 and Ezek 36f for the Johannine Farewell Discourses, cf. *F.-M. Braun*, Jean II 205, also 156; *Mollat*, Saint Jean 127f, on the 'giving' of the new commandment Jn 13,34; *Feuillet*, Mystère 95; *Cortès*, Discursos 439, with n. 193 who, however, stresses the fact that in Ezekiel the 'keeping of the commandments' is the presupposition for the sending of the Spirit.
[40] Cf. *Zimmerli*, Ezechiel II 878ff. Apparently Ezek 36,23c-38 belongs to a late post-Exilic stratum as can be inferred from its absence in old manuscripts: *Lust*, Ezekiel 36-40.

texts of the 'covenant formula': 'you shall be my people, and I will be your God (Ezek 36,28; 37,23; 37,27, in inverted form; cf. 11,20; 34,31); from the explicit announcement of a 'covenant of peace' as an 'everlasting covenant' in Ezek 37,26 (cf. 34,25); and from the double use of the catchword 'new' in Ezek 36,26.

Also in the Johannine Paraclete saying of Jn 14,16f, there is a shift from the promise of the presence of the Spirit-Paraclete 'with' (μετά v. 16, παρά v.17) to his presence 'in' (ἐν v. 17) them.[41] This might result from the fact that the Spirit is first thought of as comforter and advocate, also in the judgement (cf. Jn 15,27; 16,8; Mt 10,20), and thus takes on a function external to the disciples.[42] Even the Greek ἐν ὑμῖν ἔσται ('he will be 'in' = 'with' you') of Jn 14,17 may be understood in this external sense as the parallel in Ezek 37,27 LXX ἐν αὐτοῖς 'with them' shows. However, the close parallel in Ezek 36,27 suggests precisely the understanding of the Spirit as an inner gift. In addition, we note expressly two points of reference between our Johannine Paraclete saying and the two promises in Ezekiel: the 'abiding' of the Paraclete with the disciples in Jn 14,17 corresponds to the 'everlasting covenant' of Ezek 37,36. Moreover, although the element of knowing is certainly given, it emerges only in a varied form: whereas in Ez 37,28 the nations will know that Yahweh is the Lord because he is dwelling in the middle of his people, in Jn 14,17b, the 'world' *cannot* know the comforter. Of course, the believers can know it, something which is included in the promise of Jer 31,31-34, where the knowledge of God is precisely the essence of Jeremiah's promise of the 'New Covenant' (cf. also Jer 24,7).

EXCURSUS: The 'New Covenant' in the New Testament and in early Jewish tradition.

Our interpretation of Jn 14,16f against the background of the Old Testament promises of the New Covenant, as we find them in Jer 31,31ff and in a related form in Ezek 36,26ff; 37,26ff; cf. 11,19-21, presupposes that this promise was current in the early Christian community. This is in fact the case.

The most important place for the theology of the 'New Covenant' is the tradition of the Last Supper. This presents Jesus, in an older stratum, as speaking, in connection with Ex 24,8, of 'my blood of the covenant which is shed for many' (Mk 14,24) or 'that is shed for many for the forgiveness of sins' (Mt 26,28). However, (as already begins to be seen in Matthew), this is already being interpreted in the sense of the 'New Covenant' of Jer 31,31ff in the further developed stratum presented by Paul (1 Cor 11,25) and Luke (22,20).[43]

---

[41] Cf. *Porsch*, Pneuma 245f.

[42] The German word 'Beistand', translated here as 'comforter' brings this aspect to appropriate expression. For the origin and the theological significance of the Johannine Paraclete, cf. *Betz*, Paraklet; *Johnston*, Spirit-Paraclete; *Porsch*, Pneuma, especially 305-324.

[43] Cf. *H. Hegermann*, in: EWNT I (1980) 718-725, here 721f = EDNT I (1990) 299-301, here: 300.

With regard to content, the New Covenant is developed by Paul in Galatians as the covenant of promise by contrast with the covenant of Sinai seen as the covenant of obligation (3,15-18; 4,21-28). Ezek 36,26ff (cf. 11,19ff; 37,14) may have also influenced 2 Cor 3,1-14: „Paul views the ministry of the new covenant as the 'ministry of the Spirit,' probably in connection with a corresponding Lord's Supper interpretation (1 Cor 10:3f.) He is also dependent on OT witnesses in the context of the prophecy of Jeremiah 31, including Ezek 36:26f.".[44]

The promise of the New Covenant according to Jer 31,31-34 occupies a good deal of room in the Letter to the Hebrews: Jesus is the mediator of a new and better covenant (7,22; 8,6; 9,15ff) which is conceived, above all, in cultic terms as is shown by the repeated formula 'blood of the covenant' (9,20; 10,29: 13,20; cf. Ex 24,8). However, the author cites Jer 31,31-34 explicitly in 8,8-12 and Jer 31,33f in 10,16f, and in doing so he leads beyond the bloody offerings of the old covenant which can effect no real atonement.

Individual elements of the promise of the New Covenant of Jer 31,31-34 are found scattered throughout the rest of the New Testament such as the eschatological instruction of God mediated through Christ, at least hinted at in Mt 23,8, more explicit in Jn 6,45, and the writing of God's commandments even on the hearts of the Gentiles, in connection with Jer 31,33 in Rom 2,15.[45] At Rom 11,27, Paul cites Jer 31,33f as the scriptural basis for his hope in the final redemption of Israel.

A particular linking of the promise of a law which gives life, probably with reference to Jer 31,31ff, to the gift of the Spirit, probably with reference to Ezek 36,26ff, is made in the overloaded verse Rom 8,2, as S. *Lyonnet* has shown to be plausible.[46] Apart from 2 Cor 3,3 ('a letter from Christ delivered by us, written not with ink but with the Spirit of the living God, not on tablets of stone but on tablets of human hearts'), the gift of the Spirit in the sense of Ezek 36,26f is Paul's subject again in 1 Thess 4,8 which is in fact the oldest document of the New Testament. The eschatological purification (through the Spirit) awakens echoes (probably) of Jn 3,5.

The promise of the erection of God's sanctuary among the Israelites and his dwelling among them in the sense of Ezek 37,26ff is recalled not only in Jn 1,14[47] and 14,23 (for that, cf., *infra*, 3.2.2) but also in Rev 7,15[48] and 21,3. The 'everlasting covenant' of Ezek 37,26 par. is taken up again in Heb 13,20.

The theology of the 'New Covenant' and the 'new heart', in the sense of the promises of Jer 31,31-34 and Ezek 36,26ff (cf. 37,26ff), would probably not have found a way into the New Testament unless it had already been prepared in post-Exilic Judaism. That this was the case is demonstrated from the post-Exilic Psalms, from the theological and devotional language of Qumran, and from the partly early rabbinic texts.

In Ps 51,12-14, the promise of Ezek 36,26ff seems to have been taken up directly and transferred into the personal language of the worshipper as H.-J. Kraus has shown.[49] Just as God created (*br'*) the first man and blew the breath of life into his nostrils (Gen 2,7), so God is now requested to 'create' (*br'*) a 'pure heart' for the worshipper and to 'renew' a 'right Spirit' within him (v. 12). The prayer is further specified by the request that God may not take away his Holy Spirit (v. 13), but confer a 'ready Spirit' (v. 14). It is characteristic of this psalm that it expects God's pleasure to be not in offerings (cf. vv. 18f) but in a human spirit or

---

[44] Cf., *ibid.*, 733 = 301.
[45] Cf. the reference to these allusions to Jer 31,31-*Aland*[26].
[46] *Lyonnet*, Exegesis 145-159.
[47] Cf., again, the reference in *Nestle-Aland*[26].
[48] Here the conspicuous ἐπ' αὐτούς corresponds to the *'l* in Ezek 37,27.
[49] Cf. *Kraus*, Psalmen I ([5]1978) 541. In this case, of course, we must keep before us the suggested late dating of Ezek 36,23c-38 in *Lust* (cf., *supra*, n. 40).

heart renewed (through the Spirit of God). This links up the psalm with similar psalms such as 40,7ff (cited at Heb 10,5ff); 37,30f to which Kraus additionally refers.[50] More important here than offerings are obedience, attention to God's word, the bearing of his will in one's heart and joy thereat (cf. Ps 119,11.34.36.69 or 16.92.111.143).

However, the promise of the future New Covenant shows itself to be alive not only in the canonical psalms but also in the Dead Sea Scrolls. According to the Damascus Document, the community understands itself as the community of the New Covenant, and to enter it means 'to enter into the new covenant in the land of Damascus (CD 6,19; 8,21; 19,33; cf. 20,12; 1QpHab 2,3 *Lohse*). According to the understanding of the community, it is – in connection with Is 55,3; 61,8; Jer 32,40; 50,5; Ezek 16,60; 37,26 – an 'everlasting covenant' (1QS 4,22; 5,5; 1QM 13,7f; 1QS^b 1,2; 2,25; 3,26 *Lohse*; CD 3,13).

Especially illuminating for the development of the promise of Ezek 36,26ff is the last psalm from Qumran which seems to extend from 1QH 17,26 to 18,33.[51] Already, at the beginning, the motif of bestowal of the Spirit on the worshipper is taken up. The text is fragmentary, but the word-field of '(holy) Spirit', 'heart' and 'covenant' can be recognised (together with 'love' and 'for ever' (17,26-28). The worshipper who seems to be the 'Teacher of Righteousness' himself,[52] is able to thank God that he has 'sprinkled' his 'holy Spirit' on him. The catchword 'heart' which appears here already is taken up again at the end (18,26): 'and I, I am a creature [of clay...an ear of du]st and heart of stone. With whom will I be reckoned until these things? For [...] you have [gi]ven to the ear of dust, and you have inscribed for ever what is to happen in the heart of [stone...] you have made stop, to bring into the covenant with you...'. (18,25-28) The dependence on Ezek 36,26ff is so unambiguous here that M. Delcor can rely upon this text in fact to complete his reading.[53] The fundamental difference between the concept of the 'New Covenant' in Qumran and the New Testament is that the Essene community thinks of the New Covenant basically as the restoration of the old covenant with the fathers, Moses or David, while the New Testament sees it as something qualitatively different. Of course, the correspondence of the role of Jesus for the establishment of the New Covenant with that of the 'Teacher of Righteousness' remains important.[54]

In different ways, the promises of the 'New Covenant' and of Ezek 36,26ff are also current in the rabbinic literature. Whatever the importance of the promise of the New Covenant in Jer 31,30-33, it plays a wholly subordinate role in the rabbinic texts. The few bits of evidence we have referring to it are consistently late and of lesser importance.[55]

It is different with regard to the prophetic promise in Ezek 36,26 that God will in the future take the heart of stone out of the breast of the Israelites and replace it with a heart of flesh (with the result that they will be capable of keeping his commandments). In fact, for this

---

[50] Cf. *Kraus*, Theologie 120 and 203.
[51] Cf. the reconstruction of the opening of the hymn in 17,26 by *Maier*; *Delcor*, Hymnes; *Lohse et al.* [A new division is proposed in DSS with Puech: here 1QH 18,16-33 is found in col. XXI top, 1 QH 18,26 is found in col. XXI,10-13, see pp. 193f; 1QH 17 corresponds to 1QH DSS col. IV, p. 149].
[52] Cf. *Delcor*, Hymnes 23.290f.288.
[53] *Delcor*, Hymnes 290f.
[54] On the extent and limits of the correspondence between the 'Teacher of Righteousness' of Qumran and Jesus, cf. *Jeremias*, Lehrer, especially 319-353; *H. Braun*, Qumran II § 3, pp. 54-74; *Maier-Schubert*, Qumran-Essener 99-106, cf. ff. For the historical figure of the 'Teacher of Righteousness', cf. the controversy in: RdQ 10 (1979-81) 235-246.553-586.
[55] Cf. the reference to ShirR 1,2; QohR 2,1; PesK 107a; TanB *jtrw* § 13 (38b), *Bietenhard* 370; JalquṭSchim'oni 2 § 317 *in Strack-Billerbeck* III 704 on Heb 8,8-12 9 (= Jer 31,31-34). Tan *'qb* 8b, *ibid.* I 243.

text, there is a continuous tradition of debate: the 'heart of stone' almost always signifies the 'evil inclination' which is innate in man. This interpretation might lay claim to be much older since it is a subject of discussion at the end of the first century A.D. at the latest, that is, at the time of the composition of John's gospel.[56]

The Midrash is able to contrast the 'heart of stone' in the sense of the 'evil inclination' with the table of stone of the Law which has the function of keeping watch over the stony heart: thus, with reference to Ezek 36,26, a saying of R. Levi (about 300) in two texts of the Midrash.[57]

Especially numerous are the rabbinic instances in which, with reference to Ezek 36,26, it is expected for the 'age to come' that God will take the 'evil inclination' out of the flesh of the Israelites.[58] With few exceptions, they also belong to the Midrash, something which is not to be wondered at given the foundation of the text in the saying of the prophet and which should not be allowed to tell against the age of the tradition. The fact that this tradition is so wide-spread speaks in favour of its antiquity.

In fact, the positive idea, that God will give a new heart in the age to come is expressed only rarely but must probably be understood even in those places where, in rabbinic fashion, only one part of Ezek 36,26 is expressly cited.[59] Occasionally, the keeping of God's commandments as a result of an inner impulse, in the sense of Ezek 36,27 (cf. Jer 31,33), is also mentioned as the consequence of the endowment with a new heart.[60] A direct connection between Jer 31,31ff and Ezek 36,26ff is never made in the texts I have reviewed although one text at least comes very near to that connection in that, concerning the 'future' expulsion of the 'evil inclination', it reports two rabbinic sayings as immediately next to each other, one of which argues from Jer 31,33, the other from Ezek 36,26.[61]

A prominent difference from the perspective of the New Testament is that the bestowal of the Spirit of God according to Ezek 36,26ff gives way to the gift of the 'heart of flesh' that follows the Law. Only occasionally do we get an explicit glimpse of the bestowal of the Spirit, thus in a text in the late Psalm Midrash where it expressly forms a transition to the quotation of Joel 3,1ff (as in Acts 2,17ff).[62]

Still more important for our investigation is a text in DevR where not only is Joel 3,1 mentioned close to Ezek 36,26, but also the promise of God's dwelling among the Israelites in the Shekinah.[63] Although the text cannot be placed very early,[64] it shows the possible recipro-

---

[56] Cf. the Excursus 'Der gute und der böse Trieb' in *Strack-Billerbeck* IV 466-483. The oldest piece of evidence there (481) goes back to R. J^{e}hoschua' in Av 2,11 (c. A.D. 90).
[57] Cf. WaR 35 (132c) and the reference to ShirR 6,11 (125a) *in Strack-Billerbeck* III 90f; the (German) text of ShirR 6,11 in *Wünsche* 160.
[58] Cf. Ber 32a (*Strack-Billerbeck* III 271); ShemR 15 (76c) (*Strack-Billerbeck* III 601, *Wünsche* 107); ShemR 41 (98a) (*Strack-Billerbeck* IV 847f, *Wünsche* 293); BemR 17 (183a) (*Strack-Billerbeck* IV 474, *Wünsche* 435); TanB mqṣ § 1 (95a) (*Strack-Billerbeck* IV 481, *Bietenhard* 218); TanB mtś' §13 (57b) (*Strack-Billerbeck* IV 848, *Bietenhard* 411); PesK 148a (*Strack-Billerbeck* IV 922, in more detail *Wünsche* 210); PesK 165a (*Strack-Billerbeck* III 240, cf. *Wünsche* 238); AgBer 23 (20a) (*Strack-Billerbeck* III 94); QohR 9,15 (45a) (*Strack-Billerbeck* IV 472, cf. *Wünsche* 131).
[59] Cf. pYom 4,41 b 54 Bar (41b), *Schwab* III 2,202.
[60] Cf. MTeh 73,4 (168a) (*Strack-Billerbeck* IV 916; *Braude* II 4).
[61] Cf. ShirR 1,2 (82 b) (*Strack-Billerbeck* IV 482, more completely in *Wünsche* 15 where, in terms of content, R. Jehuda makes the same statement as R. Nechemja only with reference to Jer 31,33 instead of to Ezek 36,26).
[62] Cf. MTeh 14,6 (57b) (*Strack-Billerbeck* II 134.615; IV 850; *Braude* I 186).
[63] DevR 6 (203d) (*Strack-Billerbeck* IV 927, cf. *Wünsche* 83).

cal penetration of the promise of the alteration of human hearts, of the bestowal of the Spirit of God and of the dwelling of God among his people as gifts of the eschatological age in rabbinic thought in the area of Palestine not all that long after the New Testament era.

Looking back, we can now advance a conjecture: the promise of the gift of the Spirit by Jesus in Jn 14,16f is inserted not by accident or, in the first place, on the basis of the compositional viewpoint of the evangelist in the 'framing verses' (15.21a.23b.24a) of Jn 14 concerning 'love' for Jesus and the 'observing' of his 'commandments', but is to be understood in relation to the covenant theology of the Old Testament as it appears developed in the 'framing verses'. Above all, the promise of Ezek 36,26ff, which for its part corresponds to the promise of the 'New Covenant' in Jer 31,30-33, might have influenced the insertion and the formation of the first Johannine Paraclete saying in Jn 14,16f. This is all the more probable in that the promise of Ezek 36,26 has been shown to be current elsewhere in the New Testament and in post-Exilic and post-biblical Judaism.

3.2.2. The Coming and Abiding of Jesus and the Father (vv. 18.23)

Can we pursue the trail further? As was shown in Chapter 1 of this study, there exists a substantive connection between the promise of the Spirit-Paraclete in vv. 16f and the announcement of the coming of Jesus alone in vv. 18-20 or with the Father in v. 23. Thus we may advance the assumption that the traditional connection already demonstrated, which is already evident in the 'framing verses' and continued in the Paraclete saying of vv. 16f, also takes effect in the following verses with their promise of the coming and abiding of Jesus and the Father.

As a control on this assumption, we shall take up again a hypothetical distinction between Johannine redaction and the pre-Johannine tradition in verses 18-20.21b-23a.c.d. Only this way we can specify more precisely the character and the internal coherence of the pre-Johannine tradition.

In our passage, the opposition between the world and the disciples in seeing Jesus (v. 19),[65] the fellowship or communion between Jesus and the disciples in love (ibid.),[66] as well as the correspondence of the Father, Jesus and the disciples in indwelling (v. 20) might go back to the evangelist.[67] The interrupting question of Judas (v. 22) with the resumption of Jesus' speech (v. 23) may also be Johannine. The opposition in this question between the self-revelation of Je-

---

[64] *Strack-Stemberger*, Einleitung 282 place the composition of DevR somewhere between 450 and 800 A.D. The exegetical traditions contained in the Midrash could certainly be older.

[65] On dualism as characteristic of Johannine theology, cf., among others, *Bultmann*, Theologie 354-385; *Böcher*, Dualismus; *Schottroff*, Glaubende 228-245. On the predestinarian emphasis of Johannine dualism, cf. *Bergmeier*, Glaube.

[66] Cf., fundamentally, *Mussner*, ZΩH, especially Chapters 4 and 5.

[67] Cf. *Heise*, Bleiben 46.

sus to the disciples and that to the world similarly fits in with the Johannine dualistic pattern.[68] More difficult to allocate are the two temporal indications μικρόν 'yet a little while' v. 19 and 'in that day' v. 20: while the former can be considered as betraying the Johannine style,[69] the latter is in the traditional formulation,[70] even if it appears to have been used by John only in the Farewell Discourses. The 'knowledge' of the disciples with respect to the indwelling of the Father and Jesus or in Jesus (v. 20) requires examination from the point of view of tradition history.

The description of the disciples as 'orphans' in v. 18 cannot be classified with certainty as traditional. In the sense in which it is used, it probably came to the author rather through the genre of (wisdom) Farewell Discourses than through specific parallel texts so that scholars rightly refer, on the one hand, to Jewish and Greek parallels,[71] and, on the other hand, to the given Johannine frame and context.[72]

The subject of the impending 'coming' of Jesus (v. 18), which, in v. 23, is extended to the 'coming' of the Father, makes use of traditional material. The linking of the 'seeing' or 'manifesting' of Jesus (vv. 19.21c.22b) with the 'coming' of Jesus seems to be traditional as well, as will be shown below (cf., *infra*, 3.2.3). We would also like to assign the 'knowing' of Jesus and his gifts of love and life to the tradition as will be demonstrated presently. The erection of the home of God with the disciples (v. 23), to which the indwelling formulae of v. 20 correspond, is especially deserving of attention with regard to the determining covenant theology of the section.

We shall first of all try to shed light on the background of the promise of Jesus that he will come (v. 18) and that the disciples will see him (v. 19). As recent authors acknowledge,[73] the early Christian theology of resurrection and coming again are here being linked. An older layer in the Synoptic Gospels knows of an interpretation of Dan 7,13f's 'coming' of the Son of Man on the clouds of heaven as the awaited eschatological coming of Christ in glory (Mk

---

[68] Cf., *supra*, n. 65.

[69] *Ruckstuhl*, Einheit 214; *J. Schneider*, Abschiedsreden 106, recognises the (Johannine) genre of 'μικρόν-saying'.

[70] Cf., *infra*, n. 117.

[71] Jewish parallels are given in *Strack-Billerbeck* II 562: MekhY 13,2 (23a); pHag 1,75 d, 40; pSot 3,19a, 2; Hag 3 b; ARN 25. Greek parallels which refer to the pupils who are left behind by their teacher as orphans are listed by *Bauer* 184 and *Barrett* 463: Plato, Phaedo 116a; Lucian, de morte peregrini 6. *Bernard* 546f interprets in the sense of 'friendless' and brings forward Ps 10,14 as well as Epictetus, Diss. III XXIV 14 in support of this view.

[72] Cf., among others *Bultmann* 478 with n. 1; *Brown* 640; *Schnackenburg* III 88.

[73] Cf. *Schulz*, Untersuchungen 164-167, with a survey of the debate pursued up to 1957; *Ricca*, Eschatologie 157f; the theme of the coming again (Jesus 'comes' to take home the disciples in the sense of Jn 14,3) is overemphasised by *v. Hartingsveld*, Eschatologie 129-134.140-142; the Easter experience by *Becker* 467f. *Boismard*, Evolution 521, derives the promise of the coming of Jesus from wisdom texts (Wisd 6,12; Sir 4,14).

13,26 par; 14,62 par). The epilogue to John's gospel (21,22f) seems to be speaking of this future 'coming' of Jesus.[74] Another tradition knows of Jesus as the 'coming one', that is the promised Davidide in the sense of Ps 118,25[75] (this psalm concludes the Great Hallel for the celebration of the Passover).[76] Whether Jesus is the 'coming one' in this sense is the import of the Baptist's question according to the tradition in Q (Mt 11,3; Lk 7,19). After another tradition, it was the Baptist who announced him as the 'coming one' (Mk 1,7 par; Jn 1,15.27.30; Acts 13,25). With John here, it is rather the apocalyptic tradition of the Son of Man that seems to be in operation, as the linking of the motifs of 'coming' and 'seeing' in vv. 18f shows.[77] By contrast with the perspective of the Synoptics, this eschatological 'coming' and 'manifesting' of Jesus will be experienced in history, that is, in the real experience of the community of the disciples of Jesus. This is shown by the report of the appearance of Jesus before the ten disciples in Jn 20,19-23. It is the only Easter text that describes the Easter experience as the 'coming' of Jesus (v. 19). Corresponding to that is the fact that the disciples 'see' the Lord and thereby experience (eschatological) 'joy' (v. 20).[78] The early Christian expectation of the second coming is here thus being interpreted in the sense of Johannine 'realised eschatology'. The same thing appears to be the case in Jn 14,18f.[79]

What sense then has the reason that is given, 'because I live, you will live also?' The starting point seems to be the 'life' of Jesus after death by virtue of the resurrection (cf. Mk 16,11; Lk 24,5.23; Acts 1,3; Rom 14,9; 1 Thess 5,10), but, against this view, there speaks the fourth evangelist's conception of 'life' as the embodiment of the eschatological salvation that has its source in Jesus.[80] Moreover, the use of the present ὅτι ἐγὼ ζῶ must recommend caution here. Analogous to the 'coming' of Jesus and his 'manifestation' to the disciples, his new 'life' by virtue of the resurrection appears here to be separated from its eschatological-apocalyptic context and sense and transferred into the real experience of the community, and, beyond that, to be linked with the Johannine idea of the Incarnation, as is already clear in the Prologue to the gospel (Jn 1,1-4). The 'in that day' of v. 20 accordingly gives a new interpretation of the prophetic-apocalyptic expectation of the coming 'day of the Lord' in the 'hour of faith'. In

---

[74] *Becker* 649 recognises here the expression of the early Christian imminent expectation in the sense of 1 Thess 4,15-17; Rom 13,11.
[75] The psalm is quoted in the Johannine Triumphal Entry, Jn 12,13; cf. *Schnackenburg* II 470f; *Becker* 377f.
[76] Cf. *Strack-Billerbeck* I 845ff; IV 72; *Pesch*, Markusevangelium II 379.
[77] The oldest and fundamental text for this connection is Dan 7,13.
[78] For this eschatological gift of the Risen One, cf., *infra*, Chapter IV.3.
[79] Cf. *Schulz*, *Ricca* and *Becker* in n. 73.
[80] Cf., again, *Mussner*, ΖΩΗ, especially Chapter 5: 'Content and Essence of ζωή (αἰώνιος)'; for Jn 14,18-24, pp. 155f. Instead of a 'mystical community of life', one should, of course, speak, in the Johannine sense, of life as a reality of faith.

fact, it is this that is the subject when the 'knowing' of the dwelling of Jesus in the Father and of the mutual dwelling of Jesus and the disciples is spoken of.

Since the whole of Chapter 14 of John as Farewell Discourse focuses on the abiding link between Jesus and his disciples after the time of his departure, the weight of the three indwelling sayings is also laid on the 'being' or 'abiding' of the disciples in Jesus and Jesus in them which makes possible the 'being' of the disciples in the Father and the Father in them, mediated, on his part, by Jesus. This further step is taken in v. 23 where the subject is the 'coming' of Jesus together with the Father, and their erection of a dwelling or 'abode' with the disciples. Since the statement of v. 23 is easier to explain from the history of tradition than that of v. 20, we take it for our starting point.[81]

Within Chapter 14, the material about the 'abiding' (μονή) of Jesus and the Father with the disciples refers back first to v. 2a where Jesus speaks of there being many μοναί in the sense of 'mansions/dwellings' in his Father's house. That statement, which there was seen as a quotation from Ps 42f, is thus turned into the promise of a future 'dwelling' of the Father and Jesus with the believers if they observe Jesus' commandments, meaning by that, if they act according to the (new) covenant.

In the New Testament, the subject of God's eschatological dwelling with his people is found, above all, in the book of Revelation. In Rev 21,1-22,5, the seer unfolds his picture of the New Jerusalem which comes down from God to men. In this connection, in 21,3, the proclamation is made: 'Behold, the dwelling of God is with men. He will dwell with them, and they shall be his people,[82] and God himself will be with them'. This text for its part is referring back to the promises of the coming Jerusalem and the eschatological dwelling of God in the holy city, on Zion, in the temple and with his people.[83] The most important parallel seems to be Ezek 37,27, since here the promise of God's future 'dwelling' with the Israelites is likewise linked with the double covenant formula 'I will be their God, and they will be my people'. But the vision of the future new temple in Jerusalem of Ezek 40-44 also comes in here, above all Ezek 43,7.9 where, similarly, the subject of the 'dwelling; (*mškn*) of God with the Israelites or more precisely as a dwelling 'in the midst' (*btwk*) of them is envisaged.[84] The particu-

---

[81] Cf., already, *Holtzmann-Bauer* 251: Here, 'the theocratic idea of the dwelling of God among his people is fulfilled': Ex 25,8; 29,45; Lev 26,11f; Ezek 37,26f.

[82] The plural 'they will be his peoples' is possible here. It is accepted in *Nestle-Aland*[26] on the basis of the ancient evidence. We read in the singular with the Einheitsübersetzung and the RSV.

[83] Cf., among others, A. R. Hulst, *schkn*, in THAT II (1976) 904-909; W. Michaelis, σκηνή, in ThWNT VII (1964) 369-396, especially 373f. Both authors derive the σκηνή of the LXX from the Hebrew root škn (*Hulst* 909; *Michaelis* 372). God's dwelling has thus nothing of the provisional in the sense of a 'tent' about it.

[84] When the LXX in Ezek 37,27 reads κατασκήνωσις and in Ezek 47,7.9 κατασκηνόω, the words are again rendering the Hebrew stem *škn*: *Michaelis, loc. cit.* 373.

lar closeness of the representation in Revelation to Ezek 37,27 is shown in Rev 7,15 where the unusual expression of God's dwelling 'over' (= with?) the Israelites finds an echo (σκηνώσει ἐπ' αὐτούς; cf. Ezek 37, 27 MT *'l*).[85] In this way, Ezekiel 37 continues the modification of the promise of the New Covenant of Jer 31,31-34 by Ezek 36,26ff: God will clothe the dried up bones of Israel anew with flesh and sinews and awaken them to new life through the breath of the Spirit (vv. 1-14, cf. here the basic elements of the promise of Ezek 36,26-28!) and will restore the unity of the twelve tribes of Israel so that they will be again only one people under one shepherd (vv. 15-28). Living according to the law of Yahweh (v. 24), dwelling in his land (v. 25), an eternal 'covenant of peace' and God's dwelling with his people (vv. 26ff) belong likewise to this promise. Thus not only the double covenant formula but the context of the whole chapter refers to the covenant theology in Ezek 37,27.

For its part, the idea of a future dwelling of Yahweh among the Israelites has its pre-history and sequel in the Old Testament. At the close of 'Holiness Code' (Lev 17-26), analogous to Deut 28, blessing and cursing are promised for the Israelites on the basis of their faithfulness to the Law.[86] As chief demands, the commandment about images (as concrete faithfulness to the first and chief commandment), the Sabbath commandment and the commandment to reverence God's sanctuary are pre-eminent (Lev 26,1-2). Among God's promises are that he will keep his covenant with Israel (v. 9). After the blessing of the harvest (v. 10), there follows the promise of the dwelling of God with the Israelites (v.11) to which the double covenant formula is almost immediately connected, introduced with the renewed assurance to the 'wandering people of God': 'I will walk among you' (v. 12).

The sense of the promise in Lev 26,11 (cf. also 15,31) is just as little eschatological as the other places in the Sacerdotal Code (P)[87] which speak of the future dwelling of God with the Israelites in the Tabernacle/Tent of Meeting (Ex 25,8; 29,45.46; Num 5,3). Nevertheless, in Ex 29,45f, it is significant that here too we find the single covenant formula '(and I will) be their God' (v. 45b) and an allusion to the salvific activity of God in the manner of the opening of the Decalogue and first commandment (v. 46) in connection with the promise of God's dwelling among the Israelites.

The same promise is found in a Deuteronomistic formulation in connection with the account of the building of the temple in 1 Kgs 6,11-13.[88] Here too

---

[85] The LXX reads ἐν αὐτοῖς 'among them' here. Thus it cannot be taken as the immediate *Vorlage* of Rev 7,15.
[86] Cf. *Noth*, Leviticus 109.
[87] Cf. *Noth*, Exodus 162; 188 on Ex 29 as supplement to P; *idem*, Numeri 42, for a similar understanding of Num 5-6.
[88] According to *Würthwein*, Erstes Buch der Könige 65, vv. 11-13 constitute a later Deuteronomstic addition. *Noth*, Könige 118, speaks of a 'late addition'. In the LXX, this group of verses (up to v. 14) is missing in important old witnesses to the text.

there appears the dwelling of God in the midst of the Israelites (v. 13) depending on their obedience to his statutes, on the observing of his commandments and the following of all his ordinances (v. 12), that is, behaviour in conformity with the covenant on the part of Israel. The covenant formula here corresponds to the promise of Yahweh's help (v. 13b). All these texts are significant because, even without any regular occurrence of the word '$b^e rît$' ('covenant'), they allow the connection of the promise of God's dwelling with his people with the covenant with Yahweh and Israel's faithfulness to that covenant to be recognised.

With the post-Exilic prophets, the future dwelling of God with his people or on Zion appears more strongly as the free initiative of God. However, the formula 'know that I am God' recalls again the self-presentation of Yahweh in the first commandment. It is found in Joel 2,27 together with a reference to the unicity of Yahweh;[89] in Joel 4,17-21 together with the promise of an everlasting future for Judah and Jerusalem (v. 20).[90] In Zech 2,14f, the promise of the future dwelling of Yahweh on Zion is linked with a modified covenant formula which also includes the peoples of the world: 'they shall be my people, and I will dwell in the midst of you' (v. 15).[91] In Zech 8,3, the announcement of the future dwelling of God in Jerusalem leads to related sayings,[92] not least about the future liberation and homecoming of Israel to Jerusalem, which is concluded once again by the double covenant formula: 'they shall be my people and I will be their God, in faithfulness and in righteousness' (v. 8).[93]

We now have enough material for comparison to be able to say: the proclamation of the 'dwelling' of God with men in Rev 21,3 seems to have its traditional-historical roots in the Old Testament promises concerning the dwelling of God with the Israelites in the Ark of the Covenant, in Jerusalem, on Zion or in the Temple. There it appears almost always in connection with elements of the covenant theology, especially with the single- or double-membered covenant formula.

In Jn 1,14 such connections could again be resonant when, in the same context, the hymnic recognition of the 'dwelling' of the Logos[94] is connected with a Moses-Jesus (and hence Old-New Covenant) antithesis in vv. 17f. If the dwelling of God is replaced here by the dwelling of his 'Word' among the believers, so, with Paul (1 Cor 3,9 with the continuation in v. 16) and his school

---

[89] *Weiser*, Das Buch der Zwölf Kleinen Propheten I 102, refers to the parallel formulations in Ezekiel.
[90] According to *Weiser, loc. cit.* 109, v. 17 consists of a back reference to 2,27.
[91] According to *Elliger*, Das Buch der Zwölf Kleinen Propheten II 111, vv. 15f possibly consists of a secondary addition.
[92] *Elliger, loc. cit.*, sees a single pre-existing saying. The introduction and the independent position in the context support this.
[93] The 'dwelling' of the Israelites 'in' (*škn btwk*) Jerusalem (v. 8) corresponds to the 'dwelling' of God 'in' (*btwk*) Jerusalem.
[94] *Meagher's* speculation that Jn1.14 spoke here originally of an indwelling of the 'Spirit' instead of the Logos in the believers finds no support at all in the textual tradition.

(Eph 2,21), it is further developed into teaching about the believers as the temple and dwelling place of the Holy Ghost. Precisely in the Letter to the Ephesians, allusion is being made once more to the concept of the covenant: through God's grace, the pagan Christians are admitted into the 'covenant of promise' (v. 12) and, precisely in this way, to the sanctuary of God (vv. 11-22).

We can spare ourselves an analysis of the numerous places in the First Letter of John, in which the topic is the indwelling of God and in God or Jesus with expressions such as μένειν ἐν 'abide/remain in' and εἶναι ἐν 'be in' since this has been done in great detail by E. Malatesta.[95] From this study, we took our starting point for the interpretation of Jn 14,15-24 presented here. Malatesta's research fully confirms the internal connection of the Johannine 'indwelling formulae' with the covenant theology of the Old Testament, especially with the promises of Jer 31,31-34; Ezek 36,26ff; 37, 26ff concerning the 'New Covenant'. According to Ezek 36,26ff, God's dwelling takes shape in a concrete way through the bestowal of the Spirit who enables the Israelites to walk in accordance with the New Covenant already promised in Jer 31,31 and to fulfil his commandments in an interior way. This is probably also the starting point for the progression from the 'dwelling' of God 'among' or 'with' the believers corresponding to Jn 14,23 to Christ's 'being in' them and their 'being in' Christ and, by means of that, in God according to v. 20.

That not only the Father but Jesus also comes to his own and 'dwells' with them is prepared for not only by the Old Testament parallels for the dwelling of God among men or in Israel, especially the tradition of the holy city as the dwelling place for his name[96] and the dwelling of Wisdom with men,[97] but also through the Jewish theologoumenon of the dwelling of the Word[98] (Memra) and the divine 'dwelling'[99] (šᵉkīnāh) with men in Israel. The last concept is so widespread that it can become independent and a substitute for God's name in rabbinical Judaism.[100]

3.2.3 Love, Life, Knowledge, Sight

The supposition that the threefold promise of Jesus of the coming of the Father, his own coming and the gift of the Spirit in Jn 14,15-24 has been influenced by

---

[95] Cf. *Malatesta*, Interiority 42-77 for the indwelling formulae in the OT and their theological understanding.
[96] Cf. with the Hebrew/Aramaic root *škn* (Pi./Pa''l) Deut 12,11; 14,23; 16,2.6.11; 26,2; Ezra 6,12; Neh 1,9; Jer 7,12; more distantly Ezek 43,7 LXX.
[97] Cf., in various formulations, Prov 8,12.31; Wisd 1,4; 7,27f; Sir 1,15; 24,8.
[98] Cf., among the older literature, *Middleton*, Logos; *Hamp*, Der Begriff "Wort"; more recent is *Sabourin*, MEMRA.
[99] Cf., again, *Middleton*, Logos; *Meagher* (n. 94); *Goldberg*, Untersuchungen, as well as further titles in *Malatesta*, Interiority 34.
[100] So already the Kommentar of *Strack-Billerbeck* II 302-333 which, of course, sees the function of the MEMRA YHWH included therein.

the Old Testament promises of the New Covenant in Jeremiah and Ezekiel has been strengthened. It is thus indebted in a broader sense to the covenant theology of the Old Testament to which we have already referred back the 'framing verses' of the section about love for God/Jesus and the keeping of his commandments.

The question remains how the further promises of Jn 14,15-24 relate to the tradition-historical origin that we have given. We are talking here of the gift of the knowledge of the Spirit or the indwelling of the Father, the Son and the disciples (vv.17.20), the seeing of Jesus (vv. 19.21f; cf. v.17 for the Spirit), the receiving of the love of God or Jesus (vv. 21b.23c) and life (v. 20) Since the last two themes seem to be connected more closely with the 'framing verses', we shall begin with them.

Love

That Jesus' announcement of the receiving of the love of God or his own love in Jn 14,21b.23c goes back to traditional material becomes clear from the fact that the Fourth Gospel otherwise never speaks of the love of God for believers. Only in one place, which is not really comparable (3,16), is the love of God for the world mentioned.[101] Where the love of Jesus for 'his own' is the subject elsewhere in the second half of John's gospel, the love of God is not mentioned (13,1.34; 15,9f.12; only in 17,26 is Jesus' love for the disciples referred back to God's love in a post-Johannine way).[102]

In the Book of Deuteronomy, the promise of God's love for Israel is found precisely in the section which is devoted to the theme of the 'chief commandment' of love for God and worship of him alone (Chapters 5-11). It is situated here in immediate connection with the demand for the love of God and the keeping of his commandments. In Deut 7, the theme of the love of God appears first in connection with the promise to the patriarchs (v. 8). According to the expanded quotation of the promise in the Decalogue attached to the first commandment '[He is] the faithful God who keeps covenant and steadfast love with those who love him and keep his commandments, to a thousand generations' (v. 9) just as in a further enjoining of the commandment it says: 'And because you hearken to these ordinances, and keep and do them, the Lord your God will keep with you the covenant and the steadfast love which he swore to your fathers to

---

[101] With the majority of commentators, *Lattke*, Einheit 64-85 holds that Jn 3,16a comes from Christian tradition and interprets the verse from John's revelation theology: the world (beloved by God) is summoned to crisis by Jesus in virtue of his mission as Revealer.

[102] Cf., *supra*, Chapter 1.1 on the probably secondary nature of Jn 15-17. According to *J. Becker*, Abschiedsreden, Chapter 17 is a supplement which has been added to the speeches of Chapters 15-16, themselves later additions. Cf. also his commentary *ad loc*; additionally, *Painter*, Farewell Discourses for a similar suggestion.

keep; he will love you, bless you, and multiply you (vv. 12f)'.[103] Similarly in Chapter 10, the chief commandment of love for God and the keeping of his commandments corresponds with the remembrance of the previous love shown by God in his covenant with the Fathers (vv. 14f). Otherwise God's love for Israel appears again only once in isolated form in Deut 23,6 in a single commandment as well as later in a Deuteronomistic text (1 Kgs 10,9).[104]

All the other evidence for God's love for Israel in the Old Testament stems from the prophets.[105] With Hosea, the concept is strongly defined with the image of nuptial love (Hos 3,1; 11,1.4; 14,5); but here the reference to God's covenant with Israel is brought to expression through the naming of the prophet's son as 'Not-my-people' (1,9, with the annulment of this statement in 2,25 in a passage about a renewed covenant, 2,18-25). In Jeremiah, the love of God is already the expression of the favour and faithfulness of God (31,3[106] in the context of the promise of the New Covenant in Jer 31,31-34) and this remains the case with the Exilic and post-Exilic prophets (Is 43,4,[107] 63,9; Zeph 3,17; Mal 1,2). In this way, the correlation between the love of God or Jesus and the love shown to him in the keeping of his commandments, as it comes to expression in Jn 14,15-24, seems to be an expression of the covenant theology of Deuteronomy.

Life

The theme of 'life' as a component of the promise in Jn 14,19 could also lead to the same area of origin. 'Living' as a verb ($\zeta\hat{\omega}$) is used only seldom in John's gospel. For the receiving of the salvific gift of life, which is the key concept of the salvation received from Jesus in the Fourth Gospel, the evangelist normally uses combinations with the substantive ζωή 'life'.[108] The verb is used of 'living water' (Jn 4,10.11.38), of 'living bread' (6,51) or, in dependence on the tradi-

---

[103] According to *Lohfink*, Hauptgebot, 180f, there is a deliberate employment here of the language of the Decalogue, which originally spoke of behaviour towards God, in the context of the promise of blessing as the answering behaviour of God. This does not exclude that the love of the Great King for his vassals who 'love' him belongs already to the fixed elements of the vassal treaties of the Ancient Near East.

[104] Cf. *Würthwein*, Die Bücher der Könige I 122, who ascribes this verse to a redactor on the ground of its theological orientation.

[105] Cf. *G. Wallis 'hb* II-IV in: ThWAT I (1973) 108-128, here IV.1, 121-124.

[106] *Thiel*, Redaktion 20-28 does not ascribe Jer 31,3 to the Deuteronomistic redaction of Jeremiah, but the promise of the New Covenant in Jer 31,31-34.

[107] According to *Elliger*, Deuterojesaja 138, cf. 298, the corresponding subjects of Is 41,8 and Is 48,14 are, respectively, the love of God for Abraham (cf. LXX and Aquila) and of Abraham for God (the LXX refers the verb to the love of God for Israel). Cf., also, his textual proposal in BHS for Is 41,8; 48,14 and Zeph 3,17.

[108] Cf. the literature mentioned in n. 66 for this Johannine concept.

tion, of a sick person who has been restored to life (4,50.51.53).[109] A connection with the tradition probably lies behind those cases where life after death on being raised is spoken of (5,25; 6,51b; 11,25f),[110] even if the Johannine thought goes further to the freedom from death. Otherwise it is only the post-Johannine layer that appears to know the use of the verb for the receiving of salvation through God and Jesus (6,57f;[111] a soteriological formula seems to lie behind 1 Jn 4,9).[112] Thus a traditional link is the most likely scenario for Jn 14,19 as well.

The fourth evangelist and Paul concur in the fact that, for them, the receiving of 'life' is not bound up with the performance of the Law but with faith in Jesus Christ. Of course, for both of them, there is a fulfilling of the commandments that does lead to life. So, just as for Paul the Law is not abrogated (Rom 3,31) but rather comes to fulfilment in love of neighbour (Rom 13,8-10) because it has become the 'law of the Spirit and life in Christ Jesus' (Rom 8,2),[113] so fulfilment of the commandments and the promise of life hang together in the fourth evangelist. That is how, in Jn 14,15-24, there could be a connection between the promise of life in v. 19 and the 'keeping of the commandments' of Jesus in the 'framing verses', a connection which was already given as such in the covenant theology of the Old Testament.

The promises of the 'New Covenant' in Jer 31 and Ezek 36f do not speak explicitly of the salvific gift of 'life' but rather only of 'living in the land' (Ezek 36,28; 37,25), but Deuteronomy does. The 'chief commandment' (Deut 6,4-13) is followed by promises which focus on 'long life in the land'[114] (6,24; cf. 5,33). Love of God (6,4; cf. fear of God and serving God 6,13.24), heeding his commandments (6,17.20.24) and promise of life in the land (v. 24) belong together closely here. The same linkage recurs in Deut 8,1[115] and in the passage on bless-

---

[109] At the basis of the passage Jn 4,46-53, there certainly lies a pre-Johannine miracle story which might have its counterpart in the story of the 'Centurion from Capernaum' which is handed down in Mt 8,5-13 and Lk 7,1b-10 (Q?). Cf. the detailed discussion in *Schnackenburg* I 500-506. ζάω 'live' in this sense is found in the Synoptics, Mk 5,23 par Mt 9,18.

[110] Jn 5,25 points in this direction the apocalyptic language ('Hour', 'hearing' the 'voice' of the 'Son of Man'), Jn 6,51 the description of 'life' as 'everlasting life', Jn 11,25 the mention of 'resurrection' after 'death' which precisely requires Johannine reinterpretation.

[111] Cf. the detailed discussion of the literary origin of Jn 6,51b-58 in *Richter*, Studien 88-119; cf. 170f.

[112] Both the saying about the 'sending ' of the 'only begotten Son' and also the speech about the eschatological promise of 'life' take up common Christian parlance. Cf. *Bultmann*, Johannesbriefe 71f.

[113] Cf, *supra*, p. 61 with n. 46.

[114] *Lohfink*, Hauptgebot 81-85 has put together the 'verbs referring to blessing' in the central section of Deuteronomy. To them belong ḥyh, 'live'; 'rk ymym Hiphil, 'make your days long'; rbh 'be numerous' (referring to 'days'); yṭb l, 'to prosper'; ṭwb l, 'to be well'; as well as rbh, to be numerous (referring to 'people'). He regards the promise of life as probably grounded in wisdom. (84).

[115] Cf. also Deut 11,9.21, the promise of 'long life in the land' (with 'rk) at he end of Deut 5-11 at the conclusion of the section on the 'chief commandment' and before the transition to

ing and curse – life and death after the ensuing exile (Deut 30).[116] Here too the link between the commandment to love God (vv. 6.16.20) and the promise of life (vv. 6.15f.19f) is presented explicitly. It is at least possible that this link has also had an effect on the promise of life in Jn 14,19.

Knowledge

Among the content of the promises in Jn 14,15-24, we find that the disciples will 'know' the Spirit-Paraclete (v. 17) and that they will 'know' that Jesus is in the Father, they in him and he in them (v. 20). From the formulation in v.20, it becomes clear that here we are concerned with an eschatological promise.[117] This is confirmed by the tense in v. 17 which points to the future. The most important texts for comparison in John are, therefore, those texts in which the subject is the future 'knowledge' of the disciples. According to Jn 8,28, a future 'knowledge' of the divinity of Jesus is linked to the time of his 'lifting up'.[118] Both Jn 7,17 and 8,32 connect the knowledge of the divine origin of the teaching of Jesus or the 'truth' with the doing of the will of God or the remaining in the word of Jesus. This connection demands attention because it comes very close to the promises of Jn 14,17.20. Here too, the knowledge of the Spirit-Paraclete and of the sending of Jesus appears to be embedded in the 'framing verses' about love for Jesus and the keeping of his commandment or word/words (v. 23).

A new form of knowledge of God and his will is the object and aim of the promise of the future New Covenant in Jer 31,34: 'And no longer shall each man teach his neighbour and each his brother, saying, "Know the Lord", for they shall all know me, from the least of them to the greatest, says the Lord'.[119] Knowledge of God becomes based on the fact that God puts his Law in the hearts of the Israelites so that they are enabled to fulfil it from within. This inner

---

the individual commandments; also Deut 16,20, the promise of 'life' in a Deuteronomistic supplement to the corpus of laws: *v. Rad*, Deuteronomium 82.

[116] *V. Rad, loc. cit.* 131f, ascribes Deut 30,1-10 to the Deuteronomist and regards 30,15-20 as 'probably, after all, the last text of Dt. (= Dtn)'. More recent research sees the Deuteronomistic school at work: cf. *Schenker*, Umkehr (on vv. 1-14); *Vanoni*, Geist; *Braulik*, Gesetz, especially 152-169. Also *Smend*, Gesetz.

[117] The introductory 'in that day' adopts prophetic-apocalyptic' usage: cf. *W. Trilling*, ἡμέρα, in EWNT II (1981) 296-302, here 300ff; 301 also on Johannine reinterpretation = EDNT II (1991) 119-121: 121.

[118] The meaning is the 'hour' of his lifting up and glorification on the cross and in the resurrection, as the word-field of 'hour' (12,23.27), 'raised up' (12,32.34) and 'glorified' (12,23.28 [*bis*]) in Jn 12,20-36 shows.

[119] For *Wolff*, Wissen, a line leads from Hosea (4,6) to Deut (cf. 4,39; 7,9; 8,5ff; 9,3ff) in the recognition of the 'knowledge of Yahweh' as the basis for righteous conduct towards God. Hence the connection between knowledge of God and observing of the law in Jer 31,31-34 also becomes understandable. For the Deuteronomistic origin of this verse, cf., *supra*, n. 106.

appropriation of the Law through the gift of the Spirit in the hearts of the Israelites is also the subject of Ezek 36,27.[120]

The promise of future instruction through God himself is also found in Deutero-Isaiah (Is 54,13), where it appears in the context of the proclamation of a new Jerusalem (54,11-17) and an 'everlasting covenant' with Israel (53,3). Moreover, Jn 6,45 is alluding to Is 54,13 almost word for word.[121] Thus it is manifest that the promise of a future knowledge of the Spirit-Paraclete and of fellowship with Jesus and the Father in Jn 14,17-20 can be understood in the light of the prophetic announcement of a new covenant with Israel.

Sight

In Jn 14,17, the 'receiving', 'knowing' and 'seeing' of the Spirit-Paraclete are closely juxtaposed. Already in the dialogue with Nicodemus, it says that no one knows where the Spirit/the wind comes from and where it goes (3,8). Seeing the Spirit is thus possible only through divine revelation as indicated by Jn 1,32 where the Baptist witnesses: 'I saw the Spirit descend as a dove from heaven, and it remained on him'.

The setting in parallel of 'knowing' and 'seeing' in Jn 14,17 allows an interpretation of the 'seeing' of Jesus in v. 19 in close connection with the theme of the knowledge of Jesus - all the more, since the thought of v. 20 also returns to 'knowledge'.

For the 'seeing' of the Spirit in v. 17, one would again be able to think of the instruction promised for the end time in the sense of Jer 31,34; over against the three negative concepts of 'not receiving', 'not knowing' and 'not seeing', there stands a positive one whose probable roots in tradition we have demonstrated.[122]

4. Redaction

We have seen that the passage Jn 14,15-24 is uniformly and consistently impressed with the covenant theology of the Old Testament. The question now is how far this material was already imprinted on the material encountered by the evangelist and how far it was his own contribution.

---

[120] Cf. also Ezek 36,23 and 37,28, the knowledge of the nations that Yahweh is Lord on the basis of his conduct towards Israel or on the basis of his dwelling among the Israelites.

[121] According to *Richter*, Studien 245-261, in Jn 6,45 we are faced not with a direct quotation from the prophet but with the quotation of a haggadic tradition on Is 54,13. Cf. there the valuable material on the Jewish expectation of an eschatological teaching by God, it too on the basis of Jer 31,31-34.

[122] That the concept of a 'seeing' of God had not yet been dislodged in Judaism in New Testament times is something we have shown in Chapter II.3, n. 101. Cf. *Strack-Billerbeck* I 206-215 on Mt 5,8.

The job imposed on the evangelist in vv. 15-24 was to develop the announcement of Jesus in v. 3 πάλιν ἔρχομαι 'I will come again', an announcement stemming from the tradition, and so to create a counterpart for the section vv. 4-14 in which the announcement of the imminent 'going away' of Jesus in vv. 2f found its development (and Johannine reinterpretation). Apparently different models were at the evangelist's disposal for this task, how the Christianity of his circle pictured the 'coming' or 'coming again' of Jesus. One tradition, which comes to expression in vv. 16f, envisaged the coming of Jesus as the coming of the Paraclete who champions the community in Jesus' place (cf. Jn 15,26f; 16,13-15). With this idea there competed another, more widespread, which awaited a coming of Jesus on the basis of the coming of the apocalyptic Son of Man on the clouds of heaven, expected on the basis of Dan 7,13f. It shines through as well in Jn 14,3 in the announcement of the taking home of the believers into their heavenly dwellings with the Father. In our passage, it comes to expression laconically in v.18 (ἔρχομαι πρὸς ὑμᾶς 'I will come to you'). A third model of the expectation regarding the coming again, as we catch a glimpse of it in v. 23, is still more difficult to reconstruct. Here the expectation of the coming of Jesus is linked with that of an eschatological coming of God himself, less to judgement than to dwelling in the midst of his people. It is precisely here that the evangelist may have found the starting point for his putting this whole many-sided Parousia expectation of the early Christians under one unified perspective, thus arranging in a new way and presenting together images that are not exclusive but which complement one another. This unified perspective was provided by the traditionally central belief of the Old Testament of God's covenant with his people Israel.

Everything speaks for the fact that the creation of the 'framing verses' is to be ascribed to the evangelist, even if he made use of verbal and conceptual material from the tradition. He thereby took up a complex of motifs which – originating with the Decalogue – found its most pregnant expression in the covenant theology of Deuteronomy. This lay readily to hand as, since the Exilic and early post-Exilic age, it had shown itself to be the bearer of Israel's hope of salvation in the expectation of a 'New Covenant'. According to this expectation and promise, as they came to expression in the different forms of Jer 31,31-34; Ezek 36,26ff; 37,26ff, God would 'give' not only his Law but his Spirit within the Israelites; indeed he would even be among them and with them and live among them. They would 'know' him, and they would 'live', as could have been added from the promise of blessing in Deuteronomy. This audacious reinterpretation of the early Christian expectation of the second coming would probably not have been possible if the belief in God's promises of a New Covenant had not been current in contemporary Judaism and Christianity. That this was the case is shown by comparative texts such as those we have adduced in our Excursus on the expression.

The theologically bold step of the evangelist determined a series of additions in content to the individual sayings regarding the second coming. Whereas the community probably spoke of the 'coming' of the Paraclete (cf. Jn 15,26; 16,7.13), in Jn 14,16, the evangelist presents it as the 'gift' of the Father, probably in connection with Ezek 36,27. The abiding presence of the Paraclete with the disciples in Jn 14,16b could have been developed out of the promise of the abiding presence of God with the Israelites in Ezek 37,26ff. Furthermore, the description of the Paraclete as 'Spirit of truth' in v. 17 might be an addition of the evangelist as we have already suspected on linguistic grounds (cf., *supra*, 3.2.1), and likewise the opposition between the world and the disciples mentioned here in connection with the receiving of the Spirit-Paraclete. The 'knowing' of the Spirit could again be explained by the promise of the New Covenant in Jer 31,34; perhaps the related 'seeing' has been attached to it.

In vv. 18f, the 'seeing' of Jesus was conditioned primarily by that of the coming of the apocalyptic Son of man. The evangelist might have premised it with the earlier wisdom motif that Jesus would not abandon his own as orphans and added the antithesis of world-disciples in connection with the 'seeing' of Jesus as the coming one. In the announcement of the eschatological knowledge of the dwelling of Jesus in the Father, of the disciples of Jesus in him and Jesus in them, Ezekiel's promise of the New Covenant is brought forward again, probably added by the evangelist. The idea here shows a stage of further development by contrast with the perspective of v. 23 according to which God himself will dwell among his people or the disciples.

The dialogue between Jesus and the Apostle Judas (not Iscariot) in vv. 22f, prepared for in v. 21c, varies the theme of 'seeing' Jesus, only with a stronger emphasis on this revelation as a self-manifestation (cf. 21,1). Thus, what was said of the relation between tradition and redaction in vv. 17.19 is essentially true here. That Jesus will manifest himself not to the world but only to the disciples might here once again be the interpretation and contrast of the evangelist – on the basis of the oldest Christian Easter tradition.[123] He probably also adapts the promise of the eschatological 'dwelling' of God among the Israelites in v. 23 more powerfully to his own usage through the choice of the word μονή 'home' (cf. v.2 and the central significance of the verb μένειν 'abide' in the Fourth Gospel).[124] The linguistic variations for God's commandment, here as Jesus' 'commandments', 'words' or 'word' (cf. the 'framing verses') might similarly be ascribed to him on the basis of Deuteronomy.[125] Moreover, the re-

---

[123] Cf. the series of witnesses in 1 Cor 15,5-8, the report of the apparitions in the gospels as well as the certainly very early formula 'have seen the Lord' (1 Cor 9,1; Jn 20,18.25), which appear to refer only to the disciples.
[124] Cf. *Heise*, Bleiben.
[125] Cf. *Lohfink*, Hauptgebot 54-58: 'series building words for "Law" in Deuteronomy' to which *(dābār)* "word" and *(dᵉbārîm)* "words" also belong. For a table giving an overview to Deut 4,45-28,68, cf. *ibid.*, 295f.

ferring of the word of Jesus to the word of the Father in v. 24 is undoubtedly his work.

What theological concerns are decisive for the evangelist with his new interpretation of the early Church's expectation of the Parousia by help of the covenant theology of the Old Testament? Perhaps he was less concerned with reaching a compromise among the competing expectations of the Parousia as such and much more interested in directing the perspective from the future as the time of the consummation of the world to the post-Easter 'hour' of the faith of the young community. Just as for him possession of the Spirit was not something belonging to the next world or to the end of this one but the fruit of the 'lifting up' of Jesus (cf. Jn 7,37f) and of fellowship with him (cf. 1,33; 3,5-8; 20,22), so too were the 'seeing' of the coming one and his post-Easter presence (cf. already Mt 18,20; 28,20). What goes beyond the early Christian apocalyptic viewpoint here is the audacity not to regard the eschatological coming of Jesus as a coming both in the believing fellowship of the Church and also at the end of the age in glory, but rather to melt down and recast the apocalyptic expectation of the future into the present believing experience of the Church. In this we see a coming together of all three models in which the evangelist, as tradent of the belief of the community, brings to expression the expectation of the coming of the Lord in the literary end product which bears his stamp. Whether thought of as the coming of the Paraclete, as the eschatological coming and manifestation of the Lord himself or as the home-making together of the Father and his own – in each case the early Christian expectation of the Parousia is consistently transferred to the present of the Evangelist as the time of the Church and of salvation. It is and remains defined by the paradoxical experience – foretold by the Lord – of a salvation in which the disciples have a share but not the world. Here is the announcement of a development which in its radical form will lead to the early Christian gnosis, just as it already owes its beginning to a dualism that precedes and is found outside the New Testament.

Thus Christology and eschatology condition each other reciprocally in this central section of John 14. The determining factor appears to be the eschatological time signal which, for its part, determined the Christology taken over from early Christianity, on which depends, in the last resort, the interest and kerygmatic stance of the gospel. The concluding verses, 25-31, in Jn 14 will illuminate this relationship still further by further developing the content of the eschatological gifts of the one who is coming and the one who has already come.

IV. The Eschatological Gifts of Jesus (vv. 25-31)

The concluding section of John 14 (vv. 25-31) seems to have a recapitulatory character. In particular, verses 25-29 are dominated by the themes which build and carry the structure of the preceding verses, that is, the 'going away' and 'coming' of Jesus, the abiding link with him in 'faith' and in 'love'. Moreover, the promise of the Paraclete is taken up again (v. 26). However, new themes also ring out in these first verses – the promise of the 'peace' of Jesus in v. 27 or the theme of 'joy' in v. 28. We would surmise that, together with the renewed announcement of the Spirit-Paraclete, there is a mention of the eschatological gifts of Jesus which the one who is coming – now already in the 'hour of faith' – promises and brings to the disciples believing in him. We will, then, try to show that here too, in this description of the content of the eschatological gifts of Jesus, the evangelist is going back, by way of the early Christian tradition of the proclamation by Jesus of the kingdom of God, to the Old Testament and, above all, to its prophetic tradition. This is worth proving in detail.

1. The Structure of the Passage

The beginning and the end of the closing section of John 14 are clearly marked even if from time to time different opinions are expressed concerning the affiliation of the Paraclete saying of v. 26 and its introduction in v. 25.[1] The connection of vv. 25f to the closing section is supported, above all, by the link which the λελάληκα ὑμῖν 'I have spoken to you' in v. 25 forms with the εἴρηκα ὑμῖν 'I have told you' in v. 29. By way of conclusion Jesus now looks back on his words of farewell, and thus we have within the first Farewell Discourse of John 14 the first and only use of the perfect in verbs referred to Jesus. They are related to the aorists in vv. 26 and 28 with which Jesus refers to his previous speech.

If, then, verses 25-29 look back on the previous preaching of Jesus, verses 30-31 look to the future. To the 'These things I have spoken to you, while I am still with you' in v. 25 corresponds the 'I will no longer talk much[2] with you' in v. 30. It stands in a certain tension with the following three chapters of the Johannine Farewell Discourses and could probably have led on originally to the Passion narrative in 18,1ff.[3] Thus verses 14,30f taken together probably have the

---

[1] *Schulz* 192 and *Blank* 15.131 understand 14,25f as independent sayings; *Becker* 475 and Abschiedsreden puts 14,25f with the previous section 14,18-24. He is followed by *Schnackenburg*, Anliegen 95f.109f. Similarly *Migliasso*, Presenza 167-181, who allows the section before the last of the chapter to stretch from v. 18 to v. 27b.

[2] The π ολλά is missing in the Syrosinaiticus (cf. *Aland*, Synopsis) but it rather should be taken as original.

[3] Cf., *supra*, Chapter I.1.

original function of forming a transition to the Johannine narrative of the Passion and Resurrection of Jesus: with the 'coming' of Jesus belongs also the 'coming' of the ruler of this world (v. 30).

2. Literary Strata

That, in composing Jn 14,25-31, the fourth evangelist did not express himself freely but took over traditional material can be assumed on the basis of the vocabulary and syntax of the section even prior to any tradition-critical hypothesis.

As mentioned, verses 25-29, on the one hand, refer back in a powerful way to the previous verses of Chapter 14, on the other hand, they include nouns and verbs which in John as a whole, or at least within the Farewell Discourses, are new and conspicuous. To these belong in *v. 26* the παράκλητος 'Paraclete' (only again in 14,16; then the post-Johannine 15,25; 16,7; 1 Jn 2,1), διδάσκω 'teach' (only here in the Farewell Discourses) and ὑπομιμνῄσκω 'bring to remembrance' (only here in John's gospel); in *v. 27* εἰρήνη 'peace' (only again in Jn 16,33; 20,19.21.26), ταράσσω 'trouble' (only again in Jn 5,4 v.l.; 11,33; 12,27; 13,21; 14,1), καρδία 'heart' (only again in Jn 12,40 quotation; 13,2; 14,1; 16,6.22), δειλιάω 'be afraid' (only here in the New Testament); in *v. 28* χαίρω 'rejoice' (only again at Jn 3,29; 4,36; 8,56; 11,15; 16,20.22; 19,3; 20,20); in v. 29 γίνομαι (absolute) 'take place' (only again in Jn 13,19 [*bis*]; 16,4). In addition we have in *v. 30* ἄρχων 'ruler' (only again in Jn 3,1; 7,26.48; 12,31.42; 16,11 among which the word combination ἄρχων τοῦ κόσμου [τούτου] 'the ruler of [this] world' occurs only again in 12,31 and 16,11) and *v. 31* ἐντέλλομαι 'command' (only in the non-Johannine Jn 8,5 and in Jn 15,14.17); ἄγω (intransitive) 'go away' (only again in Jn 11,7.15.16) and ἐντεῦθεν 'hence' (only again at Jn 2,16; 7,3; 18,36; 19,18 [*bis*]).

The sentence structure also strengthens the impression that a connection with the tradition is to be supposed, particularly in verses 26-28 and 31, as has already been shown by the examination of the vocabulary. Grammatical subordination instead of coordination is encountered in vv. 26, 27 and 28 and then again in v. 31,[4] which, in fact, with the elliptical ἀλλ' ἵνα 'but so that' presents a puzzle.[5] The construction in v. 29 can also be explained as Johannine.[6]

Furthermore, the contrast between 'I' and 'you' is interrupted predominantly in these verses. Whereas the third person is absent in v. 25, it is frequently encountered in v. 26 (the 'Paraclete' as 'Holy Ghost'; the 'Father') but also in v. 27 (the 'world', 'heart') as well as in v. 28 ('Father'). In v. 29, it is

---

[4] Cf. in v. 26 the apposition and the doubled relative clause, in v. 27 the comparative clause, in v. 28 the ὅτι-clause, the unreal conditional clause and the adjoining recitative and causal ὅτι- as well as the ὅτι- and the comparative clause in v. 31.

[5] Cf. *Blass-Debrunner* 448,7 with n. 8.

[6] Cf. the almost identical construction in 13,19.

only the impersonal 'it' that appears in the third person; in v. 30, the 'ruler of the world', in v. 31, the 'world' and the 'Father'. If one puts the 'world' and the 'Father' down to the existing Johannine dualism, the striking use of the third person is reduced, above all, to verses 26, 27 and 30. In v. 31, as a striking syntactical phenomenon, mention must be made of the cohortative first person plural in the concluding 'departure signal'. Only here within the Farewell Discourses does Jesus amalgamate himself with the disciples in a 'we/us'. Here especially, the assumption of dependence on tradition can be easily confirmed.

If we keep in mind the caesura which we discovered in the previous section ('The Structure of the Passage') between vv. 25-29 on the one hand and vv. 30f on the other, it is a good idea to take the two groups of verses by themselves in the tradition-critical enquiry. Once again our concern will be not to track down the tradition-historical location of each of the concepts and ideas employed by John but rather to trace, where possible, whole word-fields and complexes of ideas to their tradition-historical roots. Our thesis proceeds along the lines that the trio 'Spirit', 'peace' and 'joy' lies at the basis of verses 26-28 as a unitary tradition-historical background which can be reckoned to be the embodiment of the eschatological promise of Jesus. With that it can be deduced, on the ground of the loose insertion of v. 26 into the context, as well as by reason of its unusual vocabulary and striking construction, that an originally independent unity that has been worked over by the evangelist lies behind this verse.[7]

In vv. 30f the evangelist seems to refer to the close of the Synoptic Gethsemane pericope as is shown by the partial verbal correspondences with Mk 14,42 par. We shall return to this later on. But next we shall turn to the theme of the promises in vv. 26-28.

---

[7] Verse 26 belongs to the five Johannine Paraclete sayings which are regularly dealt with together in research. Their individuality with respect to their context was highlighted first by *Windisch*, Parakletsprüche. In his opinion, the evangelist 'belatedly and only superficially incorporated them into his gospel': 122. He is followed by, among others, *Bultmann* 437 and *Schulz*, Menschensohn 143-146. However, post-*Windisch*, the independent working over of the Paraclete sayings by the evangelist received more attention. Also, the question of the tradition-historical background of the sayings and of the motif of the Paraclete gained in importance. In fact, *Betz*, Paraklet 210, lets the assumption of a written, fixed piece of traditional material give way and embraces the idea that the sayings were formed according to ideas that were familiar to the gospel and its readers 'and from which the gospel too is drawn'. These ideas, however, also stand in a specific tradition as his whole study tries to show. Cf., also, *Boring*, Influence 117. *Porsch*, Pneuma 320-322, does not go quite so far. In fact, he too accepts that the Paraclete sayings were not taken over as a whole from somewhere else, but he sees in them tradition which is also passed down in the Synoptics with respect to the working of the Spirit in a forensic situation which the evangelist has remodelled in his characteristic way. That traditional material lies behind the Paraclete sayings and so in Jn 14,25f is thus not disputed seriously by anyone.

3. Tradition

3.1 The Eschatological Gifts of Jesus

Even if the theme of joy in Jn 14,28 is encountered only in an unreal condition, it nonetheless forms in the Fourth Gospel, together with peace and with the gift of the Spirit, a firm complex of ideas which seems to be grounded in the tradition. This is shown above all in the comparison of the conclusion of the first Johannine Farewell Discourse with the report of the Fourth Gospel about the appearance of the Risen One before the disciples on the evening of Easter in Jn 20,19-23. Jesus' double greeting of peace structures this artistically constructed passage:[8] it leads first to the recognition scene (vv. 19f) and then on to the commissioning of the disciples (vv. 21-23). At the end of the recognition scene stands the sentence: 'Then the disciples were glad when they saw the Lord'. For its part, the commissioning of the disciples is prepared for by the fact that the Risen One breathes on them and says: 'Receive the Holy Ghost.' Against the background of the conclusion to the first Johannine Farewell Discourse which we have analysed, this coincidence of themes and motifs appears striking. Apparently, in his central Easter narrative, that of the apparition of Jesus before all the (ten) disciples on Easter Day itself,[9] the evangelist would like to announce the fulfilment of the promises which – directly or indirectly - have figured in the last testament of Jesus at the close of the first, and probably at one time the only, Johannine Farewell Discourse.[10] This interpretation fits well with Johannine 'realised eschatology' which sees the eschatological salvation as something given with faith in Jesus.

The redactional link of the first Farewell Discourse's themes of promise with the Easter narrative receives confirmation through the fact that the same themes of the promise of Jesus also appear in the concluding section of the second Johannine Farewell Discourse (Jn 16,4b-33) before the transition to the

---

[8] To Jesus' greeting of peace, the showing of his hands and side and the joy of the disciples in vv. 19f corresponds the renewed greeting of peace, the breathing and the commissioning of the disciples in vv. 21-23. Cf., on this structure, *de la Potterie*, Parole 198, who particularly elaborates the different conclusion of the two parallel sections.

[9] If one arranges the material according to groups of characters and indications of time, place and action, one can structure John 20 into seven scenes or passages: vv. 1-2.3-10.11-18.19-23.24-29.30f. The account of the appearing to the disciples on the evening of Easter Day would then occupy the middle position. Up to that point, the ascension of Jesus stands in the foreground (cf. v. 17); from v. 19, it is a question of his 'coming' again (vv. 19 and 26). Thereby a structural relationship with Chapter 14 (4-14.15-24) is revealed.

[10] The connection between the conclusion of the Farewell Discourse as promise and Jn 20,19-23 as fulfilment is most likely to be seen for Jesus' greeting of peace in Jn 20,19.21.26. Cf. *Schnackenburg* III 382f; *Blank*, Das Wort 37f who speaks of 'peace as eschatological gift of salvation'.

High Priestly Prayer of Jn 17.[11] At the beginning of this section stand the two final of the five sayings concerning the coming of the Spirit-Paraclete (vv. 7-11.13-15). Already the theme of grief is sounded here (v. 6) and then taken up in what follows (v. 20). It is contrasted with the joy which Jesus promises for the hour of the disciples' meeting again with him – under the image of the woman in travail (vv. 21f). The speech finishes then – after the promise to hear prayers made in the name of Jesus but also after the reference to the hour of the disciples' flight (vv. 23-32) – with the theme of peace and eschatological victory: 'I have said this to you, that in me you may have peace. In the world you have tribulation; but be of good cheer, I have overcome the world' (v. 33). In a striking way, Jn 16,4b-33 is also the only passage in John's gospel in which the subject is, twice (vv. 8 and 10), that of righteousness/justice (δικαιοσύνη). That here too we are dealing with an eschatological gift of salvation is shown by the comparison with Paul and the rest of the New Testament.[12]

That with the promise of the sending of the Spirit, joy and peace through the departing Jesus we are dealing with the eschatological gifts of salvation becomes clear from the context of those passages elsewhere in the Fourth Gospel in which the subject is these very gifts. Since the theme of 'peace' is confined to Jn 14,27, as well as to the texts we have already surveyed, 16,33; 20,19.21.26, we will limit ourselves here to the themes of 'Spirit' and 'joy'.

According to the Fourth Gospel, Jesus is the eschatological figure who baptises with the Spirit (1,33, cf. *infra* on Mk 1,8 par). Jesus is distinguished from the men of God who preceded him by the fact that the Spirit not only comes upon him (1,32) but also remains on him (1,33). In the dialogue with Nicodemus, the theme of 'birth from above' as 'birth again from water and the Spirit' is linked with the concept of the kingdom of God – the only mention of this idea in John (Jn 3,3.5)[13] and thus clearly an eschatological activity. Also twice in John, the bestowal of the Spirit is linked to the eschatological 'hour' (as the 'hour' of the true worship of God, 4,23f, or as 'hour' of the glorifying of Jesus, 7,39). To this corresponds the fact that the bestowal of the Spirit ('without measure') and the (eschatological) proclamation of Jesus belong together (3,34) or that Jesus' words prove to be 'spirit' and the (eschatological) gift of 'life' (6,63).[14] No wonder that the remaining texts about the promise of the Spirit as

---

[11] Cf. *infra*. The great closeness of Jn 16,4b-33 to Jn 14 contrasted with the intervening section 15,1-16,4a has long been recognised. Cf., for that, *Painter*, Farewell Discourses.

[12] The word here certainly means more than a forensic lack of guilt, as *Lindars* ΔΙΚΑΙΟΣΥΝΗ thinks. It is describing the eschatological activity of God in the Christ-event (v. 10). Cf. *Schnackenburg* III 146-150.

[13] Otherwise in John, the theme of Jesus' 'kingdom' is to be found only three times, in 18,36, in development of the given tradition of Pilate's question and Jesus' confirmatory answer in Mk 15,2 par.

[14] On the connection of 'life' with Jesus Christ according to the Fourth Gospel, cf. *Mussner*, ΖΩΗ, especially Chapter 4.

'Paraclete', that is, 'advocate' of the community for its inner growth and its outward existence, even before the courts, are reserved for the Farewell Discourses (14,16f.26; 15,26; 16,7-11.13-15).[15]

The theme of 'joy is also used in a clearly eschatological manner in John's gospel. Apart from the passages we have mentioned in the Farewell Discourses[16] and in the Easter narrative, we come across it in the discourse material of the first half of John's gospel in connection with eschatological images and motifs. Thus, in Jn 3,29, the Baptist speaks of the 'fulfilling' of his 'joy' under the image of the friend who shares in the joy of the bridegroom over the bride. The theme of the marital and nuptial love of Yahweh for Israel[17] is echoed here – as also already in the story of the marriage at Cana in Jn 2,1-11. As there, so here too, there comes to 'fulfilment' what Israel longed for under this image and what was promised to her. Another eschatological image is that of the 'harvest':[18] According to Jn 4,36, 'sower and reaper may rejoice together'. Apparently, the vision here is looking forward to the time in which the crop (of Jesus or the Apostles) in the mission field of Samaria will be fully ripe. Jn 8,56 is thinking of the eschatological 'day'[19] of Jesus: 'Abraham rejoiced that he was to see my day; he saw it and was glad.' Finally, a saying of Jesus about his joy in the face of his last journey to Jerusalem looks forward to his last sign, which prefigures his death and resurrection and will enable the faith of the disciples (Jn 11,15).[20]

Thus, 'Spirit', 'peace' and 'joy in John are the expression and concrete realisation of the salvific gifts of Jesus or God, not only when they are encountered together but also when they occur singly.

---

[15] It is disputed whether, with the 'giving over of the spirit' of the dying Jesus in Jn 19,30 may possibly be alluding to the gift of the Spirit. This opinion is represented by, among others, *de la Potterie*, Parole 191, with *D. Mollat*.

[16] Jn 15,11, the only example in Jn 15,1-16,4a, is post-Johannine.

[17] On Yahweh's marital love for Israel, cf. Hos 1-3; Ezek 16,7ff; 23,4; Is 50,1; 54,4ff. The bride-bridegroom motif also appears sporadically in the OT, thus Jer 2,2; perhaps Is 61,10; also Is 62,5. Only in Judaism does it become used more frequently for the Yahweh-Israel relationship. Cf. J. Jeremias, νύμφη, νυμφίος in ThWNT IV (1942) 1092-1099, here 1094f.

[18] On joy at the harvest, cf. Is 9,2; Ps 126,5f; in an eschatological context, only Joel 4,13; indirectly Is 27,12 where it concerns threshing. In the NT it is a frequent image for the judgement and salvation of the End Time. Cf. Mt 9,37f par Lk 10,2; Mt 13,30.39; Mk 4,29; 2 Cor 9,6; Gal 6,7ff; Rev 14,15f.

[19] 'Day' with an eschatological significance, especially as 'Day of the Lord', is a frequent expression in the OT, above all in the prophets. Cf. *M. Saebø*, jwm II-IV, in: ThWAT III (1982) 566-586, here 582-586; with individual examples, *E. Jenni*, jwm/jōm Tag, in THAT I (1971) 707-726, here: 723-726.

[20] Cf, among others, *Schnackenburg* II 104. In Jn 20,30, the evangelist looks back behind the death and resurrection of Jesus to the 'signs' of the earthly Jesus which culminate in the (symbolic) raising of Lazarus.

A close link between these themes is found not only in John but also in the rest of the New Testament – apparently through the contribution of tradition. Paul is the first to be mentioned in this connection.

Rom 14,17 Paul provides a principle by which one can arbitrate in the struggle, apparently fierce in the Diaspora communities, over the permissibility of the partaking of meat offered to idols: 'For the kingdom of God is not food and drink but righteousness/justice and peace and joy in the Holy Spirit'. In this way, a brother should not be endangered over food. Two things are significant here for our link: the belonging together of the salvific benefits of righteousness/justice, peace and joy in the Holy Spirit,[21] and their reference to the content of the proclamation of the 'kingdom of God' which Paul has taken over from the tradition. The closeness to the two texts from the Johannine Farewell Discourses which we have mentioned springs to the eyes even if in the first (Jn 14,26-28) the theme of 'righteousness/justice' is absent. That the connection of these gifts of salvation with the concept of the kingdom of God did not come to Paul out of the blue is clear from the related text, Gal 5,19-23: whoever does the 'works of the flesh' (v. 19) 'shall not inherit the kingdom of God' (v. 21). 'But the fruit of the Spirit is love, joy, peace, patience...' (v. 22).[22] Instead of 'righteousness/justice' 'love' is mentioned here; otherwise the beginning of the series corresponds exactly to the formula of Rom 14,17.

How closely for Paul righteousness/justice or love belongs with peace and joy as the fruit of the Spirit, in the sense of a description of eschatological salvation, is shown by a glance at the Letter to the Romans as a whole. After Paul has demonstrated the necessity and possibility of justification through faith in Jesus Christ in Rom 1,18-3,31 and reinforced his argument with a reference to Scripture (Abraham's justification by faith without works of the Law), he is able to describe the dimensions of salvation in Chapters 5-8. The section begins: 'Therefore, since we are justified by faith, we have peace with God through our Lord Jesus Christ' (Rom 5,1) The 'access to grace' which is made possible by faith (v. 2) is developed in what follows as the work of the love of God: 'because God's love has been poured into our hearts through the Holy Spirit which has been given to us' (v. 5).[23] A similar variation on the themes is found in Rom 8, a passage which corresponds structurally to Rom 5,1-11.[24] Thereby it shares a

---

[21] *Schlier*, Römerbrief 416 points out rightly that not only joy but also righteousness and peace are mentioned as fruit of the Holy Ghost.

[22] Cf., further, the related texts, 1 Cor 6,9-11; Eph 5,5.

[23] To joy here corresponds the 'rejoicing' in vv. 2 and 3. Cf., concerning the inner closeness of the concepts and their common occurrence in 1 Thess 2,19f, *J. Zmijewski*, καυχάομαι κτλ., in EWNT II (1981) 680-690, here: 686 = EDNT II (1991) 276-279, here: 278.

[24] Cf., for the relationship between the two passages, *Lyonnet*, Exegesis, 5-10. Thus, in Romans 1-11, the 'love of God' is the subject only in 5,5-8 and 8,35-39, the Spirit only in 5,5 and Chapter 8, Christian hope only in 5,2 and 8,18-20, corresponding to the tribulation and trial in 5,3-4 and 8,25-37, and finally 'peace' in 5,1 and 8,6 (otherwise only in the salutation formula in 1,7; also the formulaic 2,10; the quotation in 3,17).

resonance with Gal 5,19-23: 'To set the mind on the flesh is death, but to set the mind on the Spirit is life and peace' (Rom 8,6). Peace and joy occur in close combination in the concluding chapters of Romans. Above all, we can think here of the formula of blessing in Rom 15,13: 'May the God of hope fill you with all joy and peace in believing, so that by the power of the Holy Spirit you may abound in hope'.[25]

In two places in his other letters, in concluding admonitions, Paul exhorts his addressees to joy and love and, in addition, promises and desires the divine gift of peace for them. 2 Cor 13,11 commends peace, simultaneously gift and task, together with joy, readiness to accept admonition and the effort for unity. That Paul knows of the possibility of this new way of living through the triune God is shown by the blessing formula which follows almost immediately in 2 Cor 13,13 and concludes the letter definitively.

Very similar is the thought process in Phil 4,4-9. Paul first takes up once more the exhortation to 'joy in the Lord' from 3,1 in 4,4 and doubles it, goes on to the demonstration of goodness before all men (v. 5), commands a carefree attitude in view of the closeness of the Lord (v. 6) and, again, promises and desires the peace of God (v. 7) – a promise which he repeats at the conclusion of the passage after further exhortations.

What does not occur in this text explicitly we find in 1 Thess 1,6, namely that the Christian joy with which the community should occupy itself, and is indeed so doing, is the fruit and gift of the Spirit: 'you received the word in much affliction, with joy inspired by the Holy Spirit'.

From here already, certain conclusions can be drawn. We have seen that peace and joy belong closely together in Paul, that they are not principally the fruit of human effort but, also and above all, the fruit of the Spirit together with righteousness/justice, love, goodness, patience and so on. The formulation of Rom 14,17 pushes this concept very close to the passage which we have studied from the Johannine Farewell Discourses and lets us postulate that the motif complex of gift of the Spirit, peace and joy as a description of the eschatological reality was ready to hand through the tradition. This is supported not least by the pre-Pauline subject of the 'kingdom of God', something unusual in Paul, here and in Gal 5,21.

For traditional material in this connection, there is further support in the occurring of the same motif complex in other letters of the New Testament. Thus the Letter to the Ephesians (4,3) brings peace in the community into connection with the 'unity of the Spirit' which is referred to the 'one Spirit' (v. 4). A text in Hebrews (12,11), in which the subject is God's chastisement, betrays a stronger traditional impress: 'For the moment all discipline seems painful rather than pleasant; later it yields the peaceful fruit of righteousness to those who have

---

[25] Cf., also, Rom 15,33 with v. 32; 16,20 with v. 19 (even when here no immediate connection in content is given). εἰρήνη occurs again close to Rom 14,17 in v. 19.

been trained by it'. The expression (καρπὸν εἰρηνικὸν...δικαιοσύνης) is striking: since it is otherwise alien to Hebrews, the association of ideas must have been given to the author as traditional material. In this connection, we note again the theme of joy which takes us into the tradition complexes known to Paul and John.[26] We must also think of those numerous places in the New Testament which mention the (eschatological) persecution of Christians as the ground for joy.[27]

We now turn finally to the eschatological gifts of peace, joy and the Spirit of God in the Synoptic tradition. Again, the referring back of these realities to the 'kingdom of God' in Paul (Rom 14,17) can prove itself helpful. If the Pauline formula does not appear in its complete state in the Synoptics, nonetheless peace, joy and the receiving of the Spirit together with righteousness are found in them, both on their own account and also in a many faceted relationship with one another as consequences of the 'kingdom of God' and the Christ event and thereby of eschatological salvation.

The greeting of peace with which Jesus sends his disciples into the towns and villages according to Mt 10,13/Lk 10,5 (Q) corresponds not only to the common Oriental form of greeting but also, by analogy with the openings of the Epistles;[28] it is defined by the reality of Christian preaching, made concrete in Mt 10,7 and Lk 10,11 as the irrupting kingdom of heaven or of God with the coming of Christ. In the perspective of the future announced by Jesus, the 'peacemakers' are pronounced blessed according to the seventh beatitude of the Sermon on the Mount (Mt 5,9). This peace is possible because it has arrived with Jesus, the messianic king – this is shown by the account of the Triumphal Entry, above all in its Lucan version (19,38).[29]

It is in fact the Lucan account of the Triumphal Entry which permits the transition to the theme of 'joy'. The people who go out to meet Jesus and greet him as the messianic king are filled with joy (Lk 19,37). Luke already connects 'joy' and 'peace' with the birth of the messianic king as the story of the shepherds in the fields of Bethlehem indicates (Lk 2,10.14). Peace here is promised to 'men of his (God's) favour' where we are not far from the Pauline and Johannine motif complex (peace, joy, Spirit).

---

[26] Cf. *Michel*, Hebräer 445: 'The second half of v. 11 (ὕστερον δέ...) sounds strongly rhetorical and apparently stems from fixed paraenetic material'. *Ibid.*, 446 on 'peace' and 'righteousness' but also 'joy' as 'eschatological gifts of salvation' with par. from the OT and NT (Jn 16,20.22!).
[27] Mt 5,12 par Lk 6,23 (Q); Acts 5,41; 2 Cor 7,4; Phil 2,17f; Col 1,24; Heb 10,34; Jas 1,2; 1 Pet 4,13.
[28] Cf. the usage 'Grace and peace from the Father...' Rom 1,7; 1 Cor 1,3; 2 Cor 1,2; Gal 1,3; Eph 1,2; Phil 1,2; Col 1,2; 1 Thess 1,1; 2 Thess 1,2; Tit 1,4; Philem 3; cf., also, 1 Pet 2,2; 2 Pet 1,2; Rev 1,4; 'Grace, mercy, peace', 1 Tim 1,2; 2 Tim 1,2; 2 Jn 3; 'Mercy, peace and love', Jud 2.
[29] For the messianic sense of this passage, cf. *Beutler*, Friedenssehnsucht 301f.

Finally, the Spirit too appears linked with the in-breaking of the kingdom of God and the coming of Christ in the theology of the Synoptics and their sources. According to Lk 1,35 and Mt 1,18, the conception of Jesus is already the work of the Holy Spirit. According to Mk 1,8 par Mt 3,11; Lk 3,16, Jesus is the one who will baptise with the Spirit. In Mk 1,10 par Mt 3,16; Lk 3,22, the Spirit comes down on him in visible form at his own baptism in which at the same time the heavenly voice proclaims him as the Son of God in whom the Father is well pleased and the Servant of God who is bringing salvation. According to Lk 4,18, at the beginning of his inaugural sermon in Nazareth, Jesus takes up this connection of bestowal of the Spirit and commission with reference to Is 61,1f and applies it to himself. According to a saying in the Q tradition, that in its original form might go back to Jesus himself,[30] he sees that through the fact that he is casting out demons 'by the Spirit' (Mt 12,28) or 'by the finger of God' (Lk 11,20), the kingdom of God has come upon those who hear him. At least in the tradition passed on by Matthew,[31] there thus exists a connection between the bestowal of the Spirit and the coming of the kingdom of God proclaimed by Jesus.

Of course, none of the New Testament texts mentioned here leads directly to the motif complex of bestowal of the Spirit, peace and joy as the eschatological gifts of Jesus as portrayed in the Johannine Farewell Discourses and the Johannine Easter narrative. It is otherwise with a final Synoptic text which remains to be added. This is Luke's account of the appearance of Jesus before the eleven disciples on the evening of Easter Day according to Lk 24,36-43 with its conclusion vv. 44-53 which, chronologically, has only a loose attachment. References between this text and its counterpart in Jn 20,19-23 concern not least the words which we have associated with the 'eschatological gifts of Jesus'. In Lk 24,36 too, Jesus greets his disciples with the words 'Peace be with you', the probable reading according to the oldest and best manuscripts.[32] Luke also talks of the disciples' 'joy' which scarcely allowed them to believe in the reality of their Easter experience (v. 41). Finally, in Luke, the announcement of the 'promised gift' of the Father is added here (v. 49) and brings to a close Jesus' speech with his disciples. That this is a reference to the gift of the Holy Spirit is shown by the subsequent development in the first two chapters of the Acts of the Apostles (1,4.8; 2,1-4).

A judgement on the relationship of literary dependence between the two texts is subject to a series of problems. If one assumes that Jesus' greeting of

---

[30] Cf. *U. Luz*, βασιλεία, in EWNT I (1980) 481-491, here: 484 = EDNT I (1990) 201-205, here: 202.

[31] Of course, Matthew's version might be secondary to that of Lk (cf. Ex 8,15. Ps 8,4): *G. Schneider*, Evangelium nach Lukas 266.

[32] The greeting of peace is absent only in the 'Western' recension (D and its dependent Old Latin mss.) and is regarded today again as authentic. Cf. *Aland*[26] and the *Greek New Testament* who nonetheless award it the lowest level of certainty.

peace in Lk 24,36 is original, it does not follow that the relationship between the two texts is one of immediate dependence. Probably a written pre-text lay behind both the Lucan[33] and Johannine[34] texts, and this was then expanded by both evangelists. The greeting of peace and the mention of the disciples' joy must have belonged to the pre-text of Luke and that of John (or his source) (cf. also Mt 28,8), and to the latter also the receiving of the Spirit.[35] The announcement of the 'promised gift' in Luke should more likely be referred to the evangelist himself.[36] In other respects, the pre-Lucan and the Lucan text is probably still a little distant from a conscious employment of the themes of Easter peace, joy and Spirit as eschatological gifts of the Risen One. However, the (pre-)Lucan text possibly offered a starting point for the fourth evangelist to create a literary link between the Easter narrative of Jn 20,19-23 and the conclusion of the first Farewell Discourse. The author of the Farewell Discourse of Chapters 15-16 would then have further developed the theme of the eschatological gifts of Jesus in Jn 16,4b-33, especially the theme of joy.

If we pursue the tradition-historical status of the bestowal of the Spirit, peace and joy as eschatological gifts, we need not confine ourselves to the New Testament and its pre-literary layers. In fact, the motif complex has its roots in the later prophetic texts of the Old Testament. Pride of place here must go to the texts from the book of Isaiah. At the same time it does not seem necessary for all these concepts to occur verbatim. If need be, their content can be paraphrased as the reality of peace which in Old Testament and Ancient near Eastern texts is very often mentioned in connection with justice.

In the course of mentioning the eschatological gifts of Jesus in the Synoptics, we have already come up against the detailed quotation of Is 61,1f (cf. 58,6) in Lk 4,18f. As eschatological bearer of the Spirit, Jesus has been commissioned to bring the joyful news to the poor. The text from Trito-Isaiah (Is 61,1-11) is a broad development of the statement of salvation for the post-Exilic community: the one anointed with the Spirit will bring justice and righteousness (vv. 3.8.10f), but also joy (cf. vv. 1.3.7.10).[37] The relations with the neighbouring peoples will be ordered peacefully: they are astounded at Israel's redemption

---

[33] So, most recently, *Ernst*, Evangelium nach Lukas 666, who in fact (667) holds the greeting of peace as more likely to have been taken from John 20,19.
[34] So, perhaps, *Schnackenburg* III 381f, according to whom the evangelist interpolated v. 21 and appended vv. 24-29; different somewhat is *Becker* 620-625 according to whom v. 21 would have been the development of an old story belonging to the pre-Johannine Passion narrative.
[35] According to the authors mentioned in n. 34, the greeting of peace, the joy of the disciples and the receiving of the Spirit belong to the traditional account.
[36] Cf. *Ernst, loc. cit.* 668-671; G. *Schneider*, Evangelium nach Lukas 502 who interprets Jesus' 'last words' to his disciples in 24,44-49 in the context of Lucan theology.
[37] The word field for eschatological joy and rejoicing is here richly varied in the MT; the LXX is dominated by εὐφροσύνη or εὐφραίνεσθαι (v. 10), then ἀγαλλιᾶσθαι/ ἀγαλλίαμα (vv. 10f).

and are at her service (vv. 5-70. Israel's time of labour and humiliation is over (vv. 1-4). All this takes place 'for praise before all peoples' (v. 11).

The proclamation of a Spirit-filled messianic prince is used as well in Is 11,1-10:[38] again he is characterised by righteousness with equity (vv. 3-5) and the establishment of a peaceful order which extends to the realm of nature and is described in paradisial colours (vv. 6-8)[39] Without any direct mention of a messianic prince, righteousness and peace are mentioned in Is 32,15-20 as the fruit of the eschatological outpouring of the Spirit of God. This is probably a very late text of the post-Exilic period.[40] Here too paradisial motifs are echoed: the vegetable and animal worlds will be included in the Spirit-given eschatological order of salvation.

Presumably texts like these have drawn on a double source. First, there comes to expression in them Israel's hope in the reviving Spirit of God, precisely after the catastrophe of the Fall of Judah and Jerusalem in 587 BC. Deutero-Isaiah describes the new beginning of Israel in the categories of a new 'creation',[41] and so he is able to speak about the gift of God's 'Spirit' or 'breath'[42] on the children of Israel (Is 44,3). We have already seen[43] that Ezekiel understands, and at the same time theologically interprets, the bestowal of the Spirit as the revival of the whole people of Israel (cf. the prophecy of the dried-up bones, Ezek 37,1-14): in his Spirit, God teaches Israel to fulfil the Law from within and so gives her a new heart and lets the Spirit become a new and abiding presence for his covenant people (Ezek 36,26-28; 11,19f). With that there takes place at the same time purification from sins as it is called identically in Ezekiel (36,25) and Ps 51 (here as the prayer of an individual worshipper).[44]

One of the most influential Old Testament texts concerning the eschatological bestowal of the Spirit must have been Joel 3. The text announces a giving of the prophetical Spirit to the sons and daughters, the menservants and maidservants of Israel, impending judgement with a cosmic catastrophe and the possibility of redemption proceeding from Zion and Jerusalem. The passage is

---

[38] The chronological setting of the passage remains disputed. Cf. the discussion in *Wildberger*, Jesaja 1-12, 442-446, who ascribes the section to the prophet himself; for a post-Exilic origin, cf., among others, *Kegler*, Prophetisches Reden 39.

[39] On the connection between paradisial peace and the establishment of a peaceful order by the prince in the Ancient Near East and in the OT, cf. *Groß*, Idee 10.12f.16 and often; 22.24 and often. Reference to Is 11,6-8; *Schmid*, šalôm 16f.28-30.

[40] Cf. *Kaiser*, Jesaja (Kap. 13-39) 264 on Is 32,15-20: 'The composition of the apocalypse in the late post-Exilic, Hellenistic period is sufficiently established from its dependence on or relationship to texts such as 29,27ff; 30,19ff'.

[41] The verb which otherwise dominates the P account of the creation, *br'*, is found in a strong concentration in Deutero-Isaiah (15 times in Qal, once in Niphal).

[42] For this meaning of *rwḥ*, cf. Ps 104,29f.

[43] Cf., *supra*, III.3.2.1.

[44] This tradition is taken up not only in the early Christian Baptism tradition but also again in Jn 20,22ff (where the 'inbreathing' probably goes back to the creation account of Gen 2,7).

well known to readers of the New Testament through its integral adoption at the beginning of the Peter's sermon at Pentecost according to Acts 2,17-21. However it might also have influenced the self-understanding of the Pauline communities, not least with the effect that social barriers would become untenable under its influence.[45]

The other source on which our motif complex drew are messianic-eschatological texts of the post-Exilic prophets which speak of the coming joy and peace. Already, at the time of the Exile, Deutero-Isaiah (44,21-23,[46] here as the work of God's new 'creation') and Jeremiah (31,7-14),[47] speak of the coming rejoicing, Deutero-Isaiah again (54,10) and Ezekiel (34,25; 37,26) of the coming peace and 'covenant of peace'. The post-Exilic prophets can then bring these motifs together. This is especially the case with Trito-Isaiah. To the vision of the future salvation which will fall to Jerusalem's share belong both joy (Is 60.5.15),[48] as also peace and righteousness: 'I will make your overseers peace and your taskmasters righteousness' (v. 17). The motifs are repeated in Chapters 65 and 66. According to Is 65,17-25, God is creating a new heaven and a new earth. The consequence for Jerusalem is joy and gladness (v. 18).[49] The bliss in the newly established Jerusalem is described (vv. 20-24). The account is closed by a portrayal of eschatological peace that is focused on traditional images: 'The wolf and the lamb shall feed together, the lion shall eat straw like the ox...They shall not hurt or destroy in all my holy mountain, says the Lord' (v. 25). In the last chapter, 'peace' and 'joy' appear once more in an eschatological vision: 'Rejoice with Jerusalem, and be glad for her, all you who love her; rejoice with her in joy, all you who mourn over her; that you may suck and be satisfied with her consoling breasts; that you may drink deeply with delight from the abundance of her glory. For thus says the Lord: Behold, I will extend prosperity to her like a river, and the wealth of the nations like an overflowing stream' (Is 66,10-12, cf. ff).[50]

Probably from the Exilic or post-Exilic period[51] comes also a text within First Isaiah (9,1-6) which speaks of the coming salvation under a new Davidide. At the beginning stands the summons to rejoicing over the redemption that has

---

[45] Cf. *G. Lohfink*, Gemeinde 109f.
[46] Cf. Hebrew *rnn*, *rnh*, again in Greek rendered with εὐφραίνομαι, εὐφροσύνη.
[47] LXX 38,7-14. Also here vv. 7 and 12 the Hebrew *rnn* is translated by εὐφραίνομαι; v. 13 *śmḥ* qal by χαίρω, piel by ποιήσω εὐφραινομένους. For the use and synonyms of *śmḥ* in the Hebrew OT, cf. the article s.v. by *E. Ruprecht* in: THAT II (1976) 828-835.
[48] Again, a fixed terminology is lacking in the Hebrew; in v. 15 the Hebrew *g'wn* and *mśwś* is rendered by ἀγαλλίαμα and εὐφροσύνη.
[49] Here too the LXX renders a Hebrew vocabulary which recalls Is 44,21ff, by ἀγαλλίαμα and εὐφροσύνη.
[50] Here the LXX has χαίρω/χαρά for Hebrew *śwś/mśwś* (vv. 10.14), for *śmḥ*.
[51] For such a late dating, cf., among others, *Fohrer*, das Alte Testament II/III 44; *Kaiser*, Einleitung 205f, against *Wildberger*, Jesaja I 368-371 among others.

taken place (v. 2), at the close the description of the rule brought about by the coming prince: peace (vv. 5f), justice and righteousness (v. 6).

The same idea occurs in Zech 9,9,[52] the text which is taken up again in the Synoptic and pre-Johannine account of the Triumphal Entry: 'Rejoice greatly, O daughter of Zion! Shout aloud, O daughter of Jerusalem! Lo, your king comes to you; triumphant and victorious is he, humble and riding on an ass, on a colt the foal of an ass. I will cut off the chariot from Ephraim and the war horse from Jerusalem; and the battle bow shall be cut off, and he shall command peace to the nations; his dominion shall be from sea to sea, and from the River to the ends of the earth'.

It is not surprising that almost all these texts are inspired not only by royal but also by Zion theology: the eschatological salvation emanates from Zion whether it is effected by the messianic prince,[53] or brought by God himself without any intermediary figure.[54] This eschatological expectation of post-Exilic Israel has its roots already in the Psalms. The so-called 'Enthronement Psalms' (of God-the King), Pss 96-100, are already aware of joy together with justice as salvific benefits of the God of Israel who reigns out of Zion.[55] In the pilgrimage songs, Jerusalem and Zion are praised as the source of bliss, salvation, peace and righteousness; also joy or God's peace is desired for them.[56] The trail leads still further back from here; together with the establishment of an order of justice, peace and joy belong to the elements of the royal ideology of the Ancient Near East. We find it particularly in hymnic texts in the context of coronation ceremonies, especially in Egypt,[57] but also sporadically in historical texts of ancient and more recent times.[58] Texts like Ps 2; Ps 45; Ps 72 and Ps 110 show us that

---

[52] This text is wholly ascribed to a later layer in Zechariah which begins in 9,1. Cf. *Fohrer, loc. cit* 79f; *Kaiser, loc. cit.* 262, who takes the two verses to be a fragment of tradition in an early Hellenistic context.

[53] Thus in Is 61,1-11; Zech 9,9f.

[54] So in Jer 31,7-14; Is 60; 65,17-25; 66,10-14.

[55] Cf. joy and gladness Pss 96,11f; 97,1.8.11f; 98,4.8; 100,1f; justice, righteousness and equity Pss 96,13; 92,2.6.8.11f; 98,2.9; 99,4; in the related prayer of reconciliation, Ps 85, peace is also mentioned close to rejoicing (v. 7) and righteousness (12.14): 'righteousness and peace have kissed each other' (v. 11).

[56] Cf. the joy and gladness in Ps 122,1; 132,9.16; righteousness Ps 122,5; 129,4; 132,9; peace Ps 122,6ff; 125,5; 128,6. Jerusalem appears as the source of righteousness and peace also in the hymnic Ps 147,12-20 (= 147 LXX).

[57] Especially well known is the coronation hymn of Ramesses IV: ANET 378. Cf. *Groß*, Idee 13; *Schmid*, šalôm 14; further texts from both authors; also *Beutler*, Friedenssehnsucht 293. Cf., also, the hymn for the accession of Merneptah: ANET 378. For Mesopotamia, cf. the hymns of Iddin-Dagan of Isin (20th century BC): '...your kingdom makes men joyful, your shepherd's rule rejoices their hearts' (*Schmid*, 33).

[58] Cf. from ancient Egypt, the famous stele on the occasion of the wedding of Ramesses II with the daughter of the Hittite king, Ḫattušiliš; ANET 257f (the soldiers of both great kings fraternise in peace and joy); likewise, from the 13th century BC the so-called Israel-Stele of Merneptah after the successful subjugation of the Libyans and the inhabitants of the coastal

Israel adopted such ideas, and they also form the bridge to the messianic-eschatological texts of the later period.

We can summarise: the eschatological gifts which, according to Jn 14,26-29 – expressly or implicitly – Jesus promised and, in Jn 20,19-23, conferred go back to a pre-Johannine motif complex. In Paul, it describes the reality of justification, life through faith and the Spirit, in the Synoptics the reality of the 'kingdom' of God which is proclaimed by Jesus and which with his coming, his birth, his public ministry and his entry into Jerusalem has irrupted on to the scene. Peace and joy and the gift of the Spirit show themselves thus to be the description and the consequence of the reality of eschatological salvation, especially as encountered in the post-Exilic prophets. In this connection, Trito-Isaiah proves itself especially significant for the Johannine motif complex. Together with justice and righteousness, peace and joy show themselves linked with the ancient Israelite and Ancient Near East royal ideology so that the salvific gifts of the departing Jesus according to the latest, the Fourth, Gospel appear to have particularly old sources which reach back into the dim and distant past of the Near East. A similar result has already been achieved for the Old Testament covenant theology underlying Jn 14,15-24.

3.2. The Command to Leave

The tradition that stands behind Jesus' command to leave in Jn 14,30f evidently dates from a much more recent period. For a long time now, commentaries have pointed out the fact that the 'signal for departure' in v. 31, 'Rise, let us go hence', goes back to the almost verbatim command of Jesus after the prayer in Gethsemane, Mk 14,42 par Mt 26,46.[59]

This is all the more likely as the fourth evangelist does not know the Gethsemane pericope as such. The hypothesis that the evangelist has relied on the Synoptic Gethsemane tradition for the 'departure signal' of Jn 14,31 can again be strengthened through some further considerations.

First of all, we have already understood the command 'Let not your hearts be troubled' which opens the chapter and is repeated at v. 27 as a quotation from Ps 42/43 which is similarly quoted literally in the Gethsemane account of Mk

---

states of Palestine; it praises the king and the order of peace established by him: ANET 376-378; excerpts in *Schmid, loc. cit.* 19f; *Beutler, loc. cit.* From Mesopotamia, cf. a stele of Nebuchadnezzar II which promises not only peaceful dominion but also blessing and fertility to the kings who submit to him: ANET 307; Kyros as bringer of peace and joy for the inhabitants of Babylon; *ibid.,* 314f; as well as a prayer of the Seleucid ruler Antiochus Soter from the Hellenistic period in which he prays the god Nebo for dominion in righteousness, without disorder and in joy: ANET 317.

[59] *Westcott* 211 speaks of 'coincidence'; *Loisy*[2] 416 of literary dependence. Cf. *Hoskyns-Davey* 465 according to which Cyril of Alexandria already regarded Jn 14,31b as a spiritualised form of Mk 14,42 with the sense: 'Up, let us move from death to life and from corruption to incorruption'.

14,32-42 (here v. 34, par Mt 26,38).[60] Thus, the connection between John 14 and the Synoptic account of Gethsemane is not confined to the last three words of John 14. The reciprocal relationship between the two texts assumes greater weight given that we can start out from the fact that Ps 42/43 (which was also very influential on Mk 14,32-42) has left a decisive imprint on the whole section Jn 14,1-14.[61]

Connections also run from the Synoptic Gethsemane pericope to another passage in the Gospel of John which has long been recognised as close to Mk 14,32-42, namely Jn 12,27-32.[62] The subject again is the 'troubling' of Jesus' soul (v. 27). As in Mk 14,35, Jesus speaks of the prayer for the Father to let this 'hour' pass from him except that, by contrast with Mark, he does not actually make this prayer. As in Mark's gospel (14,41), the subject in the context is also the 'arrival' of the 'hour' – there with reference to the delivering of the Son of Man into the hands of sinners, here (Jn 12,23), positively, to his glorification.

The reference of the 'departure signal' of Jn 14,31 back to Mk 14,42 appears to be contradicted by the fact that in Mark (and Matthew) the command to depart is based on the arrival of the betrayer, whereas in John in v. 30, on the other hand, the close of the discourse is a response to the coming of the 'ruler of this world' (v. 30). However, this change becomes more comprehensible when understood from the point of view of the usual Johannine vocabulary and theological framework.

Thus not only is the 'ruler of this world' (ἄρχων τοῦ κόσμου τούτου) mentioned by John here in Jn 12,31 but in precisely that passage which, alongside John 14, shows connections with the Gethsemane pericope. The relationship between both these Johannine texts thereby obtains further support. What can have caused the fourth evangelist to speak of the coming of the 'ruler of this world' instead of the coming of the betrayer in Jn 14,30?

The answer permits itself to appear through a reference to the role of the 'devil' (διάβολος) in the Fourth Gospel in comparison with the Synoptics. In Jn 6,70, after the rupture among Jesus' audience over the Bread Discourse in the synagogue of Capernaum and Peter's confession 'Lord, to whom shall we go…' (v. 68) and 'You are the Holy One of God' (v. 69), Jesus says: 'Did I not choose you, the twelve, and one of you is a devil?' The latter is then openly identified in v. 71 with Judas Iscariot who was to betray him. Since John 6 shows the same structure as the 'Bread' section of Mark (6,6b-8,33),[63] a correspondence might

---

[60] Cf., *supra*, II.3, pp. 26-29.
[61] Cf., *ibid.*, pp. 26-43.
[62] So again *Westcott* 182. *Brown*, Incidents, recognises in John a basic tendency to separate in his gospel passages which constitute a single pericope in the Synoptics.
[63] Cf. *Brown* 238f in connection with *J. Weiss* among others. The correspondences are: the feeding of the 5000 (Jn 6,1-15; Mk 6,30-44), the walking on the water (Jn 6,16-24; Mk 6,45-54; after that, there is a hiatus in Mark till after the second multiplication), the seeking of a sign (Jn 6,25-34; Mk 8,11-13), sayings concerning bread (Jn 6,35-59; Mk 8,14-21), the con-

exist between the rebuffing and the rebuke of Peter as 'Satan' in Mk 8,33 and the presentation of the betrayer as 'devil' in Jn 6,70. Already Luke (cf. 9,22) allows the objection of Peter which follows on Jesus' first Passion prediction and his rebuke by Jesus to disappear. Thus the changing in John's gospel of the theme of 'devil/Satan' from Peter to Judas, who betrayed the Lord is not surprising.

In Jn 8,44, the 'Jews', 'Judaeans' or 'Judaisers'[64] who dispute with Jesus are described as 'children of the devil' (cf. Jn 8,33ff). This is intended to be a rejection of a claim of kinship with Abraham. Again, a Synoptic tradition is clearly being taken up: a false claim to kinship with Abraham is also the subject of the Baptist's call to repentance according to the sayings source (Mt 3,9; Lk 3,8). The comparison with the devil's children of those who refuse true faith in Jesus is of course made his own by the fourth evangelist.

Finally, Jn 13,2 presents as an inspiration of the devil the decision to hand Jesus over to the Jewish authorities which Mk 14,20 par Mt 26,14 ascribe to Judas himself. Here the fourth evangelist is clearly relying on tradition since the same thought returns in another formulation in Jn 13,27. Probably there exists here an older tradition which referred the inspiration of Judas' decision to betray Jesus back to 'Satan'. It has its parallel in Lk 22,3 and finds there too its confirmation in the fact that Luke also elsewhere is able to refer to 'Satan' the incitement to sin and apostasy (cf. Lk 22,31; Acts 5,3).[65]

When, in Jn 14,30, the fourth evangelist speaks of the 'coming' of the 'ruler of this world' instead of the 'closeness' of the betrayer, he is thus by this, on the one hand, following a consistent tendency to bring the role of Judas into connection with the activity of the devil, on the other hand, following the early Christian theologoumenon that sees the devil or Satan as the decisive inspirer of evil.

4. Redaction

We have already dealt with the necessary material concerning the structure and vocabulary of the closing section of John 14 (in the introduction to this chapter as well as in sections 1 and 2). So finally we have yet to ask only about the insertion of the themes recognised to be pre-Johannine into the final form of the Johannine text.

First, there is the theme of eschatological promises in vv. 25-29. The frame of this short subsection presents the eschatological gifts of Jesus clearly as

---

fession of Peter (Jn 6,60-69; Mk 8,27-30) and the subject of the Passion together with that of the betrayal (Jn 6,70-71; Mk 8,31-33).

[64] The last interpretation gains weight from the mention in Jn 8,31: it could have been meant of Jewish Christians of an inadequate Christological confession. Cf. *Brown*, Community 76ff; Gemeinde 62f.

[65] Cf. *S. Brown*, Apostasy, especially 82-114.

his legacy: Jesus has brought to a conclusion not only this Farewell Discourse but also his revealing word as such, as is expressed above all by the perfect in v. 25. With the turn of phrase 'These things I have spoken to you, while I am still with you (literally: remain with you)', the evangelist directs the attention forward to the time in which Jesus will no longer be with the disciples in his usual state. This, then, logically refers once again to the Paraclete as the one who will remain with the disciples and be with/in them in Jesus' place (v. 26). His task will be precisely that of keeping Jesus' message in their memory and developing it through his teaching. The deliberate transferring to the Paraclete of statements which elsewhere in the Fourth Gospel are applied to Jesus underlines his role as Jesus' representative.[66] Besides, the identification of the Paraclete as 'Holy Spirit' could have been advanced from Jn 20,22 where the epithet is undoubtedly more suitable in the context of the forgiveness of sins. If this is so, then it is further confirmation of the compositional connection of the conclusion of the first Farewell Discourse with John's central Easter text.

Moreover, the promise and announcement of the 'peace' of Jesus in v. 27 fits into the farewell of the departing revealer. 'Peace' can be a salutation as well as a valediction in New Testament texts.[67] That it is announced to the disciples in the hour of Jesus' departure and also conferred to them on Easter Day is part and parcel of John's particular eschatology which links the eschatological gifts of Jesus to the 'hour' of his 'lifting up' on the cross and to his Father but at the same time already grants them to the disciples at the Last Supper in which they anticipate the believing existence of the post-Easter community. As the one departing, Jesus can thus 'leave' his peace to his disciples, as the one coming again he can 'give' his peace anew – evidently 'not as the world gives'. To read out of this last limitation the fact that the eschatological peace vouchsafed by Jesus has got nothing to do with the social activity of the disciples in history, would certainly be to go beyond the text.[68] Not only do the tradition-historical roots of the Johannine concept of peace know it consistently as a social, interpersonal category and never as a purely spiritual condition; the promise of peace to the disciples as a group also excludes an individualistic misunderstanding.

When in the following (v. 27b) the command of v. 1b is taken up again: 'Let not your hearts be troubled', it is more likely that more than an exhortation to inner peace of soul is intended. The – probably LXX-oriented language – '(your hearts) may not be troubled',[69] which the evangelist inserts here, lets one think much more of a concrete threat to which the disciples will be exposed on

---

[66] Cf. *Porsch*, Pneuma 222-224, with *Bultmann, R. E. Brown* among others.
[67] Cf. Acts 15,33; Rom 15,33; 16,20; 2 Cor 13,11?; Gal 6,16?; Eph 6,23; 1 Pet 5,14.
[68] Cf. this widespread tendency today, perhaps in V. Hasler, εἰρήνη, in EWNT I (1980) 957-964, here 961 on Jn 14,27; 16,33 = EDNT I (1990) 394-397, here: 396.
[69] δειλιάω is met with in the NT only here, but more frequently in the LXX. It is found six times in the vetitive in Deut (1,21; 31,6.8) and Jos (1,9; 8,10; 10,25) and in fact is regularly coupled with φοβεῖσθαι. For the connection with καρδία, cf. Ps 119,161.

account of the departure of Jesus. Logically, then, the subject in v. 28 is once again this going away (ὑπάγειν with the emphasis on separation[70]) and coming again. The back reference reminds us of 13,33.36; 14,3f.18.23.

With the central, structural verbs of the 'going away' and 'coming' again of Jesus are associated the verbs with which the abiding link with Jesus was brought to expression in Jn 14,1-14, on the one hand, and in 14,15-24, on the other: 'believe' (v. 29) and 'love' for Jesus (v. 28b).

The separation, conceived of as the 'going away' (ὑπάγειν) of Jesus, is to take place with joy because he is 'going' (πορεύομαι, here the verb is putting emphasis on the goal[71]) to the Father. The saying that the Father is 'greater' than Jesus is not to be understood as metaphysical but rather as functional:[72] with John, the Father is consistently 'the Father who has sent him' and whose commandment Jesus carries out. Jesus' going to the Father is thus for him the fulfilling of his commission and also the conclusion of the salvific initiative of the Father. For the disciples, this event must signify – or should have signified – joy, eschatological joy.

Of course, this going away, the coming home of Jesus to the Father takes place in a concrete way in his 'lifting up' on the cross. Also for the Johannine Christians, this must have been the great scandal, and so the fourth evangelist lets this dark event be foretold not only in the words of Scripture but also in the word of Jesus (cf., also, 13,1). Faith will then recognise the imminent event as a 'sign' (cf. 20,30f).[73]

To v. 25's 'These things I have spoken to you' corresponds the 'I will no longer talk (much) with you' in v. 30. For Jesus, the time of talking is past; the time of silence has arrived. What the end of his time of revelatory discourse is bringing about is not the coming of any human being – here Judas who is betraying him – but rather the coming of the 'ruler of this world' himself. The encounter with the arresting party under Judas thus takes on cosmic dimensions. As in the parallel text, where the evangelist speaks of the 'ruler of this world' (12,31), the Adversary is spoken of here as the one over whom judgement has already been pronounced and who has been cast out of the world which he has sought to dominate. Indeed he has no power over Jesus.

The question could be asked why the Father then allows Jesus after all to embark on the way of the Passion when victory over the Adversary is already an accomplished fact. The concluding v. 31 is an attempt to answer this question. God stands in no need of this battle in order to prove himself as victor, but the unity of Jesus with the Father, in love and obedience, has to be brought before the eyes of the world – here probably still viewed as the sphere of Jesus' preaching in word and deed. On the one hand, according to John's gospel, the world

---

[70] Cf, *supra*, II.3.
[71] Cf. *ibid.*
[72] Cf. *Barrett*, Father, in dialogue with older and more recent literature.
[73] Cf., *supra*, n. 20.

does not know about Jesus and his commission (1,10; cf. 14,17 of the Spirit and 14,22 of the 'seeing' of Jesus), on the other hand, however, Jesus is the 'Light of the World' (8,12; 9,5; 12,46) and 'for this was he born and for this he came into the world, to bear witness to the truth' (18,37). In the description of the obedience of Jesus who in 'love' does as the Father has 'commanded' him, the evangelist goes back finally to the language of covenant theology.[74] He shows Jesus thus – as does the account of the Temptations in Q[75] – as the one who lives the chief commandment to the full and is ready to go to his death for it: 'Rise, let us go hence' (v. 31) – to meet the 'hour' of his own 'lifting up' and of the salvation of the new people of God (cf. 12,32).

---

[74] Cf., *supra*, III.3.1.
[75] Cf. Jesus' answers to the tempter taken from Deut 8,3; 6,13.16 in Mt 4,1-11; Lk 4,1-13.

V. Conclusions

The chief conclusion of this work has to lie in the area of tradition history. The introductory chapter was only a clearing of the ground for the specifying of the relationship between tradition and Johannine redaction in John 14 which followed in Chapters II to IV. The demarcation of John 14 as a literary unit offered no great difficulties and likewise the demonstration of the probable literary unity of the chapter. The effort to establish the basic structure of the chapter already served to prepare the way for the succeeding tradition-historical and composition-critical investigations. Useful too in this area was the genre critical definition of the chapter as 'Farewell Discourse'. Already here we demonstrated that key elements of the chapter belong to the genre of 'Farewell Discourse' which has been identified in early Jewish texts.

The result of the tradition-critical investigations of Chapters II to IV led to the discovery that the three main sections of John 14 are determined by *'Law'*, *'Prophets'* and *'Writings'*, that is, in concrete terms, the Psalms (cf. Lk 22,44).

At the beginning, the influence of a Psalm-tradition on the first fourteen verses is evident: apparently Ps 42/43, both as psalm of suffering and Pilgrimage Song, has provided the inspiration, as we speculated some years ago. This tradition-historical derivation was not weakened by the fact that we specified further individual parallels from the Old Testament for each of the concepts which occur in Jn 14,1-14. However, the argument amounted much more to explaining the collection of motifs in the said verses as a tradition-critical unity for which one cannot easily identify a parallel text. Not only do the themes of 'fear' or 'trouble', 'faith', 'house of God' and 'dwellings' with God in the first two verses appear to be defined by this tradition, but also further themes of these verses, especially the 'seeing of the countenance' of God or Jesus on which the speech of Jesus with his disciples is focused in the following verses. The eschatological interpretation of Old Testament statements about the 'house' and 'dwellings' of God in early rabbinic Judaism strengthened the hypothesis which sees the psalm tradition, which apparently came to the evangelist by way of the Gethsemane tradition, used here in John 14.

Of course, the evangelist submitted the tradition which he used to a far-reaching new interpretation corresponding to his Christology and eschatology. This is particularly the case from verse 7 onwards. Jesus not only shows the way to the Father; he is this way because he is 'the truth and the life' (v. 6). The awaited eschatological vision of God falls to the lot of the one who looks upon him in faith, and this, in fact, already in the present. The basis for this promise lies in the unity of Jesus with the Father in word and work.

For verses 15 to 24, the covenant theology of Deuteronomy (and so the *'Law'*) shows itself to be the underlying layer. This is the case, first of all, for the condition of the threefold promise of Jesus concerning his future 'coming', namely 'love' for him and the 'keeping' of his commandments. The elements of this covenant theology also show themselves alive in later texts of the Old Testament and survive also in early Jewish texts, not least in the pseudepigraphical literature and at Qumran. Also we have been able to show that, in the New Testament and in other places in John's gospel, 'love for God' is the subject almost entirely only in dependence on tradition and in connection with covenant theology and the chief commandment of Deut 6,4ff, that is to say, in connection with the confession of the unicity of God.

However, the content of the promises of Jesus in Jn 14,15-24 seems also to have been influenced by the covenant theology of the Old Testament. Above all, the texts of the future New Covenant and the new hearts bestowed therein in Jer 31 and Ezek 36 have played a role: they speak both of the 'gift' of the Spirit and also of a future 'dwelling' of God in his people, and so prepare the taking over of these promises into the Farewell Discourse of Jesus in John. The fourth evangelist could take these promises as the theological basis for Jesus' Farewell Discourse all the more since the expectation of the New Covenant promised by Jeremiah and Ezekiel and its gifts of salvation were alive both in late and post-biblical Judaism (especially among the rabbis and at Qumran) and also in the New Testament in its turn. The Excursus in Chapter III demonstrated this in detail.

The theological achievement of the evangelist in Jn 14,15-24 consists above all in having brought together, with the help of covenant theology, the three different pictures of the expected 'coming' of Jesus under a single perspective and shifting them consistently into the present. In what way Jesus 'comes' – whether represented by the Paraclete, personally at the eschatological coming or together with the Father corresponding to the expectation of the eschatological coming of God: in each case he comes here and now, that is in the 'now' of the believing community. Here, the opposition of the community to the 'world' which 'sees' and 'knows' neither the Paraclete nor Jesus belongs to Johannine eschatology with its particular perspective.

In the concluding verses 25 to 31 (especially 26 to 29), in his description of the legacy of Jesus, his eschatological gifts, the fourth evangelist clearly took up again elements of the messianic-eschatological promises in the Exilic and post-Exilic *'prophets'*. 'Spirit', 'peace' and 'joy' show themselves not only in the New Testament (above all in Paul and the Johannine parallel texts, but also in the Synoptics) but also in the later prophetic proclamation as the interlinked components of eschatological salvation mediated through God or through his appointed Messiah. Particularly close to the Johannine texts stands Trito-Isaiah. However, the description of the salvation brought by the king sent from God leads, via the Old Testament and Ancient Near East royal theology, to the route right back to the very earliest periods of the Ancient Orient.

The personal theological achievement of the evangelist again consists in representing Jesus' eschatological gifts of salvation as a reality of faith in the present. The text of the appearing of the Risen One to the disciples in Jn 20,19-

23 proves to be of fundamental significance for the consequent shift of these salvific benefits into the present of the community. The greeting of peace, the joy of the disciples and the receiving of the Holy Spirit are experienced reality there, linked with the historically experienced 'coming' of Jesus. Thus this passage too is impressed with the characteristic Christology and eschatology of the fourth evangelist.

If the opposition to the world was already mentioned in the description of the peace promised by Jesus (v. 27), it is fully developed in the closing verses 30 to 31. Once more, John goes back to tradition, here again the Gethsemane tradition of the Synoptics, but again with a free shaping of his material: behind the betrayer stands the 'ruler of this world', Satan himself. He will not be the Stronger One with regard to Jesus, no less than in the Synoptic account of the Temptations. As there, also here Jesus is the one who brings the Father's will to fulfilment in faithfulness to the chief commandment. In that the signal for departure in Jn 14,31 deliberately picks up on the Gethsemane tradition, the evangelist is closing the circle with the beginning of the chapter which was so clearly marked with this tradition.

The interpretative conclusion which we have obtained and set out here for John 14 seems to me, therefore, to be of significance for the current state of Johannine exegesis, above all because it runs counter to a trend, widespread since Bultmann, which denies an ecclesiological interest to the evangelist and ascribes it first to the so-called 'ecclesiastical' or 'deutero-Johannine' redaction. Certainly, in John 14 too, on the level of the evangelist, there are no recognisable church structures, offices, sacraments or other media of salvation. However, the evangelist shows himself deeply stamped with the central themes and concerns of the Old Testament, and this, not only here and there, but throughout the whole structure of the chapter. Thus it was probably no accident that 'Law', 'Prophets' and 'Psalms' describe and define the three main sections of the chapter. If Israel plays such a decisive role in the Johannine reproduction of the parting words of Jesus, we certainly cannot claim the support of the fourth evangelist for an individualistic viewpoint on the Christian proclamation. Against this background, we have to reconsider the question of the relevance of the Fourth Gospel for contemporary social questions.

Certainly there remains the gulf that, in the view of the fourth evangelist, separates the believers and the community from the 'world' which opposes Jesus. Instead, comparable with the other writings and perspectives of the New Testament, the horizon of the new people of God and the disciples of Jesus and with them the Church opens up. Peace and joy as the salvific gifts of the departing Jesus made possible by the Holy Spirit are promised to the community of salvation as the community of the 'New Covenant'. A step outside this circle is not taken; however, one must bear in mind that, at least from the standpoint of the Old Testament, the nations belong regularly with the process of eschatological salvation as indirect recipients.

For the present day discussion concerning the relevance of New Testament statements for Christians' work for peace today, it seems significant that, for the fourth evangelist more than for any other New Testament author, peace – together with joy and the gift of the Spirit – is a promise for the present and not for a distant future: 'Peace I leave with you; my peace I give to you; not as the world gives do I give to you. Let not your hearts be troubled' (Jn 14,27).

Postscript: John 14 in recent research

Since the publication of „Habt keine Angst. Die erste johanneische Abschiedsrede (Joh 14)" in 1984, Johannine research has continued in various fields. In general, there has been a shift from diachronic to synchronic studies. A number of recent commentaries concentrate on the existing text of the Gospel of John and either disregard its origin, sources and traditions or put the main emphasis on the existing text.[1] Other commentaries are predominantly interested in a synchronic interpretation of the text of John.[2] As for the Farewell Discourses, the same shift of paradigm can be noticed. A remarkable example of this shift is represented by Francis F. Segovia. By contrast with his earlier publications, this author now pleads for a consistent synchronic reading of the Farewell Discourses and comes to remarkable results.[3] The same approach is adopted by some recent authors from South Africa in their review "Neotestamentica".[4] The literary integrity of the Farewell Discourses is defended by L. Scott Kellum in his monograph against the widespread scepticism displayed in earlier years of Johannine research.[5]

Some authors study the Johannine Farewell Discourses, or part of them, by means of a narratological investigation.[6] Others show interest in the consolatory aspect of the Farewell Discourses, still with emphasis on the existing text,[7] or emphasize the construction of a collective identity for the community by these discourses.[8] Still other authors interpret the Farewell Discourses under the aspect of their temporal perspective. The Jesus of these discourses speaks from a post-Easter perspective, as has been pointed out convincingly by Christina Hoegen-Rohls[9], Christian Dietzfelbinger and Johanna Rahner.

---

[1] This seems to be the case with the commentaries of Francis F. Moloney, Yves Simoens and Hartwig Thyen.
[2] George R. Beasley-Murray, Udo Schnelle and Ulrich Wilckens belong to this group of authors.
[3] Cf. Francis F. Segovia, *The Farewell*.
[4] See the titles given for W. R. Domeris, R. Lemmer, H. A. Lombard and Donald F. Tolmie in the Additional Bibliography.
[5] See his title *The unity of the farewell discourse*, given in the Additional Bibliography.
[6] See the contributions of Jan du Rand, Francis F. Moloney, "The function", Gail O'Day and Donald F. Tolmie, *Jesus' Farewell*, in the Additional Bibliography.
[7] See the articles by Thomas Popp and Kari Syreeni, "Partial weaning", in the Additional Bibliography.
[8] See David M. Reis, "Jesus' farewell discourse", in the Additional Bibliography.
[9] For this author see my review in ThLZ, listed in the Additional Bibliography. For C. Hoegen-Rohls, the post-paschal perspective determines not only the Farewell Discourses, but the whole of the Gospel of John.

On the other hand, diachronic study of the Johannine Farewell Discourses has continued. Some authors still subject these discourses to the kind of classical literary criticism that distinguishes sources and layers in the text.[10]

A particular form of diachronic approach has emerged since the mid-nineties with the model of *"relecture"* – "re-reading". There seem to be examples of texts in the Gospel of John which have been "read again" and developed under the influence of a new reading situation. Different from classical literary criticism, with its distinction of original author and redactor, this model tries to determine the relation of texts among themselves, not among putative authors. The same author may have "re-read" his text and given it a new emphasis in a new situation of his reading community. Be that as it may, the question for authorship is replaced by the quest for the interrelation of the texts. Here, the influence of linguistics is discernible, and the historical paradigm is replaced by the literary one. In recent times, Andreas Dettwiler, Jean Zumstein[11] and Klaus Scholtissek[12] have promoted this approach, and the present writer has adopted it as well.[13]

Besides such literary studies, there are others which try to elaborate the Hellenistic-Roman background of the Farewell Discourses in John. Particular interest has been shown in Greco-Roman consolation literature in general[14] or in Seneca[15]. Hans-Josef Klauck studies "eschatological metaphor in antiquity and Christianity" with reference to the heavenly mansions of the believers according to John 14.[16]

The Old Testament and ancient Jewish background of the Johannine Farewell Discourses has found less attention during the past 25 years. Martin Winter studies the Farewell Discourses in the light of Old Testament and Early Jewish "Farewell words of the Fathers".[17] Neuer Wettstein lists a number of parallels to concepts and ideas in the Farewell Discourses in Philo.[18] There has been an increasing interest in rabbinical parallels to our text in recent times, perhaps owing to Jewish-Christian dialogue on the Gospel of John. Klaus Wengst shows

---

[10] See the titles given for J. Ph. Kaefer, Karl Theodor Kleinknecht and Frank Schleritt in the Additional Bibliography.

[11] See his volume *Kreative Erinnerung. Relecture und Auslegung im Johannesevangelium"*, mentioned in the Additional Bibliography under „Die Logien Jesu", and Part II of his commentary on John (ibid.).

[12] This author distinguishes between „relecture" and „réécriture" according to authorship: in the second case, the same author re-writes his previous text in order to give it a new orientation.

[13] See my article „Die Überleitung", listed in the Additional Bibliography. There (228), more examples of possible "relecture" in John are given, including John 15-17, but also John 6.

[14] Cf. the contributions by Paul A. Holloway and George L. Parsenios in the Additional Bibliography.

[15] See the article by Manfred Lang, ibid.

[16] See his article „Himmlisches Haus", ibid.

[17] See his monograph „Das Vermächtnis Jesu", ibid.

[18] See the reference to this commentary ibid.

this interest throughout his two volume commentary on John in general and also in his interpretation of John 13-14. He is joined by other authors such as James McCaffrey with his study on the Temple imagery in Joh 14,2-3[19] and John L. Ronning with his contribution on "The Targum of Isaiah and the Johannine Literature".[20] Although the extant Targums are of the Christian Era, they contain ideas older than the time of their redaction and thus remain worthy to be studied in New Testament exegesis.

How are synchronic and diachronic studies on the Gospel of John related and can they be reconciled? The question has been dealt with by the present writer[21], but also by other authors such as Hans-Josef Klauck,[22] Marinella Perroni,[23] Jean Zumstein in vol. 2 of his commentary and Jörg Frey in his three volume monograph on Johannine eschatology.[24] In fact, Frey succeeds in reconciling future and present eschatology in John, elaborating a tension between pre-Johannine early Christian and Jewish eschatology, which sees the accomplishment of history in the future, and an eschatology, more characteristic of John the Evangelist, which sees the fulfilment of the ages in the present, without falling into the trap of Bultmann's approach which attributes these two perspectives to two different authors.

There is still discussion about the beginning of the Farewell Discourse in John 14. For many authors, this discourse starts at John 13,31. Judas has left the scene, the destiny of Jesus takes its course, and Jesus begins to introduce into the mystery of his departure. For this reason, attributing the beginning of the (First) Farewell Discourse to John 13,31 makes good sense. In my monograph "Habt keine Angst", however, I identified the real beginning of this (First) Discourse rather in John 14,1, because of the fact that the preceding dialogue between Jesus and Peter is not directly linked to the subsequent themes and differs in tone and content from the dialogues of chapter 14 with Thomas and Jude. This may be the reason why Francis F. Moloney and Ulrich Wilckens also in their recent commentaries see the beginning of the (First) Farewell Discourse in John 14,1. An additional reason for this division of text may be seen in the literary coherence of John 13 which has been pointed out afresh by various authors.[25]

There are, of course, also reasons for seeing the beginning of the (First) Farewell Discourse as occurring in John 13,31. Hans-Ulrich Weidemann lists them in referring critically to my monograph.[26] Other authors favouring this di-

---

[19] See the reference ibid.
[20] Ibid.
[21] See the article "In Search of a New Synthesis" in the Additional Bibliography.
[22] See his article „Der Weggang Jesu" ibid.
[23] Ibid.
[24] See ibid.
[25] See the articles of Jean-Noël Aletti, Mary L. Coloe and R. Alan Culpepper and the commentaries of Francis F. Moloney, Yves Simoens and Hartwig Thyen in the Additional Bibliography.
[26] See his monograph *Der Tod Jesu im Johannesevangelium*, 76.

vision of text are George Beasley-Murray, Udo Schnelle, Klaus Wengst and Jean Zumstein in their commentaries and – besides Weidemann – Francis F. Segovia in his monograph of 1991.

As in other cases (one thinks of John 2,1-12 or John 11-12), there seem to be transitional passages in John which link the text in two directions, back and forwards. This may be the case as well with John 13,31-38. With its further dialogue with Peter and the resumption of subjects from the beginning of the chapter, the verses still seem to belong to chapter 13, but with the announcement of the main subjects of the subsequent discourses, they prepare as well for the following Farewell Discourse(s). It may be recorded that in my original monograph "Habt keine Angst", I spoke of John 13, "vv. 31-33.35-38 (read: 36-38) as transition and introduction".[27] This may still be a good solution to the problem. In a recent article, I chose a similar terminology.[28]

For the division of chapter 14, there seems to be a growing consensus. The distinction of the subsections vv. 1-3.4-14.15-24.25-31 (or: 25-28.29-31) is accepted by a number of authors, occasionally with reference to my monograph.[29] Most authors recognize the role of John 14,1-3 as an introduction into the main topic of the chapter: the departure and return of Christ. The former aspect is dealt with in vv. 4-14, the latter in vv. 15-24, at least according to the proposal of "Habt keine Angst". For the subunit of vv. 4-14, there is hardly a discussion; for the next subsection, authors still disagree about its extension. Udo Schnelle agrees with the proposal of my monograph in his article.[30] Klaus Scholtissek does the same, but would also include v. 26 in this section, because of an inclusion between the two promises of the Paraclete in vv. 16f. and 26.[31] Jan du Rand extends this section until v. 27, otherwise agreeing explicitly with me.[32] Here he is joined by Hans-Ulrich Weidemann, who otherwise also agrees with the proposal of my monograph.[33] For the final section, vv. 25-31, there is the formal approval of Frank Schleritt in his dissertation.[34]

In the opening section of the (First) Farewell Discourse, John 13,31-38, particular attention has been given to vv. 31-32, with the fivefold word of Jesus about his glorification and the glorification of the Father, and vv. 34-35, with Jesus' New Commandment. John 13,31-32 still remains an enigma, not only because of the unusual form of this logion of Jesus, but because of its meaning. Nicole Chibici-Revneanu is of the opinion that the author here leaves his readers

---

[27] Op. cit., 17. I omitted vv. 33f. as a possible redactional addition, with a small misprint.
[28] See my article „Die Überleitung zu den johanneischen Abschiedsreden (Joh 13,31f.)" in the Additional Bibliography.
[29] See Thomas Popp, „Die konsolatorische Kraft der Wiederholung", 538.
[30] Cf. Udo Schnelle, „Die Abschiedsreden", 67, with reference to the key terms of τηρεῖν and ἀγαπᾶν.
[31] See Klaus Scholtissek, „Relecture und réécriture", 13f.
[32] See Jan du Rand, "The Johannine 'group' and 'grid'", 125f.
[33] See Hans-Ulrich Weidemann, *Der Tod Jesu im Johannesevangelium*, 83.
[34] See Frank Schleritt, *Der vorjohanneische Passionsbericht*, 301.

intentionally in suspense, in order to invite him or her to enter more profoundly into the mystery of the mutual glorification of Father and Son.[35] Hans-Ulrich Weidemann pleads for the literary coherence of the two verses and denies the influence of tradition in this group of verses.[36] The present writer has proposed to see in v. 31 a fragment of an early Christian hymn, reinterpreted by the evangelist in v. 32, in order to adapt it to the pre-Easter situation of the Last Supper.[37]

There is also an ongoing discussion about the literary character of Jesus' New Commandment in John 13,34f. Hans-Ulrich Weidemann holds the position, frequently attested in the eighties of the last century and supposed also in "Habt keine Angst", that these verses were added by the same redactor who also added chapters 15-17.[38] In the meantime, the paradigm of "re-reading" (relecture) may offer a better solution, insofar as the relation of the verses, considered as "secondary" to their context now remains on the literary level without the hypothesis of different hands.[39]

The influence of Ps 42/43 on the beginning of John 14 has been recognized by various authors. Xavier Léon-Dufour[40] sees this influence extended until v. 11, Klaus Scholtissek[41] until v. 9. The detection of the influence of Ps 41,6.7.12; 42,5 LXX on the very beginning of John 14 "Let your heart not be troubled" is shared by other authors with the present writer.[42]

That Ps 41,5; 42,3 LXX may stand behind Jesus' words about the "heavenly dwellings" in John 14,2 is recognized as well by various authors.[43] The influence of Old Testament and Early Jewish traditions about the dwelling of God among his people is seen, with me, by Martin Hengel in his standard work on the "Johannine Question".[44]

The meaning of John 14,2-3 is still debated. With regard to v. 23 and characteristic Johannine eschatology, Andreas Dettwiler emphasizes the continuity between Jesus' announcement of his future coming to his disciples and his

---

[35] Cf. the article of the author, based on her dissertation, in the Additional Bibliography.
[36] See Hans-Ulrich Weidemann, *Der Tod Jesu im Johannesevangelium*, 93. The same position is held by Peter W. Ensor in his article listed in the Additional Bibliography.
[37] See my articles "Synoptic Jesus Tradition", 167, and "Die Überleitung" in the Additional Bibliography.
[38] See Hans-Ulrich Weidemann, *op. cit.* (note 35), 95, with reference to my monograph, p. 10, note 5.
[39] See for this proposal Jean Zumstein in his recent commentary, 49, who sees in Jn 13,34f. a "re-reading" of the First Farewell Discourse.
[40] See his commentary, p. 89f., with reference to my proposal in *NTS* 25 (1979) 33-57 and *Habt keine Angst*, 25-46.
[41] *In ihm sein und bleiben*, 232-234.
[42] See Jörg Frey, *Johanneische Eschatologie* III, 133; Francis J. Moloney, in his commentary, 397; Thomas Popp, „Die konsolatorische Kraft der Wiederholung", 531; Hartwig Thyen, in his commentary, 617f.; Jean Zumstein, in his commentary, 60.
[43] See Hans-Josef Klauck, „Himmlisches Haus", 22f.; James McCaffrey, *The house with many rooms*, 70; Hartwig Thyen in his commentary, 618.
[44] See Martin Hengel, *Die johanneische Frage*, 356f, 392.

coming in the hour of faith.[45] This position is discussed with reference to the present writer by Klaus Scholtissek.[46] This author favours a complementary understanding of Jesus' words about his future coming which combines elements of early Christian eschatology expecting the parousia of Christ with the belief that Christ comes to his disciples in faith by virtue of his resurrection and exaltation.[47]

Discussions about John 14,6 tend to deal with the exclusive claim of the Jesus of this discourse to be "the way, the truth and the life". Some authors notice possible connections of John 14,6 with Ps 43,3.4.[48] For the motif of "seeing God" in John 14,8 occasional reference is made to Ps 42,3.[49]

The influence of the deuteronomic and deuteronomistic language and thought world on John 14,15-24, which I proposed on the basis of previous literature in chapter III of "Habt keine Angst", has been more and more firmly established.[50] The starting point is always the semantic field of "love" and "keeping the commandments/words", present in John 14,15.21.23f., the so-called "framing verses". They frame Jesus' threefold promise of sending the Spirit, coming in person to his own, and coming with the Father according to John 14,16f.18-20.23. Some authors share the present writer's view of a threefold new "coming" of Jesus after Easter.[51]

The proposal to see traditional material behind John 14,16f. is shared by more than one recent author.[52] Jörg Frey also agrees with my proposal to find

---

[45] See Andreas Dettwiler, *Die Gegenwart des Erhöhten*, 118-121.
[46] „Relecture und réécriture", 17.
[47] See Klaus Scholtissek, *In ihm sein und bleiben*, 250f. The same balanced interpretation is given in the commentaries of Francis J. Moloney, 394, Udo Schnelle, 228, and Hartwig Thyen, 620-622. The complementary use of apocalyptic and present eschatology in John is at the basis of Jörg Frey's three volume work on Johannine Eschatology. For John 14,2f (with reference to *Habt keine Angst*) see his vol. III, 137, 148.
[48] See Xavier Léon-Dufour, *Lecture*, III, 100; James McCaffrey, *The house with many rooms*, 122.
[49] See Ulrich Wilckens in his commentary, 225.
[50] See Jörg Augenstein, *Das Liebesgebot*, 41-66 who nevertheless remains skeptical towards the idea of "covenant theology" in these verses; Jörg Frey, *Johanneische Eschatologie* III, 1, who accepts this idea; Xavier Léon-Dufour, *Lecture* III, 113, and Klaus Scholtissek, *In ihm sein und bleiben*, 263f, 267f, who hold the same position; Hartwig Thyen in his commentary, 630, 634, who shares the skepticism of his doctoral student Jörg Augenstein (see above) towards "covenant theology" in this section; Johns Varghese, *The imagery of love,* 340-347; Hans-Ulrich-Weidemann, *Der Tod Jesu im Johannesevangelium*, 172; Ulrich Wilckens in his commentary, 226. Only scant attention is paid to the traditional roots of "loving" and "keeping the commandments" in G. Charles A. Fernando, *The Relationship between Love and Law in the Gospel of John.*
[51] See Martin Hasitschka, „Die Parakletworte", 103; Klaus Scholtissek, *In ihm sein und bleiben*, 372f.
[52] See Jörg Frey, *Johanneische Eschatologie* III, 160; Frank Schleritt, *Der vorjohanneische Passionsbericht*, 316.

apocalyptic tradition in the motif of "seeing" Jesus from the moment of his return to his disciples.[53]

As already mentioned in connection with John 14,2f., various authors also agree with the proposal to see behind Jesus' announcement in John 14,23 that the Father and he would establish their "dwelling" among the disciples Old Testament traditions announcing God's "dwelling" among his people.[54]

In "Habt keine Angst"[55] it had been proposed to see behind the promise of "peace", "joy" and "Holy Spirit" in John 14,26-28 the eschatological gifts of Jesus. In the light of Rom 14,17 with its definition of the Kingdom of God as "righteousness (justice), peace, and joy in the Holy Spirit", "justice" may be added (cf. John 16,4e-33). The present writer has repeated this proposal on various occasions and pointed to the presence of this semantic field in John 20,19-23 as well as in John 14,26-28 and 16,4e-33.[56] Until now, this proposal has received little attention. Some authors see the relevance of Rom 14,17 for the eschatological gift of peace and the connection between the gift of the Spirit and peace and / or joy.[57] All these promises have their basis in the "peace" promised and granted by Jesus in the original sense of the Hebrew "shalom".[58]

Finally, there is still an ongoing discussion about the meaning and the relevance of Jesus' exhortation "Rise, let us go hence" in John 14,31. For many authors, these words can be understood in their plain sense and interpreted as an invitation to leave the room of the Last Supper and share Jesus' departure for his passion, narrated in John 18,1. In this case, chapters 15-17 seem to be an addition to an original Farewell in John 13,31 – 14,31 (unless one accepts the improbable hypothesis of a disturbed text which should be reconstructed by shifts of textual units). Earlier research thought of the addition of chapters 15-17, or parts of them, by one or more redactors.[59] Udo Schnelle sees a possibility of giving room for chapters 15-17 on the basis of the sequence of "Rise, let us go" in Mk 14,42 and "while he was still speaking" at the beginning of the arrest scene in Mk 14,43. According to this version, Jesus continued speaking to his disciples

---

[53] Jörg Frey, *Johanneische Eschatologie* III, 169.
[54] See Martin Hengel, *Die johanneische Frage*, 357, 392; Hans-Ulrich Weidemann, *Der Tod Jesu im Johannesevangelium*, 186. Klaus Scholtissek, „Relecture und réécriture", 27, sees in John 14,23 a „réécriture" of John 14,2f, that means, a re-writing of a previous statement by the same author under a different perspective.
[55] Pp. 90-104.
[56] See my articles "Friede nicht von dieser Welt?"; „Synoptic Jesus Tradition"; „Resurrection and the Remission of Sins".
[57] See George R. Beasley-Murray in his commentary, 262; Ulrich Wilckens in his commentary, 233; I. John Hesselink, „John 14,23-29", 176f.; Richard L. Jeske, "John 14,27 and 16,33".
[58] In this sense, Hartwig Thyen in his commentary, 635. Cf. also Jean Zumstein in his commentary, 85.
[59] See „Habt keine Angst", 9f.

between his exhortation directed to his disciples to rise and his arrest.[60] Perhaps this suggestion was too ingenious to be followed by other exegetes. A similar model is proposed by Jean Zumstein, seeing in chapters 15-17 a "relecture" of the First Farewell Discourse, after a break in reading.[61] A pause or break in reading is also supposed by other recent authors.[62] If chapters 15-17 are considered to be part of an original literary project, recent authors often attribute to the invitation of Jesus in John 14,31 a spiritual sense. The disciples are invited to rise spiritually to a higher degree of understanding Jesus and his words.[63] Repeatedly, these authors refer to Edwin Clement Hoskyns[64] and C. H. Dodd.[65] Notably in Hoskyns[66] there is found a reference to Clement of Alexandria to whom is attributed the spiritual interpretation of John 14,31 as an invitation in the sense of "Arise, let us remove from death unto life, and from corruption unto incorruption." Here, however, caution is to be recommended. A fresh study of the relevant passage[67] has led to the result that Clement of Alexandria proposes for the signal of Jesus in John 14,31 two different interpretations.[68] In the first place, these words have to be taken literally, as exhortation to rise from the Last Supper and to meet the adversary. Only secondarily, these words can be given also a metaphorical sense, and here Cyril uses more Greek philosophical than biblical language, as an invitation "to pass from death to life, from corruption to a state of incorruption", the passage quoted by E. C. Hoskyns. The transition in Clement from the first to the second interpretation is significant. He refers to the literal interpretation and goes on: "This interpretation is probable; nevertheless, it is convenient to point to a different and hidden interpretation." It may be wise to respect the text of Clement carefully.

---

[60] See Udo Schnelle, "Die Abschiedsreden im Johannesevangelium," 71-73; id. in his commentary, 238.
[61] See Jean Zumstein in his commentary, 89.
[62] See Francis F. Moloney in his commentary, 412f., with Fernando F. Segovia.
[63] See the commentaries of Thomas L. Brodie, 470f.; Xavier Léon-Dufour, 144, as a possibility of understanding the verse; Hartwig Thyen, 648; similarly H. B. H. Bevan, "Does 'arise, let us go hence' (John 14,31D) make sense where it stands?" in the Additional Bibliography.
[64] *The Fourth Gospel* (ed. Francis Noel Davey, London: Faber & Faber 1940) 548.
[65] *The Interpretation of the Fourth Gospel* (Cambridge: University Press 1953) 407-409.
[66] Loc. cit., note 63.
[67] *Sancti Patris Nostri Cyrilli Archiepiscopi Alexandrini in D. Ioannis Evangelium* (ed. post Aubertum P.H.E. Pusey; Oxford: Clarendon Press 1872; reprint Brussels: Culture and Civilization 1965) 531ff; Italian translation: S. Cirillo d'Alessandria, *Commento al Vangelo di Giovanni* (traduzione di L. Leone; Roma: Città Nuova 1995) III, 182-184 (section X,1).
[68] See my article „Levatevi".

Sources and Literature

The abbreviations of sources and literature follow the system of Siegfried M. Schwertner, *Internationales Abkürzungsverzeichnis für Theologie und Grenzgebiete. Zeitschriften, Serien, Lexika, Quellenwerke mit bibliographischen Angaben / International glossary of abbreviations for theology and related subjects. Periodicals, series, encyclopaedias, sources with bibliographical notes*, Berlin-New York: Walter de Gruyter ²1992. Biblical books are abbreviated according to the system of *The Holy Bible. The Revised Standard Version*, ibid. XXXI.

Sources

Die Bibel. Altes und Neues Testament. Einheitsübersetzung (Stuttgart 1980).
Biblia Hebraica Stuttgartensia (ed. K. Ellliger/K. Rudolph; Stuttgart 1977).
Biblia Sacra Polyglotta VT, NT III (ed. B. Waltonus Walton; London 1657).
Septuaginta. Id est Vetus Testamentum graece iuxta LXX interpretes, I—II (ed. A. Rahlfs; Stuttgart ⁷1962).
Novum Testamentum Graece (ed. E. Nestle/K. Aland; Stuttgart ²⁶1979).
The Greek New Testament (ed. K. Aland/M. Black/C. M. Martini/B. M. Metzger/A. Wikgren; Stuttgart ³1975).
Synopsis Quattuor Evangeliorum. Locis parallelis evangeliorum apocryphorum et patrum adhibitis (ed. K. Aland; Stuttgart ⁹1976).

Pritchard, J. M., *Ancient Near Eastern Texts Relating to the Old Testament* (ANET; Princeton, N. J., ²1955).

Becker, J., *Die Testamente der zwölf Patriarchen* (JSHRZ III, 1. Lieferung; Gütersloh 1974).
Brock, S. P./Picard, J.-C., ed., *Testamentum Iobi* (Brock), *Apocalypsis Baruchi Graece* (Picard) (PVTG II; Leiden 1967).
de Jonge, M., *The Testaments of the Twelve Patriarchs. A Critical Edition of the Greek Text* (PVTG 1,2; Leiden 1978).
Kraft, R. A./Purintum, A.-E., ed., *Paraleipomena Jeremiou* (SBLTT 1, Pseudepigrapha Series 1; Missoula 1972).
Riessler, P., *Altjüdisches Schrifttum außerhalb der Bibel* (Heidelberg ²1966).
Stone, M. E., ed., *The Testament of Abraham. The Greek Recensions* (SBLTT 2, Pseudepigrapha Series 2; Missoula 1972).
Baillet, M., ed., *Qumran Cave 4. III (4Q482-4Q520)* (DJD VII; Oxford 1982).
Barthélemy, D./Milik, J. T., ed., *Qumran Cave I* (DJD I; Oxford 1955).
Delcor, M., Les *Hymnes de Qumran (Hodayot). Texte hébreu - introduction - traduction - commentaire* (Paris 1962).

Lohse, E., Hrsg., *Die Texte aus Qumran. Hebräisch und deutsch. Mit masoretischer Punktation, Übersetzung, Einführung und Anmerkungen* (München 1964).
Maier, J., *Die Texte vom Toten Meer. Erste deutsche Gesamtübertragung I—II* (München-Basel 1960).
Maier, J./Schubert, K., *Die Qumran-Essener. Texte der Schriftrollen und Lebensbild der Gemeinde* (München-Basel 1973).

Bietenhard, H., *Midrasch Tanḥuma B. R. Tanḥuma über die Tora, genannt Midrasch Jelammedenu I* (Judaica et Christiana 5; Bern-Frankfurt a. M.-Las Vegas 1980).
Braude, W. G., *The Midrash on Psalms I—II* (YJS XIII; New Haven ³1976).
Goldschmidt, L., *Der babylonische Talmud. Mit Einschluß der vollständigen Mišnah, hrsg. . . . übersetzt und mit kurzen Erklärungen versehen I-IX* (Berlin-Leipzig-Haag 1899-1935).
Kautzsch, E., *Die Apokryphen und Pseudepigraphen des Alten Testaments II. Die Pseudepigraphen des Alten Testaments* (Tübingen-Freiburg i. Br.-Leipzig 1900).
Ljungman, H., *Sifre zu Deuteronomium* (RT, 2. Reihe, Tannaitische Midraschim 4; Stuttgart 1964 [ff]).
Schwab, M., *Le Talmud de Jérusalem III, 2* (Paris 1969).
Wünsche, A., *Bibliotheca Rabbinica. Eine Sammlung alter Midraschim I-V* (Hildesheim 1967; reprint).

Literature

Aalen, S., "'Reign' and 'House' in the Kingdom of God in the Gospels," *NTS* 8 (1961-1962) 215-240.
Abbott, E. A., *Johannine Grammar* (London 1906).
--, *Johannine Vocabulary. A comparison of the words of the fourth gospel with those of the three* (London 1905).
Anderson, A. A., *The Book of Psalms I. Introduction and Psalms 1-72* (NCeB 4,1; London 1972).
Augello, A., *Unità di rivelazione ed incarnazione in S. Giovanni (Giov. 14,7b—11)*: Diss. Pont. Univ. Gregorianae 1968. Cf. *LAPUG* 417 (1970) 577f.
Bacher, W., „Das Targum zu den Psalmen," *MGWJ* 21 (1872) 408-416.463-473.
Bacon, B. W., "'In my Father's house are many mansions', John 14,2," *ET* 43 (1931-1932) 477-478.
Balagué, M., "Los discursos de la última cena," *CuBi* 30 (1970) 160-164.
Balz, H./Schneider, G., Hrsg., *Exegetisches Wörterbuch zum Neuen Testament I—III* (Stuttgart-Berlin-Köln-Mainz 1980-1983).
Barrett, C. K., *The First Epistle to the Corinthians* (Harper's New Testament Commentaries; New York-Evanston 1968).

--, "'The Father is greater Than I' (Jo 14,28): Subordinationist Christology in the New Testament," in: *Neues Testament und Kirche (Fschr. R. Schnackenburg)* (ed. J. Gnilka; Freiburg 1974) 144-159.
--, *The Gospel According to St. John. An introduction with commentary and notes on the greek text* (London [^{1}1955] ^{2}1978).
Bauer, W., *Das Johannesevangelium* (HNT6; Tübingen [^{2}1925] ^{3}1933).
--, *Griechisch-Deutsches Wörterbuch zu den Schriften des Neuen Testaments und der übrigen urchristlichen Literatur* (Berlin ^{5}1958).
Becker, H., *Die Reden des Johannesevangeliums und der Stil der gnostischen Offenbarungsrede* (ed. R. Bultmann; FRLANT 68, NF 50; Göttingen 1956).
Becker, J., „Die Abschiedsreden Jesu im Johannesevangelium," *ZNW* 61 (1970) 215-246.
--, „Aufbau, Schichtung und theologiegeschichtliche Stellung des Gebetes in Joh 17," *ZNW* 60 (1969) 56-83.
--, *Das Evangelium nach Johannes I—II* (ÖTBK 4/1-2; Gütersloh-Würzburg 1979-1981).
Behler, G. M., *Die Abschiedsworte des Herrn. Johannesevangelium Kapitel 13-17* (Salzburg 1962; French 1960).
Bergmeier, R., *Glaube als Gabe nach Johannes. Religions- und theologiegeschichtliche Studien zum prädestinatianischen Dualismus im vierten Evangelium* (BWANT 6. Folge, 12; Stuttgart-Berlin-Köln-Mainz 1980).
Bernard, J. H., *Critical and Exegetical Commentary on the Gospel According to St. John II* (ed. A. H. McNeile; ICC; Edinburgh ^{2}1942).
Bernas, C, "The Activity of the Spirit-Paraclete," *BiTod* 72 (1974) 1589-1594.
Bertram, G., „Ev. Joh. 14,9 und das gnostische Christusbild," *ACIAC* 7 (1969) 379-389.
Betz, O., *Der Paraklet. Fürsprecher im häretischen Spätjudentum, im Johannes-Evangelium und in neugefundenen gnostischen Schriften* (AGSU 2; Leiden-Köln 1963).
Beutler, J., „Friedenssehnsucht - Friedensengagement nach dem Neuen Testament," *StZ* 200 (1982) 291-306.
--, „Literarische Gattungen im Johannesevangelium. Ein Forschungsbericht 1919 bis 1980," *ANRW* II 25,3 (1985) 2506-2568.
--, „Die Heilsbedeutung des Todes Jesu im Johannesevangelium nach Joh 13,1-20," in: *Der Tod Jesu. Deutungen im Neuen Testament* (ed. K. Kertelge; QD 74; Freiburg-Basel-Wien 1976) 188-204.
--, *Martyria. Traditionsgeschichtliche Untersuchungen zum Zeugnisthema bei Johannes* (FTS 10; Frankfurt 1972).
--, „Psalm 42/43 im Johannesevangelium," *NTS* 25 (1979) 33-57.
Blank, J., *Das Evangelium nach Johannes II* (GSL.NT 4/2; Düsseldorf 1977).
--, „Das Wort, der Geist und die Gemeinde. Jo 14, 23-31," *TiWo* 3 (1966) 28-44.
Blass, F./Debrunner, A./Rehkopf, F., *Grammatik des neutestamentlichen Griechisch* (Göttingen ^{15}1979).

Böcher, O., *Der johanneische Dualismus im Zusammenhang des nachbiblischen Judentums* (Gütersloh 1965).
Boismard, M.-É., "La connaissance dans l'alliance nouvelle d'après la première lettre de saint Jean," *RB* 56 (1949) 365-391.
--, "L'évolution du thème eschatologique dans les traditions johanniques," *RB* 68 (1961) 507-524.
Borgen, P., "God's Agent in the Fourth Gospel," in: *Religions in Antiquity. Essays in Memory of Erwin Ramsdell Goodenough* (ed. J. Neusner; SHR 14; 1968) 135-148.
Borig, R., *Der wahre Weinstock. Untersuchungen zu Jo 15,1-10* (StANT 16; München 1967).
Boring, M. E., "The Influence of Christian Prophecy on the Johannine Portrayal of the Paraclete and Jesus," *NTS* 25 (1979) 113-123.
Botterweck, J. G./Ringgren, H., ed., *Theologisches Wörterbuch zum Alten Testament I-III* (Mainz 1973-1982).
Bover, J. M., *Comentario al Sermón de la Cena* (BAC 70; Madrid ²1955).
Boyd, W. J. P., "The Ascension according to St John. Chapters 14-17 not prepassion but post-resurrection," *Theol.* 70 (1967) 207-211.
Boyle, J. L., "The Last Discourse (Jn 13,31-16,33) and Prayer (Jn 17). Some Observations on Their Unity and Development," *Bib.* 56 (1975) 210-222.
Braulik, G., „Gesetz als Evangelium. Rechtfertigung und Begnadigung nach der deuteronomischen Tora," *ZThK* 79 (1982) 127-160.
Braun, F.-M., "Évangile selon Saint Jean," in: *Les Saints Évangiles S. Luc - S. Jean* (SB [PC] X; Paris 1950) 293-487.
--, *Jean de Théologien et son Évangile dans l'église ancienne* (Paris 1959). *II: Jean le Théologien. Les grandes traditions d'Israël et l'accord des Écritures selon le Quatrième Évangile* (Paris 1966). *III/1: Jean le Théologien. Sa théologie. Le mystère de Jésus-Christ* (Paris 1966). *III/2: Jean le Théologien. Sa théologie. Le Christ, notre Seigneur hier, aujourd'hui, toujours* (Paris 1972).
Braun, H., *Qumran und das Neue Testament I—II* (Tübingen 1966).
Brinkmann, B., "De priore quodam sermone valedictorio Domini (Ioh 12,44-50; 15; 16)," *VD* 19 (1939) 300-307; 21 (1941) 155-156.
Brown, R. E., *The Community of the Beloved Disciple. The Life, Loves and Hates of an Individual Church in New Testament Times* (New York-Ramsey-Toronto 1979). German: *Ringen um die Gemeinde. Der Weg der Kirche nach den Johanneischen Schriften* (Salzburg 1982).
--, *The Gospel According to John I—II* (AncB 29/29A; Garden City, New York, 1966-1970).
--, "Incidents that Are Units in the Synoptic Gospels but Dispersed in St. John," *CBQ* 23 (1961) 143-160. Reprint in: id., *New Testament Essays* (Milwaukee 1965) 192-213.
Brown, R. P., "ΕΝΤΟΛΗ ΚΑΙΝΗ (St. John XIII.34)," *Theol.* 26 (1933) 184-193.

Brown, S., *Apostasy and Perseverance in the Theology of Luke* (AnBib 36; Rome 1969).
Bühner, J.-A., *Der Gesandte und sein Weg im vierten Evangelium* (WUNT, 2. Reihe, 2; Tübingen 1977).
Bultmann, R., *Das Evangelium des Johannes* (KEK 2; Göttingen [^{10}1941] ^{15}1957. Ergänzungsheft 1957).
--, *Exegetica. Aufsätze zur Erforschung des Neuen Testaments* (ed. E. Dinkler; Tübingen 1967).
--, *Die Geschichte der synoptischen Tradition* (FRLANT 29 NF 12; Göttingen ^{2}1931, Ergänzungsheft 1958).
--, *Die drei Johannesbriefe* (KEK 14; Göttingen ^{7}1967).
--, *Theologie des Neuen Testaments* (Tübingen ^{5}1965).
Burchard, C., „Das doppelte Liebesgebot in der frühen christlichen Überlieferung," in: *Der Ruf Jesu und die Antwort der Gemeinde* (Fschr. J. Jeremias) (ed. E. Lohse; Göttingen 1970) 39-62.
Calmes, Th., *L'Évangile selon Saint Jean. Traduction critique. Introduction et commentaire* (EtB; Paris-Rome 1904).
Cerfaux, L., "La charité fraternelle et le retour du Christ selon Jn 13,33-38," *EThL* 24 (1948) 321-332.
Charlier, C., "La présence dans l'absence (Jean 13,31-14,31)," *BVC* 2 (1953) 61-75.
Cignelli, L., "Giov. 14,28 nell'esegesi di Origene," *SBFLA* 25 (1975) 137-163.
Clarke, W. K. L., "Studies in Texts, Jn 14,1-4," *Theol.* 9,2 (1924) 41-43.
Clemen, C., *Die Entstehung des Johannesevangeliums* (Halle 1912).
Colunga, A., "La paz os dejo. Mi paz os doy (Jn 14,27)," *Helm.* 11 (1952) 269-288.
Computer-Konkordanz zum Novum Testamentum Graece von Nestle-Aland, 26. Auflage, und zum Greek New Testament, 3rd Edition (ed. Institut für neutestamentliche Textforschung und Rechenzentrum der Universität Münster unter besonderer Mitwirkung von H. Bachmann und W. A. Slaby; Berlin-New York 1980).
Coppens, J., "Les logia johanniques du Fils de l'homme," in: *L'Évangile de Jean. Sources, rédaction, théologie* (ed. M. de Jonge; BEThL 44; Gembloux-Leuven 1977) 311-315.
Corssen, P., „Die Abschiedsreden Jesu in dem vierten Evangelium. Mit besonderer Berücksichtigung von J. Wellhausen, Erweiterungen und Änderungen im vierten Evangelium," *ZNW* 8 (1907) 125-142.
Cortès, E., *Los discursos de adiós de Gn 49 a Jn 13-17. Pistas para la historia de un género literario en la antigua literatura judía* (Barcelona 1976).
Cullmann, O., *Der johanneische Kreis. Sein Platz im Spätjudentum, in der Jüngerschaft Jesu und im Urchristentum. Zum Ursprung des Johannesevangeliums* (Tübingen 1975).

Culpepper, R. A., "The Narrator and the Farewell Discourse in John," Paper at the annual conference of the S.N.T.S., Toronto 1980.
Dahood, M., *Psalms I. 1-50* (AncB 16; New York 1966).
De Jonge, M., "Prima oratio Jesu post coenam I (... Jo., XIV, 1-14)," *CBrug* 28 (1928) 130-135.
Dodd, C. H., *The Interpretation of the Fourth Gospel* (Cambridge 1953).
--, *Historical Tradition in the Fourth Gospel* (Cambridge 1963).
Dörpinghaus, P., *Die Abschiedsreden Jesu. Problem und Lösung* (Rottweil 1957).
Dupont, J., *Le Discours de Milet. Testament Pastoral de Saint Paul* (Actes 20,18-36) (LeDiv 32; Paris 1962).
Durand, A., "Le Discours de la Cène (Saint Jean, XIII,31-XVII,26)," *RSR* 1 (1910) 97-131.513-539; 2 (1911) 321-349.521-545.
--, *Évangile selon Saint Jean* (VSal IV; Paris [19]1930).
Elliger, K., *Das Buch der zwölf kleinen Propheten II. Die Propheten Nahum, Habakuk, Zephanja, Haggai, Sacharja, Maleachi* (ATD 25; Göttingen 1950).
--, *Deuterojesaja I* (Jes 40,1 -45,7) (BK.AT XI,1; Neukirchen 1978).
Ernst, J., *Das Evangelium nach Lukas* (RNT; Regensburg 1977).
Ernst, R., *Unseres Herrn Abschiedsreden vor seinem Leiden und seiner Himmelfahrt (Jo 13,31-17,26)* (Eupen 1948).
Estalayo Alonso, V., "La Vuelta de Cristo en el Evangelio de Juan. Análisis Literario de Jn 14,1-3," *EsT* 5,10 (1978) 3-70.
Evdokimov, P., "Étude sur Jean XIII,18-30," *EeV(M)* 3 (1950) 201-216.
Fensham, F. C., "I am the Way, the Truth and the Life," in: *The Christ of John. Essays on the Christology of the Fourth Gospel. Proceedings of the Fourth Meeting of 'Die Nuwe Test. Werkgemeenskap van Suid-Afrika'* (Neotestamentica 2; Pretoria 1968) 81-88.
Feuillet, A., *Le Mystère de l'Amour Divin dans la Theologie Johannique* (EtB; Paris 1972).
Fischer, G., *Die himmlischen Wohnungen. Untersuchungen zu Joh 14,2f* (EHS.T 38; Bern-Frankfurt/M. 1975).
Fohrer, G., *Das Alte Testament I—II/III* (Gütersloh 1969-1970).
Ford, J. Massyngberde, *Revelation. Introduction, translation and commentary* (AncB 38; Garden City, New York, 1975).
Forestell, J. T., "Jesus and the Paraclete in the Gospel of John," in: *Word and Spirit (Fschr. D. M. Stanley)* (ed. J. Plevnik; Willowdale, Ont., 1975) 151-197.
Fortna, R. T., *The Gospel of Signs. A reconstruction of the narrative source underlying the fouth gospel* (MSSNTS 11; Cambridge 1970).
Frankemölle, H., *Jahwebund und Kirche Christi. Studien zur Form- und Traditionsgeschichte des „Evangeliums" nach Matthäus* (Münster 1974).
Freed, E. D., *Old Testament Quotations in the Gospel of John* (NT.S 11; Leiden 1965).

--, "Psalm 42/43 in John's Gospel," *NTS* 29 (1983) 62-73.
Gaechter, P., „Der formale Aufbau der Abschiedsrede Jesu," *ZKTh* 58 (1934) 155-207.
Galling, K., *Die Bücher der Chronik, Esra, Nehemia* (ATD 12; Göttingen 1954).
Gallo, S., "Sermo Christi sacrificalis Jo 14-16," *VD* 26 (1948) 33-34.
Gaucho, C., "Cena, Discurso de la," *Enciclopedia de la Biblia 2* (Barcelona 1963) 266-271.
Girgensohn, H., „Worte Jesu an die ecclesia viatorum. Betrachtungen zu Johannes 14,1-6" (1947), in: id., *Heilende Kräfte der Seelsorge* (Göttingen 1966) 177-184.
Godet, F., *Commentaire sur l'Évangile de Saint Jean III. Explication des chapitres VIII-XXI* (Neuchâtel without year).
Goldberg, A. M., *Untersuchungen über die Vorstellung von der Schekhinah in der frühen rabbinischen Literatur* (SJ 5; Berlin 1969).
Gollwitzer, H., „Außer Christus kein Heil? (Johannes 14,6)," *ACJD* 2 (1967) 171-194.
Groß, H., *Die Idee des ewigen und allgemeinen Weltfriedens im Alten Orient und im Alten Testament* (TThSt 7; Trier 1956).
Grundmann, W., „Das Wort von Jesu Freunden (Joh XV, 13-16) und das Herrenmahl," *NT* 3 (1959) 62-69.
--, *Zeugnis und Gestalt des Johannes-Evangeliums. Eine Studie zur denkerischen und gestalterischen Leistung des vierten Evangelisten* (AzTh, Reihe 1,7; Stuttgart 1961).
Gryglewicz, F., „Die Aussagen über den Heiligen Geist im vierten Evangelium. Überlieferung und Redaktion," *SNTU.A* 4 (1979) 45-53.
Guilding, A., *The Fourth Gospel and Jewish Worship. A study of the relation of St. John's Gospel to the ancient Jewish lectionary system* (Oxford 1960).
Gundry, R. H., "In my Father's House are many μοναί" (John 14,2)," *ZNW* 58 (1967) 68-72.
Gunkel, H./Begrich, J., *Einleitung in die Psalmen. Die Gattungen der religiösen Lyrik Israels* (HK, Ergänzungsband zur II. Abteilung; Göttingen 1933).
Haenchen, E., *Das Johannesevangelium. Ein Kommentar aus den nachgelassenen Manuskripten* (ed. U. Busse; Tübingen 1980).
Hammer, I., „Eine klare Stellung zu Joh 14,31b," *BiKi* 14 (1959) 33-40.
Hamp, V., *Der Begriff „Wort" in den aramäischen Bibelübersetzungen. Ein exegetischer Beitrag zur Hypostasen-Frage und zur Geschichte der Logos-Spekulationen* (München 1938).
Hartman, L. F./DiLella, A. A., *The Book of Daniel. A New Translation with Notes and Commentary on Chapters 1-9 by L. F. Hartman. Introduction, and Commentary on Chapters 10-12 by A. A. DiLella* (AncB 23; New York 1978).
Haspecker, J., *Gottesfurcht bei Jesus Sirach. Ihre religiöse Struktur und ihre literarische und doktrinäre Bedeutung* (AnBib 30; Rom 1967).

Hauret, C., *Les Adieux du Seigneur (Jn 13-17)* (Paris 1952).
Heise, J., *Bleiben. Menein in den Johanneischen Schriften* (HUTh 8; Tübingen 1967).
Heitmüller, W., „Das Johannes-Evangelium," in: *SNT* 4 (Göttingen ³1920) 1-184.
--, „*Im Namen Jesu". Eine sprach- u. religionsgeschichtliche Untersuchung zum Neuen Testament, speziell zur altchristlichen Taufe* (FRLANT 1; Göttingen 1903).
Hertzberg, H. W., *Die Bücher Josua, Richter, Ruth* (ATD 9; Göttingen ²1959).
Hirsch, E., *Das vierte Evangelium in seiner ursprünglichen Gestalt verdeutscht und erklärt* (Tübingen 1936).
--, *Studien zum vierten Evangelium* (BHTh 11; Tübingen 1936).
Holtzmann, H. J./Bauer, W., *Evangelium, Briefe und Offenbarung des Johannes* (HC 4; Tübingen ³1908).
Holzmeister, U., "'Paraclitus autem Spiritus Sanctus' Ioh. 14,26," *VD* 12 (1932) 135-139.
Horton, F., "La Promesse de l'Esprit et ses effets," *EtEv* 33,4 (1973) 109-127.
Hoskyns, E. C./Davey, F. N., *The Fourth Gospel* (Plymouth ²1948).
Huby, J., *Le Discours de Jesus après la Cène. Suivi d'une étude sur la connaissance de foi dans saint Jean* (Paris 1932).
Humphries, A. L., "A Note on πρὸς ἐμαυτόν (John 14,3) and εἰς τὰ ἴδια (John 1,11): A Plea for a Revised Translation," *ET* 53 (1941-1942) 356.
Hutton, W. R., "John XIV. 17," *ET* 57 (1945-1946) 194.
Ibuki, Y., *Die Wahrheit im Johannesevangelium* (BBB 39; Bonn 1972).
Jeckel, H., „Der Garant der Kirche (Jo 14,26)," *TiWo* 3 (1966) 82-86.
Jenni, E./Westermann, C., ed., *Theologisches Handwörterbuch zum Alten Testament* (München-Zürich 1976).
Jeremias, G., *Der Lehrer der Gerechtigkeit* (StUNT 2; Göttingen 1963).
Jeremias, J., „Johanneische Literarkritik," *ThBl* (1941) 33-46.
Johnston, G., *The Spirit-Paraclete in the Gospel of John* (MSSNTS 12; Cambridge 1970).
Kaiser, O., *Einleitung in das Alte Testament* (Gütersloh ³1975).
--, *Der Prophet Jesaja. Kapitel 13 - 39* (ATD 18; Göttingen 1973).
Kegler, J., „Prophetisches Reden von Zukünftigem," in: *Eschatologie und Friedenshandeln. Exegetische Beiträge zur Frage christlicher Friedensverantwortung* (SBS 101; Stuttgart 1981) 15-58.
Kelly, J., "What Did Christ Mean by the Sign of Love?: Jn 13,34-35," *AfER* 13,2 (1971) 113-121.
Kergadarec, Y. de, "'Nul ne vient au Père que par moi.' Le premier discours de Jésus après la Cène, Jn 13,31 - 14,31," *Christus* 98 (1978) 199-208.
Kittel, G./Friedrich, G., Hrsg., *Theologisches Wörterbuch zum Neuen Testament I-X* (Stuttgart 1933-1979).

Klijn, A. F. J., "Jo 14,22 and the Name Judas Thomas," in: *Festschrift J. N. Sevenster* (Leiden 1970) 88-110.
Knabenbauer, I., *Commentarius in Quattuor S. Evangelia Domini N. Jesu Christi IV. Evangelium Secundum Ioannem* (CSS sect. III 4; Paris [6]1925).
Könn, J., *Sein letztes Wort. Die Abschiedsreden des Herrn, Jo 13-17* (Einsiedeln-Köln 1953).
Kraus, H.-J., *Psalmen I* (BK.AT XV/1; Neukirchen 1960 [[5]1978]).
--, *Theologie der Psalmen* (BK.AT XV/3; Neukirchen 1979).
Kugelmann, R., "The Gospel for Pentecost (Jn. 14:23-31)," *CBQ* 6 (1944) 259-275.
Kuhn, K.-G., Hrsg., *Konkordanz zu den Qumrantexten* (Göttingen 1960).
--, „Nachträge zur Konkordanz zu den Qumrantexten," *RdQ* 4 (1963-1964) 163-234.
Kundsin, K., „Die Wiederkunft Jesu in den Abschiedsreden des Johannesevangeliums," *ZNW* 33 (1934) 210-215.
Kuss, O., *Der Römerbrief. Erste Lieferung Röm 1,1 - 6,11* (Regensburg 1957).
Lacomara, A., "Deuteronomy and the Farewell Discourse (Jn 13:31-16:33)," *CBQ* 36 (1974) 65-84. Cf. *ThD* 22 (1974) 232-239.
Lagrange, M.-J., *Évangile selon Saint Jean* (EtB; Paris [2]1925).
la Potterie, I. de, "Parole et Esprit dans S. Jean," in: *L'évangile de Jean* (ed. M. de Jonge; BEThL 44; Leuven 1977) 177-201.
--, *La Vérité dans Saint Jean I—II* (AnBib 73/74) Rome 1977.
--, "'Je suis la Voie, la Vérité et la Vie' (Jn 14,6)," *NRTh* 88 (1966) 907-942, cf. id., *Vérité* 241-278.
Lattke, M., *Einheit im Wort. Die spezifische Bedeutung von ἀγάπη, ἀγαπᾶν und φιλεῖν im Johannesevangelium* (StANT 41; München 1975).
Le Déaut, R., *Introduction à la littérature targumique: Première partie* (Rome 1966).
Leonardi, G., "Il significato del passagio di Gesù al padre nei Discorsi d'addio di Giovanni," *ParVi* 18 (1972) 101-119.
Leroy, H., *Rätsel und Mißverständnis. Ein Beitrag zur Formgeschichte des Johannesevangeliums* (BBB 30; Bonn 1968).
L'Hour, J., *La morale de l'Alliance* (Paris 1966).
Liddell, H. G./Scott, R., *A Greek-English Lexicon. A new edition, revised and augmented by H. S. Jones/R. McKenzie* (Oxford 1953). *Supplement*, ed. by E. A. Barber (1968).
Lightfoot, R. H., *St. John's Gospel. A Commentary* (ed. C. F. Evans; Oxford 1956).
Lindars, B., "ΔΙΚΑΙΟΣΥΝΗ in Jn 16.8 and 10," in: *Mélanges Bibliques en hommage au R. P. Béda Rigaux* (ed. A. Descamps/R. R. A. de Halleux; Gembloux 1970) 275-285.
--, *The Gospel of John* (NCeB; London 1972).

--, *New Testament Apologetic. The Doctrinal Significance of the Old Testament Quotations* (London ²1973).

--, "The Son of Man in the Johannine Christology," in: id./S. S. Smalley, ed., *Christ and Spirit in the New Testament* (Festschrift C. F. D. Moule; Cambridge 1973) 43-60.

--, "Traditions Behind the Fourth Gospel," in: *L'évangile de Jean* (ed. M. de Jonge; BEThL 44; Leuven 1977) 107-124.

Lohfink, G., *Wie hat Jesus Gemeinde gewollt? Zur gesellschaftlichen Dimension des christlichen Glaubens* (Freiburg-Basel-Wien ³1983).

Lohfink, N., *Das Hauptgebot. Eine Untersuchung literarischer Einleitungsfragen zu Dtn 5-11* (AnBib 20; Rom 1963).

Lohse, E., *Die Entstehung des Neuen Testaments* (ThW 4; Stuttgart etc. 1975).

--, *Die Offenbarung des Johannes* (NTD 11; Göttingen 1960).

Loisy, A., *Le Quatrième Évangile* (Paris 1903).

--, *Le Quatrième Evangile. Les Epitres Dites de Jean* (Paris ²1921).

Lust. J., "Ezekiel 36-40 in the Oldest Greek Manuscript," *CBQ* 43 (1981) 517-533.

Lyonnet, S., *Exegesis Epistulae ad Romanos. Cap. V. ad VIII* (Except. Rom 5,12-21). Editio Altera recognita (Romae 1966).

MacRae, G., "Theology and Irony in the Fourth Gospel," in: *The Word in the World* (ed. R. J. Clifford, Festschrift F. L. Moriarty; Cambridge [Mass.] 1973) 83-96.

Malatesta, E., *Interiority and Covenant. A Study of εἶναι ἐν and μένειν ἐν in the First Letter of Saint John* (AnBib 69; Rome 1978).

Massi, P., *Die Abschiedsworte des Herrn. Jo 13-17* (Salzburg 1962).

Mateos, J./Barreto, J., en colaboración con E. Hurtado, A. Urban y J. Rius-Camps, *El Evangelio de Juan. Análisis lingüistico y comentario exegético* (Lectura del Nuevo Testamento 4; Madrid 1979).

McCarthy, D. J., *Treaty and Covenant. A Study in Form in the Ancient Oriental Documents and in the Old Testament* (AnBib 21A; Rome 1978).

Meagher, J. C., "John 1,14 and the New Temple," *JBL* 88 (1969) 57-68.

Meeks, W., "The Man from Heaven in Johannine Sectarianism," *JBL* 91 (1972) 44-72.

Michel, H.-J., *Die Abschiedsrede des Paulus an die Kirche Apg 20,17-38. Motivgeschichte und theologische Bedeutung* (StANT 35; München 1973).

Michel, O., *Der Brief an die Hebräer* (KEK XIII; Göttingen ⁶1966).

Middleton, R. D., "Logos and Shekinah in the Fourth Gospel," *JQR* 29 (NS 1, 1938-1939) 101-133.

Migliasso, S., *La presenza dell'Assente. Saggio di analisi letterario-strutturale e di sintesi teologica di Gv 13,31-14,31* (Roma 1979).

Miranda, J. P., *Die Sendung Jesu im vierten Evangelium. Religions- und theologiegeschichtliche Untersuchungen zu den Sendungsformeln* (SBS 87; Stuttgart 1977).

--, *Der Vater, der mich gesandt hat. Religionsgeschichtliche Untersuchungen zu den johanneischen Sendungsformeln. Zugleich ein Beitrag zur johanneischen Christologie und Ekklesiologie* (EHS.T 7; Bern-Frankfurt 1972).
Moe, O., "Om det nye bud Joh 13,34," *TTK* 28 (1957) 39-42.
Mollat, D., "L'Évangile selon Saint Jean," in: id./F. M. Braun, *L'Évangile et les Epîtres de Saint Jean* (SB [J]; Paris ³1973).
--, *Saint Jean. Maître spirituel* (BSpir 10; Paris 1976).
Moloney, F. J., *The Johannine Son of Man* (BSRel 14; Rome 1976).
Moran, W. L., "The Ancient Near Eastern Background of the Love of God in Deuteronomy," *CBQ* 25 (1963) 77-87.
Morgan-Wynne, J. E., "A Note on John 14.17b," *BZ* 23 (1979) 93-96.
Morris, L., *The Gospel According to John. The English text with introduction, exposition and notes* (NIC 4; Grand Rapids, Michigan, 1971).
Müller, H., "El Sermón de despedida y la oración sacerdotal," *RevBib* 31 (1969) 16-25.
Munck, J., "Discours d'adieu dans le Nouveau Testament et dans la littérature biblique," in: *Aux sources de la tradition chrétienne* (Festschrift A. Goguel; Neuchâtel-Paris 1950) 155-170.
Mussner, F., *ZΩH. Die Anschauung vom „Leben" im Vierten Evangelium unter Berücksichtigung der Johannesbriefe* (MThS.H 5; München 1952).
Myers, J. M., *Ezra - Nehemiah. Introduction, Translation and Notes* (AncB 14; New York 1965).
Nicacci, A., "Esame letterario di Gv 14," *ED* 31,2 (1978) 209-260.
Nicol, W., *The Sēmeia in the Fourth Gospel. Tradition and redaction* (NT.S XXXII; Leiden 1972).
N. N., "Le Christ a-t-il reçu de son Père un commandement de mourir sur la Croix?," *AmiCl* 49 (1932) 92-94.
Nordheim, E. von, *Die Lehre der Alten I. Das Testament als Literaturgattung im Judentum der hellenistisch-römischen Zeit* (ALGHJ 13; Leiden 1980).
Noth, M., *Könige I* (BK.AT IX/1; Neukirchen 1968).
--, *Das zweite Buch Mose. Exodus* (ATD 5; Göttingen ³1965).
--, *Das dritte Buch Mose. Leviticus* (ATD 6; Göttingen 1962).
--, *Das vierte Buch Mose. Numeri* (ATD 7; Göttingen 1966).
--, *Überlieferungsgeschichtliche Studien* (SKG.G 18,2; Halle 1943).
Oehler, W., *Das Wort des Johannes an die Gemeinde. Evangelium Johannis 15 - 17, Johannesbriefe und Offenbarung des Johannes* (Gütersloh 1938).
Onuki, T., „Die johanneischen Abschiedsreden und die synoptische Tradition. Eine traditionskritische und traditionsgeschichtliche Untersuchung," *AJBI* 3 (1977) 157-268.
Painter, J., "The Farewell Discourses and the History of Johannine Christianity," *NTS* 27 (1981) 525-543.
--, "Glimpses of the Johannine Community in the Farewell Discourses," *ABR* 28 (1980) 21-38.

Pancaro, S., *The Law in the Fourth Gospel* (NT.S 42; Leiden 1975).
Peinador, M., "Idea central del discurso de Jesús después de la Cena (Joh. XIV - XVII)," *EstB* 12 (1953) 5-28.
Pesch, R., *Das Markusevangelium II. Kommentar zu Kap. 8,27-16,20* (HThK II,2; Freiburg-Basel-Wien 1977).
Piper, O. A., "The Real Presence (John 14: 1-6)," *PSB* 51,2 (1957) 16-23.
Platino, R., "Le parole d'addio del Signore," *Fonti Vive* 9 (1963) 213-221.
Pölzl, F. X./Innitzer, Th., *Kurzgefaßter Kommentar zum Evangelium des hl. Johannes bis zum Beginn der Leidensgeschichte* (KK; Graz-Wien [4]1928).
Porsch, F., *Anwalt der Glaubenden. Das Wirken des Geistes nach dem Zeugnis des Johannesevangeliums* (GeLe Stuttgart 1978).
--, *Pneuma und Wort. Ein exegetischer Beitrag zur Pneumatologie des Johannesevangeliums* (FTS 16; Frankfurt 1974).
Rad, G. von, *Das fünfte Buch Mose. Deuteronomium* (ATD 8; Göttingen 1964).
Reese, J. M., "Literary Structure of Jn 13,31 - 14,31; 16,5-6.16-33," *CBQ* 34 (1972) 321-331.
Reim, G., „Probleme der Abschiedsreden," *BZ NF* 20 (1976) 117-122.
Rhoth, C./Wigoder, G., ed., *Encyclopaedia Judaica IV B* (Jerusalem 1971).
Ricca, P., *Die Eschatologie des Vierten Evangeliums* (Zürich-Frankfurt 1966).
Richter, G., „Die Fußwaschung Joh 13,1-20," *MThZ* 16 (1965) 13-26.
--, *Die Fußwaschung im Johannesevangelium. Geschichte ihrer Deutung* (BU 1; Regensburg 1967).
--, *Studien zum Johannesevangelium* (ed. J. Hainz; BU 13; Regensburg 1977).
Rieger, J., "Spiritus Sanctus suum praeparat adventum (Jo 14,16-17)," *VD* 43 (1965) 19-27.
Ruckstuhl, E., *Die literarische Einheit des Johannesevangeliums. Der gegenwärtige Stand der einschlägigen Forschungen* (SF NF 3; Freiburg in der Schweiz 1951).
--, „Die johanneische Menschensohnforschung 1957-1969," in: *Theologische Berichte I* (Zürich etc. 1972) 171-284.
Sabourin, L., "The MEMRA of God in the Targumim," *BTB* 6 (1976) 79-85.
Sanders, J. N., *A Commentary on the Gospel According to St John* (ed. B. A. Mastin; BNTC; London 1968).
Schaefer, O., „Der Sinn der Rede Jesu von den vielen Wohnungen in seines Vaters Hause und von dem Weg zu ihm (Joh 14,1-7)," *ZNW* 32 (1933) 210-217.
Schaeffer, F. A., "The Mark of the Christian," *ChrTo* 14 (1970) 1063-1066.
Schanz, P., *Commentar über das Evangelium des heiligen Johannes* (Tübingen 1885).
Schenker, A., „Unwiderrufliche Umkehr und neuer Bund. Vergleich zwischen der Wiederherstellung Israels in Dt 4,25-31; 30,1-14 und dem neuen Bund in Jer 31,31-34," *FZPhTh* 27 (1980) 93-106.
Schlatter, A., *Der Evangelist Johannes. Wie er spricht, denkt und glaubt. Ein Kommentar zum vierten Evangelium* (Stuttgart [3]1960).

--, „Die Sprache und Heimat des vierten Evangelisten" (1902), in: *Johannes und sein Evangelium* (ed. K. H. Rengstorf; Darmstadt 1973) 28-201.
Schlier, H., *Der Römerbrief* (HThK VI; Freiburg-Basel-Wien 1977).
Schmid, H. H., šalôm. *„Frieden" im Alten Orient und im Alten Testament* (SBS51; Stuttgart 1971).
Schnackenburg, R., „Das Anliegen der Abschiedsrede in Joh 14," in: *Wort Gottes in der Zeit* (ed. H. Feld/J. Nolte; Fschr. K. H. Schelkle; Düsseldorf 1973) 95-110.
--, *Das Johannesevangelium* (HThK IV, 1-4; Freiburg-Basel-Wien 1965-1984).
--, „Johannes 14:7," in, *Studies in New Testament Language and Text* (ed. J. K. Elliott; Fschr. G. D. Kilpatrick; NT.S 44; Leiden 1976) 345-356.
Schneider, G., *Das Evangelium nach Lukas I—II* (ÖTBK 3/1-2; Gütersloh-Würzburg 1977).
Schneider, J., „Die Abschiedsreden Jesu. Ein Beitrag zur Frage der Komposition von Johannes 13,31-17,26," in: *Gott und die Götter* (Fschr. E. Fascher; Berlin 1958) 103-112.
Schneiders, S. M., *The Johannine Resurrection Narrative. An exegetical and theological study of John 20 as a synthesis of johannine spirituality* (unpublished Dissertation, Rome, Pontifical Gregorian University 1975).
Schottroff, L., *Der Glaubende und die feindliche Welt. Beobachtungen zum gnostischen Dualismus und seiner Bedeutung für Paulus und das Johannesevangelium* (WMANT 37; Neukirchen-Vluyn 1970).
Schulz, S., *Das Evangelium nach Johannes* (NTD 4; Göttingen ^{12}1970).
--, *Komposition und Herkunft der Johanneischen Reden* (BWANT 81,5/1; Stuttgart 1960).
--, *Untersuchungen zur Menschensohn-Christologie im Johannesevangelium. Zugleich ein Beitrag zur Methodengeschichte der Auslegung des 4. Evangeliums* (Göttingen 1957).
Schwartz, E., Aporien im vierten Evangelium, in: *NGWG.PH* 1907, 342-372; 1908, 115-188.487-560.
Schweizer, E., *EGO EIMI. Die religionsgeschichtliche Herkunft und theologische Bedeutung der johanneischen Bildreden, zugleich ein Beitrag zur Quellenfrage des vierten Evangeliums* (Göttingen ^{2}1965).
--, *Das Evangelium nach Matthäus* (NTD 2; Göttingen ^{13}1973; 1. Auflage der Neufassung).
Segalla, G., "Il libro dell'addio di Gesù ai suoi (Studio della struttura di Giov. 13 - 17)," *Parole di Vita* (Roma) 15 (1970) 356-376.
Segovia, A., "El texto 'Pater maior me est' (S. Juan, 14,28). Explicado por un polemista antimacedoniano," *RET* 1 (1941) 603-609.
Seynaeve, J., "Le testament spirituel du Christ. Le(s) discours de la dernière Cène (Jn 13-17)," *Orientations Pastorales* 14,81 (Léopoldville 1962).

--, "Les Verbes ἀποστέλλω et πέμπω dans le vocabulaire théologique de Saint Jean," in: *L'évangile de Jean* (ed. M. de Jonge; BEThL 44 ; Leuven 1977) 385-389.

Siegwalt, G., "Sacrement et éthique (Étude biblique sur Jean 14,15-26)," *PosLuth* 21 (1973) 26-33.

Simoens, Y., *La gloire d'aimer. Structures stilistiques et interprétatives dans le Discours de la Cène (Jn 13 - 17)* (AnBib 90; Rome 1981).

Smalley, S. S., "The Testament of Jesus: Another Look," *StEv* 6 = *TU* 112 (1973) 495-501.

Smend, R., „Das Gesetz und die Völker. Ein Beitrag zur deuteronomistischen Redaktionsgeschichte," in: *Probleme biblischer Theologie* (Fschr. G. v. Rad; ed. H. W. Wolff; München 1971) 494-509.

Soltau, W., „Das vierte Evangelium in seiner Entstehungsgeschichte dargelegt," in: *SHAW.PH* VII Jahrgang 1916, 6. Abteilung, Heidelberg 1916.

Speyr, A. von, *Die Abschiedsreden. Betrachtungen über Kap. 13 - 17 des Johannesevangeliums* (Einsiedeln 1948).

Spitta, F., *Das Johannes-Evangelium als Quelle der Geschichte Jesu* (Göttingen 1910).

Stagg, F., "The Farewell Discourses, Jn 13 – 17," *Baptist Review and Expositor* 62,4 (1965) 459-472.

Stamm, R. T., "Courage to Face the Future (John XIV)," *LCQ* 17 (1944) 394-420.

Stange, E., *Die Eigenart der johanneischen Produktion. Ein Beitrag zur Kritik der neueren Quellenscheidungshypothesen und zur Charakteristik der johanneischen Psyche* (Dresden 1915).

Stauffer, E., „Abschiedsreden," in: *RAC* I (1950) 29-35.

--, *Die Theologie des Neuen Testaments* (Stuttgart [2]1948).

Stedman, R. C., *Secrets of the Spirits* (Old Tappan, N.J., 1975).

Stemberger, G., *Geschichte der jüdischen Literatur. Eine Einführung* (München 1977).

Stettinger, G., *Der Paraklet: Detailstudie zu den Johanneischen Abschiedsreden (Joh. 14-17)* (Wien 1923).

Stoll, R. F., "Our Lord's Farewell Discourses," *EcR* 106 (1942) 98-111.191-204.263-276.

Strack, H. L./Billerbeck, P., *Kommentar zum Neuen Testament aus Talmud und Midrasch I-IV* (München 1922-1928); *V-VI* (ed. J. Jeremias/K. Adolph; München 1956-1961).

Strack, H. L./Stemberger, G., *Einleitung in Talmud und Midrasch* (München 1982; 7. völlig neu bearbeitete Auflage).

Strathmann, H., *Das Evangelium nach Johannes* (NTD 4; Göttingen [10]1963).

Thiel, W., *Die deuteronomistische Redaktion von Jeremia 26-45. Mit einer Gesamtbeurteilung der deuteronomistischen Redaktion des Buches Jeremia* (WMANT 52; Neukirchen 1981).

Thils, G., "Explicatio Evang. S. Joannis XIII,31 - XIV,13," *CMech* 29 (1940) 33-36.
--, "De interpretatione Evang. S. Joannis, XV-XVI," *CMech* 29 (1940) 166-168.
Thüsing, W., *Die Erhöhung und Verherrlichung Jesu im Johannesevangelium* (NTA 21; Münster ²1970).
Thyen, H., „Johannes 13 und die ‚Kirchliche Redaktion' des vierten Evangeliums," in: *Tradition und Glaube. Das frühe Christentum in seiner Umwelt* (ed. G. Jeremias al.; Fschr. K. G. Kuhn; Göttingen 1971) 343-356.
--, „Aus der Literatur zum Johannesevangelium," *ThR* 39 (1974) 1-69.222-252. 289-330; 42 (1977) 211-270.
Ullendorf, E., "A Mistranslation from Aramaic? [on Joh 14,16]," *NTS* 2 (1955-1956) 50-52.
Van den Bussche, H., *Het vierde Evangelie. Jezus' woorden aan het afscheidsmaal* (Thielt 1955).
--, *Jean. Commentaire de l'évangile spirituel* (BVC; Bruges 1967).
--, "Nu is de Mensenzoon verheerlijkt (Jo. 13,31-38)," *CGan* 3 (1953) 97-105.
Van Hartingsveld, L., *Die Eschatologie des Johannesevangeliums. Eine Auseinandersetzung mit Rudolf Bultmann* (GTB XXXVI; Assen 1962).
Vanoni, G., „Der Geist und der Buchstabe. Überlegungen zum Verhältnis der Testamente und Beobachtungen zu Dtn 30,1-10," *BN* 14 (1981) 65-98.
Veenhof, J., *De Parakleet* (Kampen ²1977).
Vellanickal, M., *The Divine Sonship of Christians in the Johannine Writings* (AnBib 72; Rome 1977).
Villapadierna, C. de, "Contenido teologico-espiritual de Jn. 14,20," *EstFr* 54 (1953) 181-208.
Volz, P., *Jüdische Eschatologie von Daniel bis Akiba* (Tübingen-Leipzig 1903).
Walter, E., *Die Mysterien des Wortes und der Liebe. Auslegung der Abschiedsrede des Herrn (Joh 14-17)* (Freiburg i. B. 1964).
Walvoord, J. F., "Prayer in the Name of the Lord Jesus Christ [Jn 14,13-14]," *BS* 91 (1934) 463-472.
Wead, D. W., *The Literary Devices in John's Gospel* (ThDiss 4; Basel 1970).
Weiser, A., *Das Buch der zwölf Kleinen Propheten I. Die Propheten Hosea, Joel, Amos, Obadja, Jona, Micha* (ATD 24; Göttingen 1949).
Weiss, B., *Das Johannes-Evangelium* (KEK 2; Göttingen ⁶1902).
Wellhausen, J., *Erweiterungen und Änderungen im vierten Evangelium* (Berlin 1907).
--, *Das Evangelium Johannis* (Berlin 1908).
Wendt, H. H., *Das Johannesevangelium. Eine Untersuchung seiner Entstehung und seines geschichtlichen Wertes* (Göttingen 1900).
Wengst, K., *Christologische Formeln und Lieder des Urchristentums* (Gütersloh 1972).
Westcott, B. F., *The Gospel According to St. John: The authorised version with introduction and notes* (London 1890).

Widengren, G., "En la maison de mon Père sont demeures nombreuses, Joh 14,2," *SEÅ* 37-38 (1972-1973) 9-15.

Wikenhauser, A., *Das Evangelium nach Johannes* (RNT 4; Regensburg ³1961).

Wilcox, M., "The 'Prayer' of Jesus in Joh XI 41b-42," *NTS* 24 (1977) 128-132.

Wildberger, H., *Jesaja I (Jesaja 1-12)* (BK.AT X/1; Neukirchen 1972).

Windisch, H., „Die fünf johanneischen Parakletsprüche," in: *Fschr. A. Jülicher* (Tübingen 1927) 110-137.

Woll, D. B., "The Departure of 'The Way': The First Farewell Discourse in the Gospel of John," *JBL* 99 (1980) 225-239.

Wolff, H. W., „‚Wissen um Gott' bei Hosea als Urform von Theologie," (1953), in: id., *Gesammelte Studien zum Alten Testament* (München 1964) 182-205.

Würthwein, E., *Das erste Buch der Könige. Kapitel 1 - 16* (ATD 11,1; Göttingen 1977).

Zahn, Th., *Das Evangelium des Johannes* (KNT 4; Leipzig-Erlangen ⁶1921).

Zimmerli, W., *Ezechiel II. Ezechiel 25 - 48* (BK.AT XIII,2; Neukirchen-Vluyn 1969).

Zimmermann, H., „Struktur und Aussageabsicht der johanneischen Abschiedsreden (Jo 13 - 17)," *BiLe* 8 (1967) 279-290.

Additional Bibliography

Aletti, Jean-Noël, "Jn 13 – les problèmes de composition et leur importance," *Bib.* 87 (2006) 263-272.
Augenstein, Jörg, *Das Liebesgebot im Johannesevangelium und in den Johannesbriefen* (BWANT 134; Stuttgart: Kohlhammer 1993).
Beasley-Murray, George R., *John* (WBC 36, 2nd ed.; Nashville: Thomas Nelson 1999).
Beutler, Johannes, review of Christina Hoegen-Rohls, *Der nachösterliche Johannes*: *ThLZ* 122 (1997) 443-445.
--, review of Xavier Léon-Dufour, *Lecture de l'Évangile selon Jean. III*: *ThPh* 72 (1997) 265f.
--, "Das Hauptgebot im Johannesevangelium," in id., *Studien zu den johanneischen Schriften* (SBAB 25; Stuttgart: Katholisches Bibelwerk 1998) 107-120.
--, "Friede nicht von dieser Welt? Zum Friedensbegriff des Johannesevangeliums," in id., *Studien zu den johanneischen Schriften* (SBAB 25; Stuttgart: Katholisches Bibelwerk 1998) 163-173.
--, *Die Johannesbriefe* (RNT; Regensburg: Pustet 2000).
--, "Synoptic Jesus tradition in the Johannine farewell discourse," in *Jesus in Johannine tradition* (ed. Robert T. Fortna, Tom Thatcher; Louisville, KY: Westminster John Knox 2001) 165-173.
--, review of Klaus Scholtissek, *In ihm sein und bleiben*: *ThPh* 76 (2001) 572-575.
--, "'Levatevi, partiamo di qui' (Gv 14,31): Un invito ad un itinerario spirituale?," in: *"Il vostro frutto rimanga" (Gv 16,16). Miscellanea per il LXX compleanno di Giuseppe Ghiberti* (ed. Anna Passoni Dell'Acqua; SRivBib 46; Bologna: Edizioni Dehoniane 2005) 133-143.
--, review of Hans-Ulrich Weidemann, *Der Tod Jesu im Johannesevangelium*: *BiKi* 60 (2005) 122f.
--, *Judaism and the Jews in the Gospel of John* (SubBi 30; Roma: Editrice Pontificio Istituto Biblico 2006).
--, "In Search of a New Synthesis," in: *What We have Heard From the Beginning. The Past, Present, and Future of Johannine Studies* (ed. Tom Thatcher; Waco, Texas: Baylor University Press 2007) 23-34.
--, Resurrection and the remission of sins. John 20,23 against its traditional background," in: *The Resurrection of Jesus in the Gospel of John* (ed. Craig R. Koester, Reimund Bieringer; WUNT 222; Tübingen: Mohr Siebeck 2008) 237-251.
--, review of Hartwig Thyen, *Das Johannesevangelium*: *Bib.* 89 (2008) 131-134.
--, review of Hartwig Thyen, *Studien zum Corpus Johanneum*: *Cristianesimo nella Storia* 30 (2009) 219-222.
--, "Die Überleitung zu den johanneischen Abschiedsreden (Joh 13,31f.). Ein Beispiel der Relecture," in: *Studien zu Matthäus und Johannes / Études sur*

Matthieu et Jean. Festschrift für Jean Zumstein zu seinem 65. Geburtstag / Mélanges offerts à Jean Zumstein pour son 65ᵉ anniversaire (ed. Andreas Dettwiler, Uta Poplutz; AThANT 97; Zürich: Theologischer Verlag 2009) 221-231.

Bevan, H. B. H., "Does 'arise, let us go hence' (John 14:31 D) make sense where it stands?", *JThS* 54 (2003) 576-584.

Brodie, Thomas L., *The gospel according to John: a literary and theological commentary* (New York/Oxford: Oxford University Press 1993).

Buchhold, Jacques, "De plus grandes oeuvres que celles de Jésus! Jean 14.12-13," *Théologie évangélique* 4 (2005) 3-22.

Charlesworth, James H., "The gospel of John: Exclusivism caused by a social setting different from that of Jesus (John 11:54 and 14:6)," in *Anti-Judaism and the fourth gospel: Papers of the Leuven Colloquium, 2000* (ed. R. Bieringer, D. Pollefeyt, F. Vandecasteele-Vanneuville; Jewish and Christian Heritage Series, 1; Assen: Royal von Gorcum 2001) 479-513.

Chibici-Revneanu, Nicole, "Variations on Glorification: John 13,31f. and Johannine DOXA-language," in *Repetitions and variations in the fourth gospel: Style, text, interpretation* (ed. Gilbert van Belle, Michael Labahn, Petrus Maritz; BEThL 223; Leuven: Leuven University Press 2009) 511-522.

Coloe, Mary L., "Sources in the shadows: John 13 and the Johannine community," in *New currents through John: a global perspective* (ed. Francisco Lozada Jr.; Resources for biblical study, 54; Atlanta, GA: SBL/Leiden: Brill: 2006) 69-82.

Culpepper, Richard Alan, "The Johannine Hypodeigma: A Reading of John 13," *Semeia* 53 (1991) 133-152.

Dal Covolo, Enrico, "Argomentazioni patristiche sulla verità: 'Ego sum via et veritas' (cf. Gv 14,6) in Origene e in Agostino," in *"Il vostro frutto rimanga" (Gv 16,16). Miscellanea per il LXX compleanno di Giuseppe Ghiberti* (ed. Anna Passoni Dell'Acqua; SRivBib 46, Bologna: Edizioni Dehoniane 2005) 309-321.

Dettwiler, Andreas, *Die Gegenwart des Erhöhten. Eine exegetische Studie zu den johanneischen Abschiedsreden (Joh 13,31 – 16,33) unter besonderer Berücksichtigung ihres Relecture-Charakters* (FRLANT 169; Göttingen: Vandenhoeck & Ruprecht 1995).

Dietzfelbinger, Christian, „Die größeren Werke (Joh 14,12f.)," *NTS* 35 (1989) 27-47.

--, *Der Abschied des Kommenden: eine Auslegung der johanneischen Abschiedsreden* (WUNT 96; Tübingen: Mohr 1997).

--, „Die theologische Bewältigung von Tod und Abwesenheit Jesu in den Abschiedsreden des Johannesevangeliums," *JBTh* 19 (2004) 217-241.

Domeris, W. R., "The Farewell Discourse: An anthropological perspective," *Neotest.* 25 (1991) 233-250.

Duke, Paul D., "John 13:1-17, 31b-35," *Interp.* 49 (1995) 398-402.

du Rand, Jan A., "The Johannine 'group' and 'grid': Reading John 13-31-14,31 from narratological and sociological perspectives," in *Miracles and imagery in Luke and John: Festschrift Ulrich Busse* (ed. Joseph Verheyden; BEThL 218; Leuven [etc.]: Peeters 2008) 125-139.
Ensor, Peter W., "The glorification of the Son of Man: An analysis of John 13:31-32," *TynB* 58 (2007) 229-252.
Farrell, Shannon-Elizabeth, "Seeing the Father (Jn 6:46, 14:9). Part I. From Non-Seeing to Relational Seeing," *ScEs* 44 (1992) 1-24.
--, "Seeing the Father (Jn 6:46, 14:9). Part II. Perceptive Seeing and Comprehensive Seeing," *ScEs* 44 (1992) 159-183.
--, "Seeing the Father (Jn 6:46, 14:9). Part III. Eschatological Seeing and Memorial Seeing," *ScEs* 44 (1992) 307-329.
Fee, Gordon D., "John 14:8-17," *Interp.* 43 (1989) 170-174.
Fernando, G. Charles A., *The relationship between Law and Love in the Gospel of John. A detailed scientific research on the concepts of Law and Love in the fourth gospel and their relationship to each other* (EHS.T 772; Frankfurt am Main etc.: Peter Lang 2004).
Frey, Jörg, *Die johanneische Eschatologie, 3 vol.* (WUNT 96, 110, 117; Tübingen: Mohr I 1997; II 1998; III 2000).
Hasitschka, Martin, „Die Parakletworte im Johannesevangelium: Versuch einer Auslegung in synchroner Textbetrachtung," *SNTU.A* 18 (1993) 97-112.
Hengel, Martin, *Die johanneische Frage. Ein Lösungsversuch. Mit einem Beitrag zur Apokalypse von Jörg Frey* (WUNT67; Tübingen: Mohr – Siebeck 1993).
Hesselink, I. John, "John 14:23-29," *Interp.* 43 (1989) 174-177.
Holloway, Paul A., "Left behind: Jesus' consolation of the disciples in John 13,31-17,26," *ZNW* 96 (2005) 1-34.
Hoegen-Rohls, Christina, *Der nachösterliche Johannes: Die Abschiedsreden als hermeneutischer Schlüssel zum vierten Evangelium* (WUNT 2. Reihe 84; Tübingen: Mohr 1996).
Jeske, Richard L., "John 14:27 and 16:33," *Interp.* 38 (1984) 403-411.
Kaefer, J. Ph., "Les discours d'adieu en Jean 13:31-17,26: Rédaction et théologie," *NT* 26 (1984) 253-282.
Kellum, L. Scott, *The unity of the farewell discourse: The literary integrity of John 13.31 – 16.33* (JSNT.S 256; London: T & T Clark 2004).
Klauck, Hans-Josef, „Der Weggang Jesu: Neue Arbeiten zu Joh 13-17," *BZ* 40 (1996) 236-250.
--, „Himmlisches Haus und irdische Bleibe: Eschatologische Metaphorik in Antike und Christentum," *NTS* 50 (2004) 5-35.
Kleemann, Jürg, "'Vado a prepararvi una dimora' (Gv 14,2)," *RSEc* 18 (2000) 297-306.
Kleinknecht, Karl Theodor, „Johannes 13, die Synoptiker und die ‚Methode' der johanneischen Evangelienüberlieferung," *ZThK* 82 (1985) 361-388.

Köstenberger, Andreas J., "The 'greater works' of the believer according to John 14:12," in id. *Studies on John and gender: A decade of scholarship* (Studies in Biblical Literature 38; New York etc.: Peter Lang 2001) 117-128.

Koester, Craig, R., "Jesus as the way to the father in Johannine theology (John 14,6)," in *Theology and Christology in the fourth gospel: Essays by the members of the SNTS Johannine Writings Seminar* (ed. Gilbert van Belle, Jan G. van der Watt, Petrus Maritz; BEThL 184; Leuven: University 2005) 117-133.

La Gioia, Fabio, *La glorificazione di Gesù Cristo ad opera dei discepoli: Analisi biblico-teologica di Gv 17,10b nell'insieme dei capp. 13-17* (Tesi Gregoriana – Serie Teologia 101; Roma: Pontificia Università Gregoriana 2003).

Lang, Manfred, „Johanneische Abschiedsreden und Senecas Konsolationsliteratur. Wie konnte ein Römer Joh 13,31-17,26 lesen?," in *Kontexte des Johannesevangeliums: Das vierte Evangelium in religions- und traditionsgeschichtlicher Perspektive* (ed. Jörg Frey; WUNT 175; Tübingen: Mohr Siebeck 2004) 365-412.

Lemmer, R., "A possible understanding by the implied reader, of some of the *coming-going-being sent* pronouncements, in the Johannine Farewell Discourses," *Neotest.* 25 (1991) 289-310.

Léon-Dufour, Xavier, *Lecture de l'évangile selon Jean. III. Les adieux du Seigneur (chapitres 13-17)* (Parole de Dieu; Paris: éditions du Seuil 1993).

Lombard, H. A., "A working supper in Jerusalem: John 13:1-38 introduces Jesus' Farewell Discourses," *Neotest.* 25 (1991) 357-378.

McCaffrey, James, *The house with many rooms: The temple theme of Jn. 14,2-3* (AnBib 114; Roma: Editrice Pontificio Istituto Biblico 1998).

Menken, Maarten J. J., *Old Testament Quotations in the Fourth Gospel: Studies in Textual Form* (Contributions to Biblical Exegesis & Theology, 15; Kampen, NL: Kok Pharos 1996).

Moloney, Francis J., "A Sacramental Reading of John 13:1-38," *CBQ* 53 (1991) 237-256.

--, *Glory not dishonor: Reading John 13-17* (Minneapolis, MN: Fortress 1998).

--, "The function of John 13-17 within the Johannine narrative," in *What is John?* II (ed. Fernando F. Segovia; SBL Symposion Series; Atlanta, GA: Scholars 1998) 43-66.

--, *The gospel of John* (Sacra Pagina Series, 4; A Michael Glazier Book; Collegeville, MN: The Liturgical Press 1998).

Neuer Wettstein: Texte zum Neuen Testament aus Griechentum und Hellenismus. Band I/2 Texte zum Johannesevangelium (ed. Udo Schnelle unter Mitarbeit von Michael Labahn und Manfred Lang; Berlin/New York: de Gruyter 2001).

Neugebauer, Johannes, "Zu den Abschiedsreden im Johannesevangelium," in *"Methodenstreit zum Johannesevangelium": Dokumentation des Symposions vom 29. und 30. Juni 1990 in Kelkheim* (ed. J. Hainz; Darmstadt: Weihert-Druck 1991) 154-161.

O'Day, Gail R., "'I have Overcome the World' (John 16:33): Narrative Time in John 13-17," *Semeia* 53 (1991) 153-166.
Parrinder, Geoffrey, "Only One Way? John 14:6," *ET* 107 (1995) 78-79.
Parsenios, George L., *Departure and consolation: The Johannine farewell discourses in the light of Greco-roman literature* (NT.S 117; Leiden: Brill 2005).
Pastorelli, David, *Le Paraclet dans le corpus johannique* (BZNW 142; Berlin/New York 2006).
Perroni, Marinella, "È possible una convergenza tra sincronia e diacronia? Il caso di Gv 13," *RdT* 47 (2006) 585-599.
Pöttner, Martin, „‚Im Hause meines Vaters gibt es viele Aufenthaltsorte..': Erwägungen zur räumlichen Symbolik des johanneischen Sprechens in Joh 13,33-14,7," *Mitteilungen für Anthropologie und Religionsgeschichte* 14 (1999) 141-150.
Popp, Thomas, „Die konsolatorische Kraft der Wiederholung: Liebe, Trauer und Trost in den johanneischen Abschiedsreden," in *Repetitions and variations in the fourth gospel: Style, text, interpretation* (ed. Gilbert van Belle, Michael Labahn, Petrus Maritz; BEThL 223; Leuven: Leuven University Press 2009) 523-587.
Rahner, Johanna, „Vergegenwärtigende Erinnerung: Die Abschiedsreden, der Geist-Paraklet und die Retrospektive des Johannesevangeliums," *ZNW* 91 (2000) 72-90.
Reis, David M., "Jesus' farewell discourse, 'otherness', and the construction of a Johannine identity," *SR* 32 (2003) 39-58.
Renwart, Léon, "'Je suis la voie e la Vérité et la Vie'," *NRTh* 115 (1993) 886-899.
Ronning, John L., "The Targum of Isaiah and the Johannine Literature," *WThJ* 69 (2007) 247-278.
Schleritt, Frank, *Der vorjohanneische Passionsbericht: Eine historisch-kritische und theologische Untersuchung zu Joh 2,13-22; 11,47-14,31; 18,1-20,29* (BZNW 154; Berlin: de Gruyter 2007).
Schnelle, Udo, „Die Abschiedsreden im Johannesevangelium," *ZNW* 80 (1989) 64-79.
--, *Das Evangelium nach Johannes* (ThHK 4; Leipzig: Evangelische Verlagsanstalt 1998).
--, „Die johanneischen Abschiedsreden und das Liebesgebot," in *Repetitions and variations in the fourth gospel: Style, text, interpretation* (ed. Gilbert van Belle, Michael Labahn, Petrus Maritz; BEThL 223; Leuven: Leuven University Press 2009) 589-608.
Scholtissek, Klaus, *„In ihm sein und bleiben": Die Sprache der Immanenz in den johanneischen Schriften* (HBS 21; Freiburg etc.: Herder 1999).
--, „Abschied und neue Gegenwart: Exegetische und theologische Reflexionen zur johanneischen Abschiedsrede 13,31-17,26," *EThL* 75 (1999) 332-358.

--, „Relecture und réécriture: Neue Paradigmen zu Methode und Inhalt der Johannesauslegung aufgewiesen am Prolog 1,1-18 und der ersten Abschiedsrede 13,31-14,31," *ThPh* 75 (2000) 1-29.

Segovia, Fernando F., "The Structure, Tendenz and Sitz im Leben of John 13,31-14,31," *JBL* 104 (1985) 471-493.

--, *The Farewell of the Word: The Johannine Call to Abide* (Minneapolis: Fortress Press 1991).

Sheridan, Ruth, "The Paraclete and Jesus in the Johannine farewell discourse," *Pacifica* 2 (2007) 125-141.

Simoens, Y., *Selon Jean, 3 vol.* (Bruxelles: Éditions de l'Institut d'Études Théologiques 1997).

Söding, Thomas, „Die Wahrheit des Evangeliums: Anmerkungen zur johanneischen Hermeneutik," *EThL* 77 (2001) 318-355.

--, „Gottes Wohnung für die Menschen: Eine neutestamentliche Annonce," *IKaZ* 33 (2004) 236-244.

Syreeni, Kari, "Incarnatus est? Christ and community in the Johannine farewell discourse," in *Testimony and interpretation. Early Christology in its Judeo-Hellenistic milieu. Studies in honour of Petr Pokorný* (ed. Jiří Mrázek and Jan Roskovec; JSNT.S 272; London: T & T Clark 2004) 247-264.

--, "Partial weaning: Approaching the psychological enigma of John 13-17," *SEÅ* 72 (2007) 173-192.

Tait, Michael, *Jesus, the divine bridegroom in Mark 2:18.22. Mark's Christology upgraded* (AnBib 185; Rome: Gregorian & Biblical Press 2010).

Thyen, Hartwig, *Das Johannesevangelium* (HAT 6; Tübingen: Mohr Siebeck 2005).

--, „Joh 13,1ff als Objekt literarkritischer Analysen," in id. *Studien zum Corpus Iohanneum* (WUNT 214; Tübingen: Mohr Siebeck 2007) 591-594.

--, „Das Neue Gebot Jesu, einander zu lieben (Joh 13,34), im Streit der Auslegungen," in id. *Studien zum Corpus Iohanneum* (WUNT 214; Tübingen: Mohr Siebeck 2007) 623-630.

--, „Joh 14,2-4 im Streit der Auslegungen," in id. *Studien zum Corpus Iohanneum* (WUNT 214; Tübingen: Mohr Siebeck 2007) 631-634.

--, „Joh 14,6 und ein Absolutheitsanspruch des Christentums?," in id. *Studien zum Corpus Iohanneum* (WUNT 214; Tübingen: Mohr Siebeck 2007) 635-637.

--, „Joh 14,28: ‚Der Vater ist größer als ich': Indiz einer subordinatianischen Christologie?," in id. *Studien zum Corpus Iohanneum* (WUNT 214; Tübingen: Mohr Siebeck 2007) 638-643.

Tolmie, Donald François, "The function of focalization in John 13-17," *Neotest.* 25 (1991) 273-287.

--, *Jesus' Farewell to the Disciples: John 13,1 – 17,26 in Narratological Perspective* (Biblical Interpretation Series 12; Leiden etc.: Brill 1995).

Trudinger, Paul, "In my father's house: Expository note on a Johannine theme," *ET* 112 (2001) 229-230.

Varghese, Johns, *The Imagery of Love in the Gospel of John* (AnBib 177; Rome: Gregorian & Biblical Press 2009).

Vetrali, Tecle, "'Io sono la via, la verità e la vita' (Gv 14,6)," *RSEc* 18 (2000) 279-296.

Weidemann, Hans-Ulrich, *Der Tod Jesu im Johannesevangelium: Die erste Abschiedsrede als Schlüsseltext für den Passions- und Osterbericht* (BZNW 122; Berlin etc.: de Gruyter 2004).

--, „Der Gekreuzigte als Quelle des Geistes," in *The death of Jesus in the fourth gospel* (ed. Gilbert van Belle; BEThL 200; Leuven: University Press etc. 2007) 567-579.

--, "Eschatology as liturgy: Jesus' resurrection and Johannine eschatology," in *The resurrection of Jesus in the gospel of John* (ed. Craig R. Koester, Reimund Bieringer; WUNT 222; Tübingen: Mohr Siebeck 2008) 277-310.

Wengst, Klaus, *Das Johannesevangelium*, 2 vol. (Theologischer Kommentar zum Neuen Testament 4,1-2; Stuttgart: Kohlhammer I ²2004 II 2001).

Wilckens, Ulrich, *Das Evangelium nach Johannes* (NTD 4; Göttingen: Vandenhoeck & Ruprecht 1998).

Winter, Martin, *Das Vermächtnis Jesu und die Abschiedsworte der Väter. Gattungsgeschichtliche Untersuchung der Vermächtnisrede im Blick auf Joh. 13-17* (FRLANT 161; Göttingen: Vandenhoeck & Ruprecht 1994).

Yarid, John R. Jr., "Reflections of the upper room discourse in 1 John," *BS* 160, 673 (2003) 65-76.

Zumstein, Jean, "The farewell discourses (John 13:31-16:33) and the problem of Anti-Judaism," in *Anti-Judaism and the fourth gospel: Papers of the Leuven Colloquium, 2000* (ed. R. Bieringer, D. Pollefeyt, F. Vandecasteele-Vanneuville; Jewish and Christian Heritage Series, 1; Assen: Royal von Gorcum 2001) 461-478.

--, „Die Logien Jesu in der ersten Abschiedsrede und die joh Schule," in id. *Kreative Erinnerung: Relecture und Auslegung im Johannesevangelium* (AThANT 84; Zürich: Theologischer Verlag ²2004) 177-187.

--, „Die Abschiedsreden (Johannes 13,31 – 16,33) und das Problem des Antijudaismus," id. *Kreative Erinnerung: Relecture und Auslegung im Johannesevangelium* (AThANT 84; Zürich: Theologischer Verlag ²2004) 189-205.

--, *L'évangile selon Saint Jean (13-21)* (Commentaire du Nouveau Testament. Deuxième série IVb; Genève: Labor et Fides 2007).

--, "L'interprétation de la mort de Jésus dans les discours d'adieu," in *The death of Jesus in the fourth gospel* (ed. Gilbert van Belle; BEThL 200; Leuven: University Press etc. 2007) 95-119.

--, „Die Deutung der Ostererfahrung in den Abschiedsreden des Johannesevangeliums," *ZThK* 104 (2007) 117-141.

--, "Jesus' resurrection in the farewell discourses," in *The resurrection of Jesus in the gospel of John* (ed. Craig R. Koester, Reimund Bieringer; WUNT 222; Tübingen: Mohr Siebeck 2008) 103-126.

Index of Authors

Aalen, S., 31
Aletti, J.-N., 105
Anderson, A. A., 42
Augenstein, J., 108
Augustine, 41, 42

Bacher, W., 33
Barrett, C. K., 13, 25, 36, 40, 65, 97
Bauer, W., 16, 18, 24ff, 29, 31, 36f, 40, 45f, 59, 65, 67
Beasley-Murray, G. R., 103, 106, 109
Becker, H., 15, 42
Becker, J., 13f, 16, 25f, 32, 36, 46, 55, 65f, 71, 79, 89
Begrich, J., 31
Behler, G. M., 13, 25f, 36
Bengel, J. A., 41
Berger, K., 50
Bergmeier, R., 64
Bernard, J. H., 24, 27, 31, 36, 38, 40, 45, 65
Betz, O., 60, 81
Beutler, J., 24, 26f, 33, 45, 59, 87, 92f, 103f, 106f, 109f
Bevan, H. B. H., 110
Bietenhard, H., 46, 62f
Billerbeck, P., 34f, 41, 62f, 65f, 70, 75
Blank, J., 17, 79, 82
Blass, F., 80
Böcher, O., 64
Boismard, M.-É., 16, 31f, 37, 50, 65
Borgen, P., 44
Boring, M. E., 81
Braulik, G., 74
Braun, F.-M., 13, 16, 59
Braun, H., 59, 62
Brinkmann, B., 13
Brodie, Th. L., 110
Brown, R. E., 14, 17, 25, 27, 32, 36, 38, 40, 43-46, 50, 54, 65, 94ff
Brown, S., 95

Bultmann, R., 13-18, 25f, 30, 36, 40, 42, 45f, 64f, 73, 81, 96, 101, 105
Burchard, Ch., 55

Calmes, Th., 13, 16
Charlier, C., 16
Chibici-Revneanu, N., 106
Clarke, W. K. L., 36, 38
Coloe, M. L., 105
Cortès, E., 18-21, 54f, 59
Culpepper, R. A., 105

Dahood, M., 26, 42
Davey, F. N., 93, 110
Debrunner, A., 80
Dettwiler, A., 104, 107f
Dietzfelbinger, Ch, 103
DiLella, A., 54
Dodd, C. H., 18f, 27f, 40, 110
Domeris, W. R., 103
Dupont, J., 19
Du Rand, J., 103, 106
Durand, A., 13, 16

Elliger, K., 69, 72
Ensor, P. W., 107
Ernst, J., 89
Estalayo Alonso, V., 31, 37, 40

Fernando, G. Ch. A., 108
Feuillet, A., 59
Fischer, G., 25, 30f, 33, 35f, 38
Fohrer, G., 91f
Frankemölle, H., 56
Freed, E. D., 27-30
Frey, J., 105, 107ff

Gaechter, P., 13
Galling, K., 54
Gallo, S., 16
Godet, F., 13
Goldberg, A. M., 70

Gollwitzer, H., 42
Groß, H., 90, 92
Grundmann, W., 19
Guilding, A., 31, 36f
Gundry, R. H., 31
Gunkel, H., 31

Haenchen, E., 7, 13, 24ff, 36
Hammer, I., 13
Hamp, V., 70
Hartman, L. F., 54
Hasitschka, M., 108
Hasler, V., 96
Hegermann, H., 60
Heise, J., 31f, 64, 77
Heitmüller, W., 36, 38, 40, 46
Hengel, M., 107, 109
Hertzberg, H. W., 54f
Hesselink, J., 109
Hirsch, E., 13f
Hoegen-Rohls, C., 103
Hoffner, H. A., 31
Holloway, P. A., 104
Holtzmann, H. J., 16, 24ff, 37, 41, 45f, 67
Hoskyns, E. C., 19, 38, 40, 46, 93, 110
Huby, J., 13
Hulst, A. R., 32, 67

Ibuki, Y., 44
Innitzer, Th., 13

Jenni, E., 84
Jepsen, A., 29
Jeremias, G., 62
Jeremias, J., 15, 84
Jeske, R. L., 109
Johnston, G., 60

Kaiser, O., 91ff
Kaefer, J. Ph., 104
Kellum, L. S., 103
Klauck, H.-J., 104f, 107
Kleinknecht, K. Th., 104

Knabenbauer, I., 13
Kraus, H.-J., 26, 31, 42, 61f
Kundsin, K., 38

Lacomara, A., 54
Lagrange, M.-J., 13, 16, 25, 45f
Lang, M., 104
la Potterie, I. de, 24, 31, 37, 40ff, 44, 82, 84
Lattke, M., 71
Le Déaut, R., 33
Lemmer, R., 103
Léon-Dufour, X., 107f, 110
Leroy, H., 23, 40
Liddell, H. G., 32
Lightfoot, R. H., 25
Lindars, B., 13, 17, 19, 21, 25ff, 31, 36, 38, 40ff, 83
Lohfink, G., 91
Lohfink, N., 7, 53, 57, 72f, 77
Loisy, A., 14, 16, 25f, 36, 46, 93
Lombard, H. A., 103
Lust, J., 59, 61
Luz, U., 88
Lyonnet, S., 61, 85

Malatesta, E., 52, 57, 70
McCaffrey, J., 105, 107f
McCarthy, D. J., 53
Meagher, J. C., 69f
Meeks, W., 44
Michaelis, W., 67
Michel, H. J., 18f, 55
Michel, O., 58, 87
Middleton, R. D., 70
Migliasso, S., 13, 16, 79
Miranda, J. P., 44
Mollat, D., 13f, 36, 54, 59, 84
Moloney, F. F., 103, 105, 107f, 110
Moran, W. L., 53
Morris, L., 25, 36
Munck, J., 18, 20f
Mussner, F., 64, 66, 83
Myers, J. M., 54

Neuer Wettstein, 104
Nordheim, E. von, 18f
Noth, M., 54f, 68

O'Day, G. R., 103
Onuki, T., 14

Painter, J., 71, 83
Pancaro, S., 54
Parsenios, G. L., 104
Perroni, M., 105
Pesch, R., 50, 66
Pölzl, F. X., 13
Popp, Th., 103, 106f
Porsch, F., 59f, 81, 96

Rad, G. von, 74
Rahner, J., 103
Reis, D. M., 103
Ricca, P., 65f
Richter, G., 13ff, 73, 75
Ronning, J. L., 105
Ruckstuhl, E., 15, 39, 43, 65
Ruprecht, E., 91

Sabourin, L., 70
Saebø, M., 84
Sanders, J. N., 24f, 31, 36, 38
Schaefer, O., 24, 31, 36ff, 41
Schanz, P., 13
Schenk, W., 58
Schlatter, A., 25
Schleritt, F., 104, 106, 108
Schlier, H., 85
Schmid, H. H., 90, 92f
Schnackenburg, R., 13f, 16, 18, 25, 29, 32, 36, 38, 43-46, 57, 65f, 73, 82ff, 89
Schneider, G., 88f
Schneider, J., 19, 65
Schnelle, U., 103, 106, 108ff
Scholtissek, K., 106, 108f
Schottroff, L., 64

Schulz, S., 15, 17, 24ff, 36, 38, 40, 65f, 79, 81
Schweizer, E., 56
Scott, R., 32, 103
Segovia, F. F., 103, 106, 110
Simoens, Y., 103, 105
Smend, R., 74
Soltau, W., 15
Spitta, F., 15
Stauffer, E., 18
Stemberger, G., 33f, 64
Strack, H. L., 34f, 41, 62-66, 70, 75
Strathmann, H., 13, 16, 25, 36
Syreeni, K., 103

Thiel, W., 72
Thyen, H., 13f, 103, 105, 107-110
Tolmie, D. F., 103
Trilling, W., 74

Van den Bussche, H., 13
Van Hartingsveld, L., 65
Vanoni, G., 74
Varghese, J., 108
Volz, P., 34

Wallis, G., 72
Weidemann, H.-U., 105-109
Weiser, A., 69
Weiss, B., 13, 16, 25, 36
Wellhausen, J., 13ff
Wendt, H. H., 15
Wengst, K., 104, 106
Westcott, B. F., 13, 16, 25, 31, 36, 44f, 93
Widengren, G., 30f
Wikenhauser, A., 16, 25, 40, 46
Wilckens, U., 103, 105, 108f
Wildberger, H., 90f
Windisch, H., 15, 81
Winter, M., 104
Wolff, H., 74
Würthwein, E., 68, 72

Zahn, Th., 13, 25f, 36, 38, 46
Zimmerli, W., 59
Zmijewski, J., 85
Zumstein, J., 104-107, 109f

Index of References (selection)

Old Testament

Gen
2,7	*61*
5,22.24	*21*
27,1-45	*21*
35, 27-29	*21*
49,1f	*20*

Ex
19,5	*54*
20,5f	*53*
24,7f	*54*
24,8	*60f*
25,8	*67f*
29,45f	*68*

Lev
15,31	*68*
17-26	*68*
26,1-2.9-12	*68*

Num
5,3	*68*

Deut
1,31-33	*36*
5-11	*53, 73*
5,6-21	*54*
5,9f	*53*
5,33	*73*
6,1	*54*
6,4-13	*58, 73*
6,4ff	*53, 58, 100*
6,4	*57*
6,5	*53*
6,6	*54*
6,13	*56, 73*
6,17.20	*73*
6,24	*73*
7,8-13	*71f*
7,9	*53f, 56*
7,21	*54*
8,1	*73*
10,12	*53*
10,14f	*72*
11,1.13.22	*53*
13,4f	*53*
18,18(f)	*43, 46*
19,9	*53*
23,6	*72*
28	*68*
30,(1)6-20	*74*

Jos
22,5	*54*
23,11	*55*

1 Kgs
2,3f	*55*
3,3	*54*
6,11-13	*68*
10,9	*72*

Neh
1,5	*54*

Tob
14,7.9	*55*

Ps
2	*92*
6,4(f)	*27*
22	*26*
23	*37*
25-27	*37*
37,30f	*62*
38,11	*28*
40,7ff	*62*
42/43	*7, 23f, 26-35, 37, 40ff, 49, 67, 93f, 99, 107*
42	*27, 43*

42,3	*41f, 108*	61,1f	*89*
42,4	*43*	61,8	*62*
42,5	*32, 107*	63,9	*72*
42,6	*26-29, 31, 107*	65,17-25	*92*
42,7	*27f, 32, 107*	66,10-14	*92*
42,9	*41*	Jer	
42,11	*43*	24,7	*60*
42,12	*26-29, 31, 107*	31	*58f, 73, 100*
43,3	*32, 35, 41, 107f*	31,3	*72*
43,4	*108*	31,7-14	*92*
43,5	*26-29, 31, 107*	31,30-33	*62, 64*
43,9	*41*	31,31-34	*57, 59, 60ff, 68, 70, 72, 74ff*
45	*92*		
46,5	*33*	31,31ff	*60f, 63*
51	*90*	31,33f	*61*
51,12-14.18f	*61*	31,33	*61, 63*
69	*26*	31,34	*74f, 77*
69,10	*31*	32,40	*62*
72	*92*	50,5	*62*
73	*37*	Ezek	
96-100	*92*	11,19-21	*59f*
110	*92*	11,19f	*90*
118,25	*66*	11,20	*60*
119	*62*	16,60	*62*
122	*92*	34,25	*60, 91*
Sir		34,31	*60*
2,15f	*54*	36f	*58f, 73*
Is		36	*100*
9,1-6	*91*	36,24-28	*57*
11,1-10	*90*	36,25	*90*
32,15-20	*90*	36,26-28	*59, 61-64, 68, 70, 76, 90*
40,3	*40*		
43,4	*72*	36,27	*60, 63, 75, 77*
44,3	*90*	36,28	*60, 73*
44,21ff	*91*	37	*57, 68*
54,10	*91*	37,1-14	*90*
54, 11-17	*75*	37,14	*61*
55,3	*62*	37,23	*60*
58,6	*89*	37,25	*73*
60	*91f*	37,26-28	*59, 70, 76f*
60,5.15	*91*	37,26	*62, 91*
60,17-25	*91f*	37,27	*60, 67f*
61,1-11	*89*	37,28	*60, 75*

37,36	*60*	22,37	*56*
40-44	*67*	23,8	*61*
43,7.9	*67*	24,12	*56*
Dan		24,41	*38*
7,13f	*65, 76*	26,14	*95*
9,4	*54*	26,28	*60*
Hos		26,38	*26, 94*
1,9	*72*	26,46	*27, 93*
2,18-25	*72*	28,8	*89*
3,1	*72*	28,20	*78*
11,1.4	*72*	Mk	
14,5	*72*	1,7	*66*
Joel		1,8	*83, 88*
2,27	*69*	1,10	*88*
3,1ff	*63*	6,6b-8,33	*94*
4,17-21	*69*	11,23f	*43*
Zeph		12,28	*53*
3,17	*72*	12,30	*56*
Zech		12,40	*51*
2,14f	*69*	13,26	*65f*
8,3.8	*69*	14,20	*95*
9,9f	*92*	14,24	*60*
Mal		14,32-42	*93f*
1,2	*72*	14,34	*26f*
		14,36	*28*
		14,41	*28, 94*
New Testament		14,42	*27, 81, 93f, 109*
		14,43	*109*
Mt		14,62	*66*
1,18	*88*	16,11	*66*
3,9	*95*	Lk	
3,11	*88*	1,35	*88*
3,16	*88*	2,10.14	*87*
4,5.8	*38*	3,8	*95*
4,10	*56*	3,16	*88*
5,9	*87*	3,22	*88*
10,7	*87*	4,8	*56*
10,13	*87*	4,18(f)	*88f*
10,20	*60*	7,19	*66*
11,3	*66*	9,22	*95*
12,28	*88*	10,5	*87*
18,20	*78*	10,11	*87*
21,21f	*43*	10,27	*56*

11,20	*88*	4,46-54	*45*
11,42	*56*	4,50f.53	*73*
17,35	*38*	5	*36*
19,37f	*87*	5,1-30	*45*
22,3	*95*	5,4	*80*
22,20	*60*	5,17f	*32*
22,31	*95*	5,25	*45, 73*
22,44	*99*	5,36	*45*
24,5	*66*	5,37	*42*
24,23	*66*	5,42	*57f*
24,27	*26*	5,44	*57*
24,36-43	*88*	5,45	*29*
24,36	*88f*	6,1-21	*45*
24,44	*26*	6,35	*44*
24,49	*88*	6,36	*36*
Jn		6,38	*44*
1,1-4	*66*	6,45	*61, 75*
1,4.10-13	*59*	6,51	*72f*
1,10	*98*	6,57f	*73*
1,11	*38*	6,63	*83*
1,14	*61, 69*	6,65	*36*
1,15.27.30	*66*	6,68-71	*94*
1,17f	*69*	6,69	*44, 94*
1,18	*42*	7,3	*80*
1,23	*40*	7,17	*74*
1,32	*75, 83*	7,26f	*44*
1,33	*78, 83*	7,26.48	*80*
1,40.48	*44*	7,33-36	*37, 44*
2,1-11(12)	*45, 84, 106*	7,35f	*40*
2,16	*31f, 80*	7,37f	*78*
2,17	*31*	7,39	*46, 83*
3,1	*80*	8,5	*80*
3,3.5	*83*	8,12	*44, 98*
3,5-8	*78*	8,19	*32*
3,8	*75*	8,22	*40*
3,13.31f	*44*	8,23	*44*
3,16	*71*	8,24	*36*
3,29	*80, 84*	8,28f	*45*
3,34	*83*	8,28	*44, 74*
4,10f.38	*72*	8,32	*74*
4,23f	*83*	8,33ff	*95*
4,23	*44f*	8,35	*32*
4,36	*80, 84*	8,41	*57*

8,42	*44, 57f*	13,31-35	*14*
8,44	*95*	13,31-33	*19, 106*
8,55	*44*	13,31f	*14, 28, 106, 107*
8,56	*80, 84*	13,31	*13, 105*
9	*45*	13,33	*14, 19f, 37, 44, 97*
9,5	*98*		
10	*57*	13,34f	*14, 20, 106f*
10,14f	*44*	13,34	*59, 71, 107*
10,16	*57*	13,36-38	*13f, 24, 29, 37, 44, 106*
10,18	*32*		
10,25	*32, 36, 45*	13,36	*14, 44, 97*
10,29	*32*	13,37f	*29*
10,36	*36*	15-17	*13, 15, 71, 107, 109f*
10,37	*32*		
10,38	*44f*	15-16	*71, 89*
11-12	*106*	15,1-8	*13, 16*
11	*46*	15,9-17	*20*
11,1-47	*45*	15,9f.12	*71*
11,7.15f	*80*	15,14.17	*20, 80*
11,15	*80, 84*	15,22	*45*
11,25f	*73*	15,25	*80*
11,25	*44*	15,26f	*76*
11,33	*27f, 31, 80*	15,26	*51, 58, 77, 84*
11,40	*36*	15,27	*60*
12,23	*74, 94*	16,3	*44*
12,24	*39*	16,4-33	*82f, 89, 109*
12,27-32	*94*	16,4	*80*
12,27f	*27f*	16,5f	*44*
12,27	*27f, 31, 80*	16,6	*29, 80, 83*
12,31	*80, 94, 97*	16,7-11	*83f*
12,32	*37, 74, 98*	16,7	*51, 77, 80*
12,42	*80*	16,8-11	*46*
12,46	*44, 98*	16,8	*60, 83*
13,1ff	*20*	16,10	*83*
13,1	*44, 71, 97*	16,11	*80*
13,2	*80, 95*	16,13ff	*76, 83f*
13,3	*44*	16,13	*58, 77*
13,19	*80*	16,15	*36*
13,21	*27f, 31, 80*	16,17	*36, 44*
13,27	*95*	16,20	*80, 87*
13,30	*28*	16,21f	*83*
13,31-14,31	*13, 109*	16,22	*29, 80, 87*
13,31-38	*106*	16,23-33	*83*

16,28	*44*	11,27	*61*
16,33	*80, 83, 96, 109*	13,8ff	*73*
17	*13*	14,9	*66*
17,1	*28*	14,17	*85ff, 109*
17,3.8.23.25	*44*	15,13	*86*
17,13	*44*	1 Cor	
17,24	*39*	2,9	*56*
17,26	*13, 71*	3,9.16	*69*
18,1ff	*79*	8,3f	*57*
18,1	*13, 109*	10,3f	*61*
18,11	*28*	11,25	*60*
18,36	*80, 83*	2 Cor	
18,37	*98*	3,1-14	*61*
19,3	*80*	3,3	*61*
19,16	*38*	13,11.13	*86*
19,18	*80*	Gal	
20,19	*80, 82f, 89*	3,15-18	*61*
20,19-23	*66, 82, 88f, 93, 100f, 109*	4,21-28	*61*
		5,19-23	*85f*
20,20	*80*	5,21	*86*
20,21.26	*80, 82f*	Eph	
20,22	*78, 96*	2,11-22	*70*
20,30f	*97*	4,3f	*86*
21,15ff	*57f*	Phil	
21,22f	*66*	3,1	*86*
21,22	*38*	4,4-9	*86*
Acts		1 Thess	
1,3	*66*	1,6	*86*
1,4.8	*88*	4,8	*61*
2,1-4	*88*	4,17	*38f*
2,17-21	*91*	5,10	*66*
2,17ff	*63*	Heb	
5,3	*95*	7,22	*61*
13,25	*66*	7,25	*40, 58*
Rom		8,6	*61*
1,18-3,31	*85*	8,8-12	*61*
2,15	*61*	9,15ff.20	*61*
3,31	*73*	9,24	*58*
5-8	*85*	10,5ff	*62*
5,1-11	*85*	10,16f.29	*61*
8,2	*61, 73*	12,11	*86*
8,6	*85f*	13,20	*61*
8,28	*56*		

Jas		19,1f	*56*
1,27	*51*	19,33	*62*
1 Pet		20,12	*62*
1,8	*57*	20,21	*56*
1 Jn		1QpHab	
2,1	*51, 58, 80*	2,3	*62*
4,6	*51, 59*	1QH	
4,7-5,3	*52, 57*	16,7.13.15	*56*
4,9	*73*	17,26-18,33	*62*
Rev		18,25-28	*62*
7,15	*61, 68*	1QM	
21,1-22,5	*67*	13,7f	*62*
21,3	*61, 67, 69*	1QS	
		4,21	*59*
Apocrypha and Pseudepigrapha		4,22	*62*
		5,5	*62*
Hen(aeth)		1QS[b]	
93,2	*21*	1,2	*62*
Hen(sl)		2,25	*62*
XIIf	*21*	3,26	*62*
Jub			
20,1-20	*21*	*Rabbinic texts*	
20,7	*55*		
36,5ff	*55*	Targum	
36,7-10	*21*	Gen	
37,4	*21*	49,1f	*20*
TestXII		Ps	
TestBen		46,5	*33*
3,1.5	*55*	65,5	*33*
TestDan			
5,3	*55*	Midrash	
TestIs		SifDev	
5,1f	*55*	1,10	*34*
7,6	*55*	DevR	
TestJud		6	*63*
20,1.5	*59*	Ps	
		11	*34*
Qumran texts		43,3	*34f, 41*
CD		*Apostolic Fathers*	
3,13	*62*		
6,19	*62*	Herm(m)	
8,21	*62*	3,4	*59*

New Testament Studies in Contextual Exegesis
Neutestamentliche Studien zur kontextuellen Exegese

Edited by / Herausgegeben von Johannes Beutler, Thomas Schmeller
und Werner Kahl

Band 1 Joseph Osei-Bonsu: The Inculturation of Christianity in Africa. Antecedents and Guidelines from the New Testament and the Early Church. 2005.

Band 2 Werner Kahl: Jesus als Lebensretter. Westafrikanische Bibelinterpretationen und ihre Relevanz für die neutestamentliche Wissenschaft. 2007.

Band 3 Fergus J. King: More Than A Passover. Inculturation in the Supper Narratives of the New Testament. 2007.

Band 4 Anthony Iffen Umoren: Paul and Power Christology. Exegesis and Theology of Romans 1:3–4 in Relation to Popular Power Christology in an African Context. 2008.

Band 5 Solomon Wong: The Temple Incident in Mark 11, 15-19. The Disclosure of Jesus and the Marcan Faction. 2009.

Band 6 Johannes Beutler: *Do not be afraid.* The First Farewell Discourse in John's Gospel (Jn 14). 2011.

www.peterlang.de

Wilson Paroschi

Incarnation and Covenant in the Prologue to the Fourth Gospel (John 1:1–18)

Frankfurt am Main, Berlin, Bern, Bruxelles, New York, Oxford, Wien, 2006. XV, 238 pp.
European University Studies: Series 23, Theology. Vol. 820
ISBN 978-3-631-54830-1 · pb. € 50,80*

This study deals with the structural and exegetical relationship between pre-existence and incarnation in the dynamics of John's Prologue (John 1:1–18). It discusses the point in the narrative at which the shift from the pre-existent Logos to the incarnate Christ takes place and, therefore, the perspective from which the individual parts of the passage (vss. 1–5; vss. 6–13; vss. 14–18) should be interpreted. By making a detailed and comprehensive analysis of the text and evaluating all contrasting views on the subject, the book shows the essential chronological order of the narrative, whose climax (vss. 14–18) is not the announcement of the incarnation proper, but rather a profound theological reflection on the significance of that event based on the covenantal traditions of the exodus story and later prophetic expectations.

Contents: The Pre-existent Mode of the Logos (John 1:1–5) · The Ministry of the Incarnate Logos (John 1:6–13) · The Covenantal Meaning of the Incarnation (John 1:14–18)

Frankfurt am Main · Berlin · Bern · Bruxelles · New York · Oxford · Wien
Distribution: Verlag Peter Lang AG
Moosstr. 1, CH-2542 Pieterlen
Telefax 00 41 (0) 32/376 17 27

*The €-price includes German tax rate
Prices are subject to change without notice

Homepage http://www.peterlang.de

www.ingramcontent.com/pod-product-compliance
Ingram Content Group UK Ltd.
Pitfield, Milton Keynes, MK11 3LW, UK
UKHW021829210426
5322IPUK00004B/91